MODERN VOICE

Date Due

MODERN VOICE

Working with Actors on Contemporary Text

Catherine Weate

OBERON BOOKS
LONDON

WWW.OBERONBOOKS.COM

First published in 2012 by Oberon Books Ltd
521 Caledonian Road, London N7 9RH
Tel: +44 (0) 20 7607 3637 / Fax: +44 (0) 20 7607 3629
e-mail: info@oberonbooks.com
www.oberonbooks.com

Full acknowledgement for extracts reproduced in this book can be
found on pages 291-2.

A catalogue record for this book is available from the British Library.

ISBN: 978-1-84943-171-2
Digital ISBN: 978-1-84943-537-6

Cover design by James Illman

Printed and bound by CPI Group (UK) Ltd, Croydon, CR0 4YY.

For

Mum

(who was a brilliant teacher, ahead of her time)

Acknowledgements

My mother was a classroom teacher who believed in the power of the imagination as a teaching tool. She passed away while I was working on this book but the thought of her educational foresight kept me writing. Thanks Mum for teaching me about teaching.

Trying to untangle my specific vocal sources is virtually impossible after so many years of coaching. My solution is to thank everybody I have ever worked with who have provided me with such wonderful inspiration.

Writing a book may appear to be a solo task but there was always someone around the corner for motivation, encouragement and support.

Special mention must be given to Francesco and Max for their loving patience (particularly when I was in silent mode trying to think through an idea: I'm sure it was deeply frustrating).

My test readers, Les Cartwright, David Shirley and Mia Ball, offered up invaluable reassurance and advice. Some very lengthy drafts were shaped from their feedback.

And, of course, none of this would have been realised without James Hogan, Charles Glanville and the fantastic team at Oberon Books, particularly Andrew Walby for his incisive editorial eye.

I couldn't have done it alone. Thank you.

CONTENTS

PART TWO: REALISTIC DRAMA

PART THREE: NON-REALISTIC DRAMA

Chapter 10 – Expressing the Absurd

PREFACE

Modern Voice: Working with Actors on Contemporary Text has been designed to follow on from *Classic Voice: Working with Actors on Vocal Style* published in September 2009 by Oberon Books. *Classic Voice* provides a comprehensive preparation for the vocal demands within classical texts: *Modern Voice* focuses on the less defined demands of contemporary text.

Most actors think there isn't as much to work on vocally when they approach a contemporary text, particularly if there aren't any specific dialect demands. However, lifting written rhythms off the page can be a huge challenge. Sometimes these rhythms are realistic, resembling or mirroring the speech patterns of real human beings: sometimes they are non-realistic, distorting speech patterns for particular effect. *Modern Voice* provides directors, lecturers, teachers, trainers and coaches with a myriad of ideas to explore these demands in rehearsal.

Part One (Chapters 1 and 2) unpacks contemporary vocal realism. Chapter 1: 'Rhythm in Speech' focuses on the rhythmic features that create spontaneous speech. What are the characteristics of a real voice? And, what makes speech believable?

Chapter 2: 'Rhythm in Writing' focuses on the rhythmic features in contemporary writing and how they can be brought to life for an audience. There are practical exercises and activities at the end of the chapter that can be implemented as part of a workshop/rehearsal plan. Prose is used as sample text so that the rhythmic values of written text can be explored without the over-complication of character dialogue or direct speech. Some of the exercises are technical, artificial and a little unfashionable: they ask actors to think about specific rhythmic elements *whilst* they are reading aloud, rather than just concentrating on communicating meaning and emotion. However, the pay-offs are considerable. By completing work like this prior to working (more organically) on dramatic text, an actor's voice can become rhythmically focused and precise.

Chapters 1 and 2 are the backbone of *Modern Voice*, providing important information for the dramatic processes that follow. You may be tempted to skip them so that you can get to the heart (and point) of the book but Chapters 3 through to 11 have been designed with the assumption that you already know about the technical nuts and bolts of the work from these initial pages.

Part Two (Chapters 3, 4, 5, 6 and 7) introduces dramatic text that contains realistic content and relies on true-to-life speech rhythms to communicate that content. Defining 'realism' isn't easy and there is a great deal of confusion and disagreement in the academic world about it. Chapter 3: 'Journeys, Demands and Challenges' characterises realistic text through its socio-political context and focuses on its rise in selected parts of the English-speaking world (specifically the late nineteenth century to the mid-1960s). Information about the vocal demands and challenges that actors face when working on realism is then considered from within these cultural frameworks.

Chapter 4: 'Creating Character', Chapter 5: 'Dealing with Dialogue/ Revealing Relationships', Chapter 6: 'Capturing the Colloquial' and Chapter 7: 'Voicing the Verbatim' provide practical processes for working on realistic drama. Each chapter includes an overview of the vocal/verbal demands, samples of text and a workshop plan. Although verbatim texts can be non-realistic in presentation, the speech rhythms are naturalistic, having been edited from real-life interviews, first-hand testimonies and documented public inquiries.

Part Three (Chapters 8, 9, 10 and 11) deals with non-realistic drama: meaning text that stretches the boundaries of realism in plot, time, character, presentation, rhythm and/or language. Chapter 8 unpacks the nature, demands and challenges of such texts and provides information on some of the major non-realistic theatrical movements throughout the twentieth century. Chapter 9 focuses on text that, at times, feels realistic but treats word and rhythm non-realistically, such as works written by Harold Pinter and Howard Barker. Chapter 10 discusses the vocal demands of absurdist drama, using the texts of Samuel Beckett and Eugene Ionesco as working examples. Finally, Chapter 11 takes a look at contemporary verse plays, such as those written by Sarah Kane and Glyn Maxwell, which brings us back (full circle) to some of the processes required when working on classical verse plays, like those outlined in *Classic Voice*. These last three chapters provide information on the vocal/verbal demands of the text samples and workshop plans for practical experimentation.

Like *Classic Voice*, the term 'actor' is used throughout but encompasses students from secondary schools, performing arts courses, universities and drama schools, as well as the amateur performer, the untrained professional and the trained professional. The exploratory exercises and activities listed in *Modern Voice* are appropriate for all.

If you are an actor and have picked up this book then you will find that the information/exercises/activities are relevant to your rehearsal processes, although you may need to adjust the workshop plans to meet your individual needs rather than those of a group/ensemble.

Each workshop starts with a brief vocal warm-up, appropriate for the work to come. Open, free and flexible voices will help your actors explore a sample text in detail. Of course, there is no reason why you can't include your own warm-up exercises, particularly those that you feel more comfortable working with. However, be aware that most of the warm-ups in *Modern Voice* have a pay-off for the work to come. If you do decide to make changes then make sure it is relevant for the particular vocal demands of the text you are using. Information on how to structure your own vocal warm up can be found in Chapter 1 of *Classic Voice: Working with Actors on Vocal Style*.

The workshops in *Modern Voice* are offered as a starting point for dealing with the text as a whole and, therefore, can be used as an initial vocal exploration prior to embarking on a full-scale project or rehearsal. However, they shouldn't replace in-depth one-to-one exploration of text in preparation for performance. None of the workshops are constructed within a particular time frame (given the variations in timetabling between schools, colleges, training academies, conservatoires, universities, amateur groups and professional companies). Longer workshops can be broken up into smaller units and separate sessions if need be.

The sample texts have been included to provide a starting point for exploration and there is no need to feel limited by them (particularly if the gender breakdown doesn't work for your group). The workshop exercises and activities can be applied, just as easily, to other similar types of texts.

Although there is technical information within this book, do work to ensure that your classes, workshops and rehearsals remain practical (just underpin them with a strong technical base). Bring knowledge about the voice and the text to the classroom or rehearsal room floor and use that knowledge in practical ways to help your actors bring the drama to life.

PART ONE:
VOCAL REALISM

CHAPTER 1: RHYTHM IN SPEECH

Understanding how rhythm works in conversational speech can help us lift dramatic dialogue off the page. As a teacher, coach, lecturer or director, you will need to spend time listening to the ways in which human beings use rhythm to communicate so that you can help your actors accurately recreate truthful human speech for an audience, whilst using somebody else's words.

This chapter unpacks, in detail, all the elements that combine to form the vocal realism inherent in contemporary speech rhythm. At times, it may seem quite technical and divorced from the reality of spoken communication. For this reason, it's a good idea to speak any examples out loud and apply what's been written to your own way of talking in order to have a point of reference. There will always be exceptions to the 'rules', given the idiosyncratic nature of our speech. However, I am sure you will recognise many familiar patterns.

1. SPEECH RHYTHM: SEPARATING THE ELEMENTS

In English, speech rhythm is created by a combination of *phrasing*, *pausing*, *stressing*, *pitching*, *tuning* and *pacing*.

- *Phrasing and Pausing* – When we speak we communicate in groups of words, separating them out with silences of various lengths, in order to clarify more precisely what we want to say

- *Stressing* – When we speak we bring some information into the foreground and place some into the background, depending on what we're trying to communicate. One of the ways in which we do this is by placing 'stress' on a particular syllable or syllables (by using extra breath energy, a lift in pitch and by lengthening the sound itself) and weakening the other surrounding syllables

- *Pitching and Tuning* – When we speak we combine different pitch levels with contours of pitch, creating a tune or intonation pattern (linked to the stresses across the phrase)

CATHERINE WEATE

- ***Pacing*** – When we speak we vary the pace, lengthening some sounds, speeding up others, depending on their relative importance within a phrase. Faster pacing will also blur sound, changing the rhythmic energy

2. SPEECH RHYTHM: CONNECTING THE ELEMENTS

Phrasing, pausing, stressing, pitching, tuning and pacing *work together* in connected speech in order to express meaning and emotion. As we speak, we simultaneously group the words together, define these groups with pauses, stress some syllables, weaken others and marry them with a specific intonation tune. In fact, phrasing, pausing and stressing *decide* the intonation pattern.

Take a look at the following examples and then speak all three of them aloud, noting the differences between them.

> I went to the supermarket | after the meeting.

> I | went to the supermarket after the meeting.

> I | went to the supermarket | after the meeting.

'I went to the supermarket after the meeting' could be said as one phrase but then again the grouping of words could be broken down further so that there are two or three pieces of information presented. This not only changes where the stresses are placed but also the tune or intonation pattern, dividing it into two or three different tunes. The elements are interdependent.

3. SPEECH RHYTHM: FORMING THE ELEMENTS

What influences and, ultimately helps to form, our speech rhythm? There are a series of variables that (unconsciously) shape the way in which we use phrasing, pausing, stressing, pitching, tuning and pacing in our speech. We are all affected by:

- ***The grammatical rules of the language we are speaking*** – grouping particular words together and giving them a specific tune helps us to maintain grammatical structures in speech, just as punctuation does in writing (although the two don't necessarily follow the same patterns). For example, often we use pauses to mark the beginning and end of grammatical units, such as clauses and sentences.

- ***The drive and energy of our own internal rhythm*** – each of us has our own unique internal rhythmic energy that drives us physically and vocally. Rhythm is a part of our core: our hearts beat in a rhythm, we breathe in a rhythm, we eat in a rhythm, we walk in a rhythm and, of course, we speak in a rhythm.

- ***The drive and energy of the world in which we live*** – our own internal rhythms are adjusted to the world in which we live. For example, how many of you, living in a rural setting, find the tempo of city dwellers different to your own when you visit a large metropolis. You may even find the movement of crowds along a sidewalk/ pavement, at odds with your own movement. If there are physical differences then there will be vocal/speech differences as well.

- ***The drive and energy of the culture in which we live*** – our culture and language also adjusts our own internal rhythm. For example, an Italian speaker, living in a very verbal culture, may tend to use less and/or smaller silences between groups of words, giving an impression of longer, unbroken phrases. Stress and intonation patterns are very different between languages. In many Indian languages, syllables are stressed with a lowering of pitch, whereas in English we use a rise of pitch to bring a syllable into focus. Transferring an Indian intonation pattern to an English phrase will define the speaker as foreign and may lead to misunderstanding (despite the correct grammatical words being used).

- ***The drive and energy of the accent-dialect we speak*** – the way in which we use individual sounds within our accent-dialect, will also create a distinctive rhythm. For example, Italian vowels are shorter than many English vowels, creating a much more staccato rhythm.

Australians and Americans often use greater vowel energy than their English cousins, who prefer a little more bite to their consonants, thereby creating a completely different rhythm. There are also lexical stress differences between accent-dialects (lexical, meaning the standard dictionary stress for a word). For example, an American may place the primary stress on the first syllable of '*laboratory*' and elongate the *-ory* ending, whilst English speakers may place the stress on the second syllable and shorten or weaken the *-ory* ending. So, American and English speakers who use phrases with this word will have different intonation patterns (and therefore, rhythms).

- *The context in which we are speaking* – the difference between delivering a lecture to a large group of students and having a quiet gossipy conversation with a friend in the pub, will give you an idea of how much context affects our rhythmic delivery.
- *The importance of the information we are communicating* – important information will be rhythmically different to inconsequential information. Perhaps in an effort to over-clarify, there will be smaller (and more frequent) phrases, longer silences, stronger stressing, a wider intonation range and a slower pace.
- *Our familiarity with the information we are communicating* – our words always flow more easily (there are less hesitations) when we are familiar with the information we are communicating.
- *Our emotional relationship with the information we are communicating* – how we feel about the information may create a smooth, rapid delivery or pepper it with hesitations and emotive pauses. For example, human beings tend to deliver information more quickly when they are excited and slow it down when they need to think their way, emotionally, through the information.

4. SPEECH RHYTHM: ANALYSING THE ELEMENTS

In order to come to an in-depth understanding of contemporary vocal realism, we need to analyse and clarify each of the elements that combine to form speech rhythm. Here are some initial questions that may help you to focus your thoughts in the right direction:

(a)   How do we break up our thoughts? (Phrasing and Pausing)

(b)   Where do we place the stresses within these thoughts? (Stressing)

(c)   Where do we pitch the tune across these stresses? (Pitching and Tuning)

(d)   How does our pace affect phrasing, stressing, tuning? (Pacing)

(a) PHRASING AND PAUSING

Everybody in the world breaks up their thoughts into phrases. But how do we know where the breaks occur? How do we divide the words up? How do we decide on the grouping?

SENSE-GROUPS

How we phrase is dependent on how we think. Written punctuation can give us some idea of how to group our words together (if we are reading from the printed page) but we certainly don't think in written punctuation when we are speaking conversationally. We tend to think and speak in **sense-groups** (groups of words linked together by sense). The boundaries of a sense-group are marked by silence or a pause in sound (oral punctuation). Sometimes this is a conscious process, when we are measuring out our words carefully, but most of the time it is an unconscious process.

The size of the sense-group is defined by which information the speaker wants to focus the listener's attention on, bringing some of it into the foreground and placing some of it into the background (technically speaking, stressing certain syllables to make them more prominent and weakening other syllables to lessen their impact). A sense-group usually has one or two primary stresses, sometimes three and, very occasionally, four or five. We keep them fairly short as we speak because we don't always know where we are heading so our brain needs to break up the information into small, manageable chunks. Context and emotional state are key, however.

A speaker may use more pauses, and therefore sense-groups, in order to create greater impact when making an announcement. Retelling a story about a thrilling personal experience may mean a speaker uses longer sense-groups to create a flowing sense of excitement.

Here are a few rules often (unconsciously) followed by native speakers of the English language when formulating sense-groups:

- **Nouns** – Sentences and clauses that contain a lot of nouns tend to be broken down into smaller sense-groups, so that the heavily loaded information can be presented in more manageable chunks. The break or pause usually occurs after one of the nouns. For example:

  The books on the library shelf | were in many different languages.

- **Contrasts** – When we contrast one idea or subject with another we tend to break the contrasting information up into two separate phrases. For example:

  The deli closes at noon | but the supermarket is staying open.

- **Subjects** – Sometimes we separate out a topic or subject into a phrase all of its own, giving it extra emphasis and making it more distinct. For example:

  The books | on the library shelf…

  The deli | closes at noon…

- **Adverbials** – The type of adverbials that modify the meaning of a thought within a clause (for example: *technically, unfortunately, fortunately, apparently, seriously*) tend to be separated out with a pause into their very own phrase. For example:

  Technically | the library was open. (**beginning**)

  The party | surprisingly | was over before it began. (**middle**)

  We didn't hear the phone | unfortunately. (**end**)

However, the type of adverbials placed at the end of a clause that are separated out with a comma in writing (for example: *though, then, too*) aren't separated out with a pause in speech. For example:

He isn't well, though.

I'll go to the shop, then.

I have qualified all these examples with 'tend to' or 'sometimes' because although I am sure you will have recognised most of these phrasing features in your own speech, likewise you will know of instances when you will have bypassed them.

BREATH-GROUPS

A sense-group doesn't necessarily coincide with the way in which we breathe. Sometimes, in actor training, students are taught 'one thought to one breath'. However, human beings have quite a large breath capacity (unless struck down with illness) and if we took a breath each time we started a new sense-group then there would be far too much oxygen in the bloodstream, causing dizziness and (possibly) physical panic. Taking a breath also takes time, which would mean creating a long-ish pause at the end of each sense-group, ruining the overall rhythmic tempo and flow of our speech. Test it out and you will find it sounds quite stilted and plodding.

Therefore, we often have a number of sense-groups within one breath-group. This is an unconscious and natural process whereby our bodies synchronise with our brains in order to maintain the flow of our spoken information as well as provide us with enough oxygen to live comfortably. It's also the reason why our physical and vocal rhythms synchronise.

LISTS

What if we speak words that can't be linked together by sense? Do we still phrase? The answer again is 'sometimes'. Lists of numbers, items, ideas and concepts are a good example. Sometimes, we separate them out with a pause between each word, sometimes we do not. If we are speaking quickly or we are listing information that we instinctively know is familiar to the listener (for example: *Monday, Tuesday, Wednesday* … or *1, 2, 3, 4, 5*…) then we won't separate the words out into individual phrases. However, if it is unfamiliar information (*I think we should meet on Thursday | Sunday | and Monday* or *My telephone number is 020 | 1234 | 5678*) then we will indeed phrase. We will always phrase when we are listing items that we don't want the listener to forget. Phrasing lists helps us to create greater impact. We will also phrase if a list is extremely long, separating the list out into manageable chunks (rather than pausing between each individual word).

BREAKING THE SENSE

Sense-groups don't always remain intact in our everyday speech. There are times when we need to break the sense (i.e. pause for a moment) for a variety of different reasons.

- *Parenthesis* – The definition of spoken parenthesis is a thought within a thought, or, a sense-group within a sense-group. We interrupt the flow of one thought (almost as if we are sidetracked) to insert another and then return to the continuation of the original thought. In writing, brackets or commas are often used to mark a parenthetic thought. When speaking, we tend to use pauses (as well as a change in pitch level and intonation pattern) to separate out and make the sense-groups clear. Spoken parenthesis is very common in everyday speech as our brains move rapidly from one thought to another, triggering off complimentary or contrasting thoughts that need to be added into the spoken framework.

- *Emphatic Emphasis* – Sometimes, for extra emphasis, we will surround a word with pauses. This will be married to strong stressing and an extreme lift in pitch on the word itself. For example:

    It will be | *the* | event of the decade!

- **Emotional Emphasis** – Emotional moments often require extra pauses. We may break the sense-group because we find it difficult to verbalise a piece of emotionally charged information or because we need a moment to (emotionally) collect our thoughts together before we can go on or we may want to emphasise the importance of the emotional moment. Usually this takes the form of a pause before and sometimes after the word that is emotionally charged. For example:

    He | died | in that car crash.

- **Sarcasm** – Often we break sense-groups with a pause when we are being sarcastic. The pause usually comes before the word that will carry the sarcasm in an attempt to over-emphasise that we mean the opposite of the truth. In the following example, clearly the speaker didn't receive any help at all.

    I really appreciated your | help.

- **Hesitations** – Sense-groups can also be broken up at odd and random points in their delivery because human beings are not always fluent. Sometimes our brains and mouths lose their synchronicity (our thoughts can run along quite quickly and our articulating muscles can't always keep up) so we need a moment to rebalance before we continue. Or we hesitate over a choice of word or we are tentative about the information we're bringing forth into the world. These hesitations can take the form of a silence or we can use a sound or word to cover our hesitation so that we can maintain the rhythmic flow of our speech. A repeated word, a repeated sound at the start of a word (like a small stutter), or a 'filler' sound, such as '*um*', '*ah*', '*uh*', '*er*' or '*mh*' are all common and frequent in the course of spontaneous speech.

TIMING THE SILENCES

Pauses interrupt the flow of sound but also contribute to the overall rhythmic timing of our speech by providing beats of silence. So, if the rhythm of our speech is to be maintained, the size of the pause is important.

We tend to use quite brief *sense pauses* between most sense-groups so that the rhythmic flow isn't interrupted. This is particularly true if we are speaking quickly in rapid, spontaneous, conversational speech. When we come to the end of a breath-group (possibly after a series of sense-groups) we tend to take a longer *breath pause* so, physically, there is enough time to take oxygen into our body.

The timing of *emphatic pauses* (where particular words are emphasised or made distinct by a pause) depends on the size of the impact we wish to make, whilst the size of the *emotional pause* (where the emotional moment is held by a silence) is dependant on the strength of our emotion at the time of speaking. Likewise, the timing of a *sarcastic pause* will vary depending on the impact we want to make with our sarcasm.

Hesitation pauses are entirely different. The size of the silence will differ, depending on the reason behind the hesitation. However, as human beings we don't particularly like silence when we are in conversation, which is why we tend to repeat words and/or use filler sounds, rather than hesitate without sound.

(b) STRESSING

Highlighting certain words in our speech helps us to be more specific with the information that we want to convey to the listener. But how do we go about doing this? Through the use of stress, which (in English) is a combination of extra breath energy, a lift in pitch and a lengthening of sound, placed on the strong syllables of a word that we wish to make prominent for the listener. This means there are patterns (often fairly irregular, but patterns nonetheless) of strong and weak syllables that create a rhythmic beat.

But how do we know what to stress? On which syllables do we place the stress?

WORD STRESS OR LEXICAL STRESS

In order to answer these questions we need to understand the lexical stress of each word in our own particular accent-dialect. By lexical I mean the standard dictionary stress of a word, something that we start learning through imitation from the day we are born.

In English, every word of more than one syllable has its own particular lexical stress, its own rhythmical value, outside of connected speech. For example, a strong stress sits on the first syllable of 'never and the second syllable is weakened: in the word a'llowed, the strong stress sits on the second syllable. We wouldn't even think of changing these stresses: stressing the second syllable of *never* or the first syllable of *allowed* would be odd and lead to misunderstandings (although there are a number of words in English that can change meaning with a simple shift in the placement of the stress, for example, 'subject/sub'ject, 'contract/con'tract and 'present/pre'sent).

Some words have more than one stressed syllable: a primary stress (the strongest stress) and a secondary stress (the runner-up). In English, you can find both in the word *pro‚nunci'ation*. The remaining weakened syllables are either shortened versions of the vowel, or, the vowel is replaced by a schwa, a neutral sound which is centrally located in the mouth. Phonetically, the schwa is represented by an upside down 'e', as in / ə /. Try saying the word *actor* and the word *annoyed*. The second syllable of *actor* and the first syllable of *annoyed* are both weakened syllables and the same sound is used to represent them – the schwa.

In compound nouns, words that are created by the linking together of two nouns (for example, 'toothbrush, 'newspaper and 'keyboard), the lexical stress tends to sit on the first syllable/noun. This means that we make it clear to the listener that a 'toothbrush is a brush for *teeth* (rather than just any old brush), a 'newspaper is paper with *news* (rather than just a piece of blank paper) and a 'keyboard is a board with *keys* on it (rather than just a non-descriptive piece of board). Some compounds are written as two separate words, others are hyphenated, but they operate in exactly the same way (for example: 'time frame, 'credit card and 'absent-minded). However, there are exceptions, known as double-stressed compounds. They usually start with a secondary stress and the main primary stress occurs in the second part of the compound. This includes names of people (ˌCatherine 'Weate), names of roads and public places (ˌPiccadilly 'Circus) and names of institutions (ˌLondon 'Library). There are also some double-stressed compounds where the first part of the compound names a place or time (ˌTown 'Hall and ˌChristmas 'Day) and some where the first part names a material or ingredient (ˌfur 'coat and ˌegg 'sandwich) although this excludes any compounds ending in *juice* or *cake*. Strange but true.

Accent-dialect, as we learnt earlier, has a bearing on lexical word stress. There are variations as you cross the English-speaking world. Remember the word *laboratory*? Americans tend to place the primary stress on the first syllable and a secondary stress on the second last syllable, which lengthens out the *-ory* ending. English speakers stress the second syllable and weaken everything else. Because of these differences and, in order to avoid confusion, I'll need to focus on just one accent-dialect. For the moment this will be Standard British Speech or Received Pronunciation.

SENTENCE STRESS OR CONNECTED SPEECH STRESS

When we speak and group words together in phrases, word stress is often adjusted because of the need to highlight and focus on particular parts of our communication, whilst placing other parts into the background. This doesn't mean that lexical word stress changes, it just means that some of the lexical word stresses are less prominent than others. Traditionally, this has been called 'Sentence Stress' but, as we learnt earlier, we don't think in sentences, we think in phrases or sense-groups. So I prefer to talk about 'Connected Speech Stress' rather than 'Sentence Stress'.

Connected speech stress depends on meaning and context; the more important the word, the stronger its stress. For example: *I ˌneed to take a 'very ˌlong 'bath.* The speaker is clarifying the content of his message by placing a primary stress on *bath* and indicating how dirty he feels by placing another primary stress on the lexically stressed syllable of *very*. As you can see the pattern of weak and strong stresses is irregular (rather than the regular pattern you might find in a piece of metrical verse or music).

However, there is still a strong rhythm, created by the variation between strong and weak syllables. Phrases with lots of stressed syllables tend to create a stronger rhythm and slow speech down. Phrases with less stressing tend to flow more rapidly.

J.C. Wells in his excellent book *English Intonation* describes the way in which we use stress across a phrase, breaking it down into the ***Nucleus***, the ***Tail***, the ***Onset***, the ***Head*** and the ***Pre-Head***. This framework helps us create a specific tune or intonation pattern (but more on that later).

- ***The Nucleus*** is the last stressed syllable in a phrase and occurs on or near the last word. It's usually the most important, being the key to the meaning we're trying to communicate. For example (with the nucleus in bold): *That 'must have been **'painful***.

- ***The Tail*** is the part of the phrase that follows the nucleus and so isn't accented. For example (with the tail in bold): *That 'must have been **'painful***. Sometimes there might be a few words in the tail (depending on where the nucleus sits) and sometimes the tail doesn't exist at all (if the nucleus falls on the final syllable). For example: *That 'must be a 'pain*.

- ***The Onset*** is a stress placed somewhere before the nucleus. If there are a number of stresses before the nucleus then it is the first stress. For example (with the onset in bold): *That **'must** have been 'painful*.

- ***The Head*** is the section of the phrase, starting at the onset and finishing just before the nucleus. For example (with the head in bold): *That **'must have been** 'painful*.

- ***The Pre-Head*** is the first part of the phrase where there might be unstressed syllables that occur before the first stressed syllable. For example (with the pre-head in bold): ***That** 'must have been 'painful*.

Here's how it works in order:

Pre-head | Onset | Head | Nucleus | Tail

That 'must have been 'painful.

That – pre-head
must – onset
must have been – head
pain – nucleus
ful – tail

It 'doesn't 'suit me.

It – pre-head
does - onset
doesn't - head
suit - nucleus
me - tail

MORE ABOUT THE NUCLEUS

The nucleus helps us to make our meaning and emotions specific and distinct for listeners so we tend to drive through phrases to get to it. However, it's also the key to the way in which we use stress across the whole phrase (and therefore, the key to the overall rhythmic pattern). For this reason it's important to focus on how we (consciously or unconsciously) decide on its placement. We've already learnt that it is the last lexically stressed syllable in a phrase and sits on or near the last word but how do we decide *which* is the last lexically stressed syllable? Here are just a few rules that we tend to follow in our speech. The examples indicate the nucleus in bold type. Of course there are often other primary and secondary stresses across these sample phrases but, for the moment, let's just focus on the nucleus.

- *Key Content* – As speakers, we need to highlight the key information/ content that will bring our words to the attention of the listener. We do this by placing the nucleus on the lexically stressed syllable of the last *content* word in the phrase, favouring nouns but sometimes using verbs, adverbs and adjectives, depending on what we're trying to get across. For example: *Let's go for a walk in the **park**.*

When verbs occur at the end of the phrase, the nucleus tends to fall on the noun that occurs before it. For example: *Is the **water** running?* Likewise, if an adjective occurs at the end of the phrase, the nucleus tends to fall on the noun that occurs before it. For example: *The **food** is ready.* If there isn't a noun present then the nucleus will occur on the lexically stressed syllable of the final verb or adjective. For example: *That must have been **painful**.*

- ***Fresh Content*** – Stressing across a phrase is influenced by whether we are introducing fresh, new content to the listener. We tend to highlight that new information and weaken (place into the background) any old information that we believe the listener is aware of or has heard before. The nucleus will sit on the last lexical stress in a phrase that contains fresh content. If the last lexical stress in the phrase contains old (familiar) content, then the nucleus will occur earlier, on content that contains new information. For example:

    Speaker 1 – *Let's order fish and **chips**.*

    Speaker 2 – *I'd prefer **chick**en and chips.*

Because *chips* have already been mentioned the nucleus is placed on the lexically stressed syllable of *chicken* by Speaker 2, which is fresh content in the conversation. This not only occurs when the same words are repeated, it can also occur when different words are used for the same content. For example:

    Speaker 1 – *Have you read this **book**?*

    Speaker 2 – *Yes, it's a **great** story.*

Even though Speaker 2 substituted the word *story* for *book*, it is pretty much the same content so there is no need to place the nucleus there. Instead, the nucleus sits on the new information i.e. what the speaker thought about the book/story.

- **Shared Content** – In conversation, there is usually content that is shared knowledge between speakers and listeners. Speakers don't need to highlight this shared knowledge if the listener already knows about it. Instead, the speaker will place the nucleus on the lexically stressed syllable of the word that highlights the content that isn't shared. For example, *This **bus** | is going to **London**.* In the first phrase, the nucleus doesn't need to be placed on *bus*, because the passenger/listener knows they're on a bus and so the information doesn't need to be clarified with the nucleus.

- **Contrasting Content** – When we contrast one idea or subject with another we tend to break the contrasting information up into two separate phrases. The nucleus is placed on the lexically stressed syllables of the contrasting information in each of those phrases, making the contrast distinct. For example:

  *The **deli** | is open on a **Thursday** | but on **Friday** it's closed.*

- **Pronouns** – The nucleus usually doesn't occur on personal pronouns and prepositions (for example: *It doesn't **suit** me.*) although there are exceptions to this rule. The nucleus might occur on a pronoun when:
  - contrasting information is highlighted using pronouns. For example: *You're as upset as **I** am.*
  - a possessive pronoun (*mine, yours, his, hers, ours* and *theirs*) occurs at the end of a phrase and highlights new information. For example: *Which glass is **yours?*** The exception would be phrases that end in *of mine* and *of yours*. For example: *a **friend** of mine.*
  - a reflexive pronoun (*myself* and *yourself*) is used for emphasis. For example: *I'll do that **myself.***
  - a pronoun is used at the end of a commonly used idiomatic phrase. For example: *Good for **you*** and *Search **me**.*

- **Adverbs of Degree** – These are the words that tell us about the intensity or degree of an action (such as *very, nearly, quite, just, too, enough, extremely, completely*). They consistently attract the nucleus because their inclusion in a phrase adds weight, emphasis or intensity to the content. For example: *These plates are **extremely** hot.*

- ***Letters and Numbers*** – When we use a series of letters or numbers, the nucleus usually falls on the last one. For example: *Let's watch the BBC* and *The serial number is 365.* The exception occurs when the final letter or number has already been used: we don't need to draw attention to the repeated number so the nucleus falls on its unfamiliar predecessor. For example: *The serial number is 3656.*

- ***Reporting Clauses*** – The nucleus doesn't occur in reporting clauses (such as *he asked, she said*) that come after quoted direct speech. The nucleus will occur in the direct speech and *he asked/she said* will become the tail.

(c) PITCHING AND TUNING

Each phrase we utter has its own particular tune or melody, otherwise known as intonation.

WHY DO WE NEED TUNEFUL SPEECH?

Intonation has a number of important functions. We use it to:

- Communicate meaning and express emotion more specifically. The words we use have particular meanings and definitions but intonation helps us to put them into a context, making them specific and real for listeners.

- Avoid monotony. Intonation makes our speech interesting. I'm sure you'd agree that the most boring speakers are the ones who tend to flatten their tunes, making them much less distinct and, therefore, difficult to listen to. Without intonation we'd all sound like automated robots from some bad science fiction movie.

- Clarify our grammatical structures. Different intonation patterns often help our listeners understand when we are making a statement or asking a question.

- Define the rhythm of our conversations. Intonation helps us to indicate for the listener when we are coming to the end of a point (and making a space for a response) or if we'd like to continue talking.

- Give us a particular identity. We all have our own, individual intonation patterns, peculiar to ourselves. However, these are also adjusted to the accent we speak, the social group we associate with and the culture we belong to. It is believed that many of these patterns are set in place whilst we are in the womb, listening to our mothers' speech melodies.

> The psychologists Jacques Mehler and Peter Jusczyk have shown that four-day-old French babies suck harder to hear French than Russian, and pick up their sucking more when a tape changes from Russian to French than from French to Russian. This is not an incredible proof of reincarnation; the melody of mothers' speech carries through their bodies and is audible in the womb. The babies still prefer French when the speech is electronically filtered so that the consonant and vowel sounds are muffled and only the melody comes through. But they are indifferent when the tapes are played backwards, which preserves the vowels and some of the consonants but distorts the melody. Nor does the effect prove the inherent beauty of the French language: non-French infants do not prefer French, and French infants do not distinguish Italian from English. The infants must have learned something about the prosody of French (its melody, stress and timing) in the womb, or in their first days out of it. [1]

However, some intonation patterns cross the boundaries of culture, accent and society. For example, in the English-speaking world newsreaders and journalists have their own particular, recognisable intonation pattern. Another example is the particular intonation patterns of mothers world-wide, also known as 'Motherese'. There are common, recognisable tunes for approving, comforting, prohibiting and directing attention.

HOW DO WE CREATE A TUNE?

The intonation pattern or tune or melody is formed out of a series of pitch changes created by the vocal folds. As we get ready to speak, our outgoing breath moves up the trachea and into the larynx. Inside the larynx, the breath pressure causes the vocal folds to vibrate and create sound. Different pitches are determined by how fast or slow the vocal folds vibrate: fast vibrations create higher pitches, slower vibrations create lower pitches. Because we change our pitch constantly across each phrase we utter, the vocal folds work rapidly to adjust position, tense, relax, speed up and slow down, allowing us to lift, leap and dive, lunge and plunge in our speech.

These changes in pitch are already partially decided for us because of the particular syllables we have chosen to stress in a phrase (dependant, of course, on the meaning we want to make clear). As we've already learnt, English stress is partially created by lifts in pitch. These stress/pitch patterns then become, as J.C. Wells in *English Intonation* puts it, the 'hooks on which the intonation pattern is hung'.[2] Therefore, deciding the stress pattern (and particularly, the placement of the nucleus) decides the tune or melody of our speech. They're all interconnected.

Take, for example, the phrase *I don't believe it*. Here's how it might be stressed:

> *I 'don't be'**lieve** it.*

> *I* – pre-head
> *don't* – onset
> *don't be* – head
> *lieve* – nucleus (in bold)
> *it* – tail

Speak this phrase aloud and whatever type of meaning or emotion you choose to use, you'll hear pitch changes across all of its elements – the pre-head, the head, the nucleus and the tail. However, the greatest pitch change or pitch movement occurs on the nucleus because it holds the most stress weight.

HOW DO WE DECIDE ON THE TYPE OF TUNE TO USE?

So, having decided where the stresses are placed across a phrase, how do we know what type of tune to use with them? There are a variety of different options, depending on the meaning and emotion we want to communicate. We need to focus on the nucleus first (despite the fact it often lives at or towards the end of a phrase). This is because it holds the greatest pitch change or pitch movement in a phrase. The nucleus can have a Falling Tone or a Non-Falling Tone.

- **The Nucleus – Falling Tone**

This starts on a high pitch and moves downwards *on* the nucleus. If there is a tail after the nucleus then those syllables remain low-pitched. Falling Tones are usually used for:

> Complete statements
> Commands
> Agreement
> Aggression
> Questions starting with a 'wh' word (*who, what, which, where, when, why, how*)
> Questions not requiring a 'yes' or 'no' answer
> End of breath-groups

Try the following statement aloud with a Falling Tone on the highlighted nucleus.

> *I don't be**lieve** it.*

The level of fall depends on how emotionally excited the speaker is. So a high fall will occur across a wider pitch range, starting on a higher note than a low fall, given the speaker's heightened state of excitement or involvement. For example:

> *I know how it **works**.* (low fall – a matter of fact)

> *I know how it **works**.* (high fall – excited about the discovery)

- **The Nucleus – Non-Falling Tones (Rise and Fall-Rise)**

In a Rising Tone, the pitch starts low and moves upwards *on* the nucleus. If there is a tail after the nucleus then the rise is spread over those syllables as well.

In a Fall-Rise Tone, the pitch of the voice moves down and then up *on* the nucleus. If there is a tail after the nucleus then the Fall-Rise Tone is spread over the tail as well.

Non-Falling Tones are usually used for:

> Doubt
> Anxiety
> Surprise
> Pleading
> Threats
> Incomplete statements
> Questions requiring a 'yes' or 'no' answer
> The end of a single sense-group within a larger breath-group

Try the following statement aloud with doubt and/or surprise in your voice. A Rising Tone or Fall-Rise Tone will occur on the highlighted nucleus.

> *I don't be**lieve** it.*

A WORD OF WARNING

Categorising intonation patterns according to sentence/phrase type can be difficult as there is no definitive set of rules. There will always be special circumstances that create exceptions. Certainly I found it confusing learning all this as an Australian teenager, where a Non-Falling Tone for complete statements is built into much of the accent. However, these categories can be useful as a ***fall-back position*** for speakers of Received Pronunciation (meaning that they are the most commonly used categories) as long as teachers don't try to impose them as the ultimate, definitive standard for students to attain. Intonation patterns need to remain flexible and free so that speakers can adjust them to their needs and the context of their situation. They should remain as loose guidelines.

I won't be discussing all the special circumstances that differ from this fall-back position as it would take up too many pages and not be of particular use to actors as part of their rehearsal process. However, we do need to focus on what happens to intonation in the part of the phrase that comes before the nucleus (pre-nuclear tones).

WHAT HAPPENS BEFORE THE NUCLEUS?

We've already established that the **pre-head**, **onset** and **head** come before the nucleus and the tail. For example:

> *That* – pre-head
> *must* – onset
> *must have been* – head
> *pain* – nucleus
> *ful* – tail

The pitch of the *pre-head* can either be high or low.

The pitch movement of the *head* is launched by the *onset* and could be high level or low level (where stressing is like a series of level steps), falling (where stressing falls in pitch) or low rising (where stressing rises in pitch).

Both pitch movements of the *pre-head* and the *head* are independent from the nucleus. The only part of the phrase that isn't independent is the tail, which relies on the nucleus to determine its rise or fall.

WHAT ARE KEY CHANGES? WHY DO WE USE THEM?

We've already learnt that the pitch of our voice moves around considerably on each phrase to create particular tunes or intonation patterns, depending on the meaning we're trying to convey. However, we can also change the overall level of our pitch (the key). Here are a few reasons why we might use a key change.

- **To clarify our subject matter**: We may abruptly change to a higher or lower key during conversation to indicate that we're speaking about a completely new subject. This lets the listener know, automatically, that we are changing tack.

- **To highlight our subject matter:** Sometimes we use a key change (higher or lower) to indicate that a piece of information is more important than the previous one.

- **To include a new listener:** During the course of a conversation we may turn to involve a new listener in our subject matter. A key change (higher or lower) will help us to draw them in.

- **To indicate parenthesis:** We use a key change to mark parenthesis in our speech. In 'Phrasing and Pausing' I discussed how we often interrupt the flow of one thought by inserting something additional (almost like being sidetracked) and then continue on with the original thought. In writing, we usually put brackets, commas or dashes around the insertion and call it parenthesis. In speech, a key change occurs, indicating to the listener that it's an addition/insertion. When we continue on with our original thought, after the insertion, we will automatically return to the original key that we were speaking in. Usually we use a lower key change for the addition/insertion but it can sometimes be a high key change, depending on the subject matter.

(d) PACING

The terms 'pace' and 'tempo' refer to how fast or slow we speak. This doesn't happen at a fixed rate but varies, depending on the meaning or emotion we are trying to convey. We do this by lengthening certain sounds (which slows us down) and shortening certain sounds (which speeds us up). Sound length is decided by which syllables we choose to stress in a phrase as stress is partially created by a *lengthening of sound on the strong syllable* of a word that we wish to make prominent for the listener (combined with extra breath force and a lift in pitch). Take for example: *That 'must have* *been **painful**.* The 'uh' sound in 'must' and the 'ay' in 'painful are longer than the other sounds because they live in stressed syllables. Of course there are different types of length depending on whether the sound is in a primary or secondary stressed syllable, whether the syllable is in an onset or nucleus position in the phrase or whether the sound is a short or long vowel.

This means that English is a ***stress-timed language***, where syllables can last different amount of times depending on their context and meaning. Strong syllables occur at fairly regular intervals but their value is still different to weak syllables with the schwa. The alternative is a ***syllable-timed language***, where each syllable takes up roughly the same amount of time, creating a quick, staccato-like rhythm that tends not to vary (like in Italian, French and Spanish). This means that English ears often find Italian, French and Spanish speech quite fast.

So, in English, when we slow down, we lengthen out the long stressed sounds further than usual: when we speed up, we shorten them. But why do we do this? Here are just a few reasons.

- **We speed up our speech (shortening strong syllables)**
    - if we are in a physical hurry (our thoughts, and therefore our speech, tend to operate in conjunction with the speed in which our bodies are moving)
    - if we are in a particular emotional state (such as being nervous or excited)
    - if there is unimportant information to deliver that doesn't need particular emphasis
    - if there is content that is light-hearted in tone

- **We slow down our speech (lengthening strong syllables)**
    - if we are in a sleepy or relaxed physical state (again, our thoughts, and therefore our speech, tend to operate in conjunction with our bodies)
    - if we are in a particular emotional state (such as being sad or depressed)

- if we are being careful with our words (thinking things through as we speak)
- if we wish to create an impact with our words (the bigger the impact, the stronger the stress, the longer the sounds in those strong stresses and, therefore, the slower the pace)
- if we wish to highlight particular content in our speech

However, within this there will still be small changes of pace, dependant on the very tiny and specific meanings that we want to make clear.

So if 'pace' and 'stress' are interdependent, how does a change in pace affect phrasing, pausing, pitching and tuning? Faster paces will affect the timing of our silences, giving less definition to our phrasing and clarifying less of the information we wish to convey. Faster paces will also give us less time to formulate a pitch movement over stressed syllables, so the tune of our speech can tend to flatten. This all seems a bit negative but faster speeds are still an important part of how we make our communication distinct and specific.

We also have a tendency in intense moments to combine a faster pace with a louder volume and a higher pitch key (just listen to individual voices in a football crowd) but a faster pace can still operate in conjunction with a softer volume and a lower pitch key. The options are endless.

BLURRING

Word boundaries don't exist in the flow of conversational speech: blurring is a natural consequence, however clear and articulate the speaker may be. If you listen to a speaker of a language you don't understand it is almost impossible to tell where one word starts and another finishes. It is the same with English despite the fact we might think we are speaking or hearing fully formed individual words. As we speed up, blurring occurs more frequently. Some accents use blurring more widely than others.

This is one of my favourite examples of blurring that a speaker of Broad Australian might use:

Have you learnt your things?

becomes

flernchuhthingz?

Similitude, Assimilation and Elision are particular types of blurring that you might recognise in your own speech or the speech of others around you.

- **Similitude** occurs when a sound is slightly modified under the influence of one of its neighbours. Take, for example, the phrase '*The cat moved quickly*'. We simply cannot pronounce the full weight of the '*t*' at the end of '*cat*' when it is followed by an '*m*'. To do so would be over-pedantic and disrupt the rhythmic flow of the phrase. Another example would be in the word '*month*', where the '*n*' isn't formed (as it would be in isolation) by placing the tongue up to the hard palate. Instead, the tongue comes forward to the teeth in readiness for the '*th*', which is a dental sound, changing its value.

- **Assimilation** occurs when a sound is changed into something completely different because of one of its neighbours (A is replaced by B under the influence of C). For example, in the phrase '*does she*', the '*z*' is replaced with a '*zh*' (as in the middle sound of '*measure*') because of the influence of '*sh*'.

- **Elision** is where a sound or a syllable is lost in the flow of conversational speech. There is absolutely nothing wrong with eliding sounds, it just makes it easier for the speaker to maintain rhythmic flow. For example, in the phrase '*take care*' we tend to lose the '*k*' sound in '*take*' under the influence of the '*k*' sound at the start of '*care*'. Another example would be the loss of the '*d*' in the phrase '*blind mice*'.

5. REVISITING THE BASICS

Here are three important points to remember from this chapter:

- English speech rhythm is formed by a combination of phrasing, pausing, stressing, pitching, tuning and pacing.

- It is the interdependence of these elements that creates contemporary vocal realism. You can't focus on one without focusing on the others.

- Their particular attributes vary depending on the language, grammar, accent, culture, context, content, emotional state and individual energy of each speaker.

CHAPTER 2: RHYTHM IN WRITING

This chapter is all about what happens when we try to lift somebody else's words off a page of text, whether it be reading aloud or performing from memory. We've already established how rhythm operates when we are speaking spontaneously but now our task is to apply this to the written word.

Current thinking in actor training is that if we connect to the meaning/emotion of a text then natural speech rhythm (i.e. vocal realism) will automatically follow. However, this isn't always the case. Writers create specific rhythms to draw out character, story, culture, meaning and emotion for an audience. It is tempting for actors to superimpose their own idiosyncratic speech rhythms onto this, or, they aren't sufficiently aware of how rhythm operates in order to lift words off the page and create spontaneous speech. This doesn't mean that they should consciously think about rhythm *every* time they speak or read or present a memorised text but they do need to open up their ears to the way in which other people use rhythm as well as understand the basic principles of how their own rhythms work. A process of discovery, analysis and practical experiment will help them to adapt their own rhythms to the rhythm of the text and, at the same time, establish a recognisable vocal realism. In this way they will 'serve' the text, bringing it rhythmically to life.

Before we start, it's important to note that this chapter operates on the assumption that you've already read Chapter 1: 'Rhythm in Speech'.

1. SPEAKING AND WRITING: WHAT'S THE DIFFERENCE?

Both speaking and writing are skills that require practice but we learn them in vastly different ways. Our brains are wired for speech and our bodies have evolved muscular mechanisms for its delivery. Once we enter into the world it is then a matter of listening to the people around us and practising what we've learnt. However, writing usually requires specific and formalised study of some sort. All human beings speak (unless there is a problem that prevents them from doing so) but not everybody writes if there aren't opportunities available for them to learn.

Although both speaking and writing are communication tools, allowing us to express thought, idea and emotion, the end results are often worlds apart for a variety of different reasons. Focusing on these differences will help you and your actors understand the leap that needs to be made in order to speak a written text aloud for an audience.

- **Transience vs. Permanence**
  - Speaking is a transient activity so that once words are spoken they are immediately lost (unless recorded by a technological device).
  - Writing is a permanent activity so that when words have been transferred onto a page they can be reviewed and re-read many times.

- **Time vs. Space**
  - Speaking is restricted by the boundary of time.
  - Writing is restricted by the boundary of space.

- **Spontaneous vs. Planned**
  - Speaking usually happens spontaneously, in the moment. This means it can be hesitant, tentative and littered with repetitions and fillers ('ums' and 'ahs').
  - Writing is always planned and structured so it can be revised and edited before an audience sees it.

- **Known vs. Unknown**
  - Speakers know their audience and tailor their language accordingly. They rely on a shared understanding with their listeners who can fill in the gaps.
  - Writers don't (necessarily) know who is going to read their text so they need to clarify and structure their language to suit a diverse audience.

- **Interactive vs. Isolated**
  - Speaking is an interactive process. Listeners feed into the process immediately with body language that can encourage or reject.
  - Writing is carried out in isolation and feedback is delayed.

- **Informal vs. Formal**
  - Speakers tend to make more use of contractions (can't for cannot/ it's for it is), slang and swearing.
  - Writers tend to use more formal syntactic constructions (unless they're writing for a specific character)*

- **Non-Verbal vs. Verbal**
  - Speakers use body language and facial expression to define, clarify and emphasise their words.
  - Writers need to clarify and structure their language so that it can live outside of physical embodiment.

- **Verbal Rhythmic Devices vs. Written Rhythmic Devices**
  - Speakers use rhythmic devices such as phrasing, pausing, stressing, pitching, tuning and pacing to convey meaning and emotion to an audience.
  - Writers use rhythm to convey meaning and emotion as well but focus on choice of word/image, punctuation, sentence length and paragraph structure (i.e. the patterns on the page).

Stephen Pinker in *The Language Instinct* talks about the differences between speech and writing and uses, as an example, the Watergate tapes, where President Nixon was recorded in conversation with White House staff in the 1970s. The tapes were transcribed and because these written transcriptions could not include the intonation patterns and timing of the speakers, many of the partial phrases and hesitations created a great deal of confusion. It became quite difficult to clarify what the President and his staff actually meant.

> …whether a man would end the year as president of the United States or as a convicted criminal literally hinged on the meaning of *get it* and on whether *What is it that you need?* was meant as a request for information or as an implicit offer to provide something.[3]

What does all this mean for the actor, who is attempting to draw the features of speech from the written word? First of all, it depends on the writing and whether the author has included speech features in his/her text. *Playwrights who create dialogue and novelists who include direct speech or write in first-person prose often use contractions, hesitations, fillers, elisions, assimilations and dialect on the written page to provide a degree of vocal realism. These two examples are from contemporary texts (although their subjects are historical). Both writers utilise dialect and colloquial speech (but in different ways) to bring their characters to life.

This extract is dialogue taken from the play Our Country's Good *by Timberlake Wertenbaker. Liz is a convict transported for seven years to Australia in the late eighteenth century. Here she explains how she came before the judge.*

LIZ: Luck? Don't know the word. Shifts its bob when I comes near. Born under a ha'penny planet I was. Dad's a nibbler, don't want to get crapped. Mum leaves. Five brothers, I'm the only titter. I takes in washing. Then. My own father. Lady's walking down the street, he takes her wiper. She screams, he's shoulder-clapped, says, it's not me, Sir, it's Lizzie, look, she took it. I'm stripped, beaten in the street, everyone watching. [4]

This extract is written in the first person and is taken from the novel Remarkable Creatures *by Tracy Chevalier. Mary lives in nineteenth-century Lyme Regis and survives by collecting and selling fossils from the local cliffs.*

MARY: I don't remember there ever being a time when I weren't out upon beach. Mam used to say the window was open when I was born, and the first thing I saw when they held me up was the sea. Our house in Cockmoile Square backed onto it next to Gun Cliff, so as soon as I could walk I'd be out there on the rocks, with my brother Joe but a few years older to look after me and keep me from drowning. Depending on the time of year, there'd be plenty of others about, walking to the Cobb, looking at the boats, or going out in the bathing machines, which looked like privies on wheels to me. Some even went in the water in November. Joe and me laughed at them, for the swimmers come out wet and cold and miserable, like dunked cats, but pretending it was good for them. [5]

Here is another example from a contemporary text. This dialogue attempts to mirror the rhythm of spontaneous speech on the written page by including hesitations, partial phrases, abrupt thought changes, as well as colloquialisms.

CATHERINE WEATE

It gives us the impression that the character is thinking his thoughts through (spontaneously) as he speaks.

> *This extract is dialogue taken from the play* Talkin' Loud *by Trevor Williams. Carl grew up on a London estate, became a celebrity boxer then fell into a life of crime. Here he explains how the fighting started.*
>
> CARL: The man that prowls the estate like he owns it. Him and his dog, keeping us in check. The man we all wanna take out. I do, me little Carl. One day when he's got no dog wid him, one of my spars decides to say something. Next thing I'm on the floor. My spars run off and left me and I'm there on the floor not knowing what's happened. And down there I swear I hear something. Like nothing I've ever heard, like all the thoughts in my head got words for them all at once. It's drilling through my skull louder and louder like…God's thunder or…then I'm on him thumping him, lick after lick. He can't touch me now cos all I'm hearing is…laughter from thunder. I beat him, beat him bad but the words all gone now, just calm and sweet. Next day I'm somebody, the yout' that's mashed down big man. He can't look at me again and everyone else is looking at me different. That's the start. [6]

For some actors, this makes it easier. They can tap into these speech rhythms quite quickly. For other actors it is more difficult. Because these rhythms might be very different to their own rhythms the text becomes a stumbling block. They cannot speak it aloud without tripping themselves up. Finding the character then becomes complicated.

There are a whole different set of concerns when writing has been constructed in a more formal manner (perhaps long stretches of descriptive narrative). Some actors will find this easier as there is a more logical pattern to follow. Others may find it more difficult because it is less like rhythmical speech. These actors may not be used to reading (in their heads) material such as this outside of the rehearsal room so their brains are unfamiliar with the composition. Here are examples of more formal descriptive passages of writing.

The following three extracts of descriptive narrative are taken from *The Children's Book* by A.S. Byatt.

Extract 1

The Exhibition could be seen as a series of paradoxes. It was gigantic and exorbitant, covering 1,500 acres and costing 120 million francs. It attracted 48 million paying visitors, took over four years to build and included the elegant new Alexander III Bridge, arching over the Seine, the glass-roofed Grand Palais, and the pretty pink Petit Palais. But it had the idiosyncratic metaphysical charm of all meticulous human reconstructions of reality, a charm we associate with the miniature, toy theatres, puppet booths, doll's houses, oilskin battlefields with miniature lead armies deployed around inch-high forests and hillocks. It had the recessive pleasing infinity of the biscuit tin painted on the biscuit tin. [7]

Extract 2

So they went into the dark, leather-scented shop, and Elsie sat on an upholstered chair, with Herbert Methley kneeling on one side of her and the shoe-shop boy on the other, bringing more and more shoe-boxes from his store behind his counter. Methley stroked her feet as she inserted them carefully into black shoes and brown shoes, shoes with little heels and shoes with punched trimmings, and serviceable brogues. He was uncannily accurate about which shoes would prove to fit her feet comfortably, rejecting those that were too heavy, and also those that might prove to pinch. He made her walk in the shoes, and turn her body round so that he could see from all angles, and asked where the tips of her toes reached, and whether her heels scrubbed. It was oddly intimate. [8]

Extract 3

The rain blew chill and horizontal across the flat fields and liquefied the mud, and deepened it, so that movement was only possible along duckboard planks – the 'corduroy' road, laid across it. The men at the front crouched in holes in the ground and the holes were partly filled with water, which was bitterly cold, and deepening. The dead, or parts of the dead, decayed in and around the holes, and their smell was everywhere, often mingled with the smell of mustard gas, a gas which lay heavily in the uniforms of the soldiers, and was breathed in by nurses and doctors whose eyes, lungs and stomachs were damaged in turn, whose hair was dyed mustard yellow. [9]

Each of these extracts possesses different formalised, rhythmic demands, dependent on the meaning and mood that is being conveyed. The first extract describes the Paris Exhibition of 1900 and includes some factual information; the second is set in a shoe shop and provides us with a glimpse of a private, personal scene; whilst the third extract features strong, evocative images from trench warfare.

It is important that actors familiarise themselves with all types of writing so that their brains and mouths can keep up with different rhythmic patterns. Therefore, they need to spend time reading as many different types of writing as they can, outside of the rehearsal room, silently in their head *and* speaking it aloud.

2. RHYTHM IN WRITING: ANALYSING THE ELEMENTS

Writers create rhythm in their prose by choosing particular words and images, deciding on an order for these words and images, using punctuation creatively, varying the length of clauses and sentences, and, structuring their paragraphs into specific shapes. In most cases, the patterns they've created on the page mirror the progression of their thoughts. As we read through these patterns silently, we 'hear' different rhythms in our head.

- **Paragraphs**
  - Writers organise their thoughts into units on the page (paragraphs).
  - Paragraphs mean that a writer can subdivide the main focus of the writing into separate sections in order to clarify the meanings and emotions they wish to convey. A little like stepping stones, making their way to a final point or conclusion.
  - Paragraphs always start on a new line and often have the first few words indented on the page. Sometimes a line space is inserted between paragraphs for extra clarity.
  - The start of a new paragraph usually marks a change in thought progression. The end of a paragraph usually marks the point when a thought has been sufficiently developed. Paragraphs, at their climax, often prepare the way for the paragraph that follows.

- ○ Separate paragraphs are also used to quote the continuous words of a speaker.
- ○ Short paragraphs create succinct, concise, sharp, direct thoughts. Longer paragraphs allow the writing to flow so that an idea can be developed more fully. Most writers will use a combination of shorter and longer paragraphs to vary the rhythmic value of their writing.

This extract is taken from the short story, A Serious Talk by Raymond Carver. Burt and Vera are no longer together: Vera has a new boyfriend. However, she invites Burt over at Christmas to see the children and give his gifts. She has warned that he can't stay long because her boyfriend and his family will be arriving shortly for dinner. Notice how Carver varies the size of his paragraphs. In fact, one paragraph is so small that it only contains a single, short, bald, sentence. It rhythmically marks the moment when Burt is left all alone.

Vera served sodas, and they did a little talking. But mostly they looked at the tree. Then his daughter got up and began setting the dining-room table, and his son went off to his room.

But Burt liked it where he was. He liked it in front of the fireplace, a glass in his hand, his house, his home.

Then Vera went into the kitchen.

From time to time his daughter walked into the dining room with something for the table. Burt watched her. He watched her fold the linen napkins into the wine glasses. He watched her put a slender vase in the middle of the table. He watched her lower a flower into the vase, doing it ever so carefully.

A small wax and sawdust log burned on the grate. A carton of five more sat ready on the hearth. He got up from the sofa and put them all in the fireplace. He watched until they flamed. Then he finished his soda and made for the patio door. On the way, he saw the pies lined up on the sideboard. He stacked them in his arms, all six, one for every ten times she had ever betrayed him. [10]

- **Sentences**
  - Writers organise their paragraphs into smaller units (clauses and sentences).
  - A sentence is usually defined as a grammatically complete group of words (often containing a subject, verb and object) beginning with a capital letter and ending with a full stop, exclamation point or question mark.
  - A clause is usually defined as a group of words that contains a subject and a verb and forms part of a sentence. There may be a number of clauses within the one sentence.
  - Too many sentences with the same construction can be boring so writers use different types of sentences to express their thoughts. Here are some examples:
    - A simple sentence contains a subject and a verb and expresses a complete thought.
    - A compound sentence contains two independent clauses joined by a coordinator (such as '*and*' or '*so*'). For example: *I went to buy a tomato and the shop wasn't open today.* The two clauses are called 'independent' because they could stand alone and still make sense.
    - A complex sentence contains an independent clause, which is joined by one or more dependent clauses. There will be a subordinator (such as '*because*', '*although*', '*since*', '*when*') or a relative pronoun (such as '*that*', '*which*'). When a subordinate starts a complex sentence (such as '*when*') then a comma is required at the end of the dependent clause. For example: *When he cleaned the car, he scratched the windows.* The first clause is dependant, the second is independent.

o   Rhythm is created by the construction and length of these sentences, creating a particular drive and energy. A writer may use short, simple phrases or sentences to suggest immediacy and directness or long complicated sentences to strengthen evaluation or reflection.

This extract is taken from the novel, The Slap by Christos Tsiolkas, describing the key moment in the novel when the child, Hugo, is slapped by Harry. Notice how Tsiolkas varies the length of his sentences. They become shorter and sharper as the slap occurs, drawing extra attention to the moment.

The boy's face had gone dark with fury. He raised his foot and kicked wildly into Harry's shin. The speed was coursing through Hector's blood, the hairs on his neck were upright. He saw his cousin's raised arm, it spliced the air, and then he saw the open palm descend and strike the boy. The slap seemed to echo. It cracked the twilight. The little boy looked up at the man in shock. There was a long silence. It was as if he could not comprehend what had just occurred, how the man's action and the pain he was beginning to feel coincided. The silence broke, the boy's face crumpled, and this time there was no wail: when the tears began to fall, they fell silently. [11]

- **Punctuation**
    o   Punctuation helps writers to organise their thoughts into paragraphs, sentences and clauses, by dividing up the writing into manageable chunks.
    o   Punctuation provides readers with a visual aid that clarifies the sense of the text as they read silently in their heads.
    o   On the page, it takes the form of a mark, sign or symbol (as opposed to a letter of the alphabet or a word).
    o   Different types of punctuation have different time values (even if we are reading in our head and not speaking aloud). For example, commas create a shorter interruption than full stops, providing space between one thought and the next.
    o   There are very specific rules for the use of punctuation – far too many to outline here – but there is also quite a bit of room for creativity. In other words, there are times when writers have an opportunity to choose how they use punctuation in their writing (sometimes even deciding to break the rules).

CATHERINE WEATE

o   Writers can choose to use punctuation to create a rhythmic effect. For example, if a writer decides to use a lot of punctuation, breaking up his/her thoughts into very small units, then the rhythm may become abrupt, spiky and pointed (depending on the words they've used and the thoughts they want to get across).

This extract is taken from the novel, True History of the Kelly Gang by Peter Carey, a fictional autobiography of the life of Ned Kelly, the outlawed Australian bushranger, who was hanged at the age of 25. Carey has used very little punctuation throughout the novel and is grammatically 'creative', creating a style similar to the only surviving letter actually written by Ned Kelly. This not only establishes an authentic voice but also allows the text to flow, particularly in action scenes. However, it also means that the reader has to work a little harder to clarify the meaning.

Hall raised his revolver he snapped 3 of 4 caps but the Colt's patent refused the gun would not fire. When I heard the snapping I thought I were a dead man I stood until Hall came close the pistol shaking in his hand. I feared he would pull the trigger again so I duped and jumped at him and caught the revolver with one hand and himself by the collar with the other.

It were only then he cried out the mare were stolen and he were arresting me for horse stealing. I did not believe him and I tripped him and let him take a mouthful of dust I could of done worse but were bound to keep the peace. Hall still had his gun but I had learnt a thing or 2 in Beechworth Gaol and I kept him rolling in the dust until we got to the spot where Mrs O'Brien were erecting brush fencing outside the hotel and on this I threw the big cowardly policeman. I chucked him on his belly and I straddled him and rooted both spurs into his thighs. He roared like a big calf attacked by dogs and I got his hands at the back of his neck and tried to make him let the revolver go but he stuck to it like grim death to a dead volunteer.

He called for assistance to some men who were looking on I dare not strike any of them on account of my bond. These men got ropes tied around my hands and feet and then the great cowardly Hall smote me over the head with his 6 chambered Colt.[12]

- **Word/Image**
  - Writers choose their words carefully in order to create particular images, ideas, thoughts and emotions in the mind of the reader. The sounds and syllables that help form these words will have an effect on the rhythmic pattern of the writing as well, reinforcing the image, thought or emotion that the writer is trying to convey. For example:
    - If writers choose to use a series of words that contain short vowels and/or only have a single syllable, then the writing may become sharp and direct.
    - If writers choose to use a series of words that contain long vowels and/or have a number of syllables, then the writing tends to flow more smoothly.
  - The type of words a writer chooses to use can also have an effect on the rhythm. Lots of verbs and active words will pace up the text. Lots of passive words may slow the tempo down.
  - How writers choose to order their words in a clause or sentence is important to the rhythm as well. Sometimes they may leave a key word that contains an important point to the end of the clause or sentence, creating suspense: sometimes they start with a key word to signpost the important point. Either way this changes the rhythm of the writing.

This extract is taken from the novel, The Kite Runner *by Khaled Hosseini, which tells the story of Amir, who grows up in Kabul. Here, he describes the moment before a traditional kite fight. Notice how Hosseini uses active words to create movement, excitement and anticipation. The fact that most of these active words are more than one-syllable ('-ing' words) also helps to drive the text forward.*

I had never seen so many people on our street. Kids were flinging snowballs, squabbling, chasing one another, giggling. Kite fighters were huddling with their spool holders, making last-minute preparations. From adjacent streets, I could hear laughter and chatter. Already, roof-tops were jammed with spectators reclining in lawn chairs, hot tea steaming from thermoses, and the music of Ahmed Zahir blaring from cassette players. [13]

This extract is taken from the short story Tricks *by Alice Munro, published in* Runaway. *Notice how the single-syllable words in 'And her purse was not there' pull the reader up sharply. This abrupt rhythmic change contrasts with the fluidity of the swan and the restaurant dream. The last two sentences incorporate many single-syllable words (like the repeated 'no'), some short vowels (like the repeated 'i' sounds in 'ticket' and 'lipstick') and some hard consonants (like the repeated 'k' in 'ticket', 'lipstick' and 'comb'), which reinforce a blunt feeling of loss.*

Last year, she saw *Antony and Cleopatra*. When it was over she walked along the river, and noticed that there was a black swan — the first she had ever seen — a subtle intruder gliding and feeding at a short distance from the white ones. Perhaps it was the glisten of the white swans' wings that made her think of eating at a real restaurant this time, not at a counter. White tablecloth, a few fresh flowers, a glass of wine, and something unusual to eat, like mussels, or Cornish hen. She made a move to check in her purse, to see how much money she had.

And her purse was not there. The seldom-used little paisley-cloth bag on its silver chain was not slung over her shoulder as usual, it was gone. She had walked alone nearly all the way downtown from the theater without noticing that it was gone. And of course her dress had no pockets. She had no return ticket, no lipstick, no comb, and no money. Not a dime.[14]

3. SPEAKING TEXT ALOUD: PHRASING AND PAUSING

When we speak text aloud, we often use sentences, clauses and punctuation as markers for our oral phrasing and pausing. However, it's important to note that written punctuation should only be used as a guide because it doesn't always coincide with oral punctuation (phrasing and pausing). There are times when writers use punctuation to make grammatical sense of a clause and/or sentence where there wouldn't be a pause in spontaneous speech. Take, for example, Single-Word Introductions. When a clause starts with words such as *oh, yes, no, well,* there is usually a comma placed after them in written text. However, we tend not to separate them out into a separate phrase with a pause in speech (*Oh, I'm not sure about that* or *Well, don't do it*). Likewise, there are times when a writer hasn't used punctuation (there is no grammatical need) but a pause is required to make sense of the text for a listener.

This is one reason why we tend to use longer sense-groups when we are reading aloud or speaking texts from memory and shorter sense-groups when we are speaking conversationally. The other reason for this is because we tend to know what we're going to say next when reading aloud or speaking somebody else's words, whereas in conversational speech we might not necessarily know where we are headed so our brain needs to break up the information into smaller, more manageable chunks.

Playwrights who write informal speech rhythms into their text, often use written punctuation that coincides with oral punctuation and shorten sense-groups to give the impression of spontaneous speech. Harold Pinter is a particular master of it.

This extract is dialogue taken from the play Betrayal *by Harold Pinter. Jerry is talking to Emma, with whom he is having a long-term affair. The text is broken up into small sense-groups marked by written punctuation in the rhythm of spontaneous speech. This helps give us the illusion of a real character, living in the moment, as well as emphasising Jerry's sense of discomfort about how their relationship has changed over time.*

JERRY: You see, in the past. . .we were inventive, we were determined, it was. . .it seemed impossible to meet. . . impossible. . .and yet we did. [15]

Another problem can occur when we are trying to synchronise our sense-groups and our breath-groups (see Chapter 1). In spontaneous speech, this is an organic process whereby we create a number of sense-groups (marking them with short pauses) before we come to the end of a breath-group (where there is space to take a longer pause and, therefore, a breath). In this way, our bodies can synchronise with our brains in order to maintain the flow of our spoken information as well as provide us with enough oxygen to live comfortably.

When we read aloud or speak somebody else's words, we are using a rhythm different to our own so the organic and unconscious nature of this process is interrupted and we can find ourselves running out of breath before there is an appropriate place/space to breathe. Therefore, finding the rhythmic flow of somebody else's words is just as important as building up breath capacity for an actor. You can build up enormous reserves of lung capacity but if your body and brain and mouth are rhythmically out of sync then you may still run out of breath before the end of the breath-group.

SUMMING UP: THE PITFALLS

- Avoid pausing at every written punctuation mark. Instead, think in sense-groups as you speak, not in written text.

- Avoid breathing at inappropriate points (where there isn't the space or time to do so, destroying rhythmic flow and sense). Instead, know where you are headed in the text so that your body knows how far it has to go before it can get to the end of the breath.

- Avoid lengthening out sense-groups beyond what is used in spontaneous speech. Instead, think about your listener and group the thoughts into more manageable chunks.

4. SPEAKING TEXT ALOUD: STRESSING

When we speak spontaneously in our native speech patterns, word stress and connected speech stress come naturally to us. When we read aloud or speak a text from memory, we are required to use stress that may be unfamiliar to us, rhythmically. Therefore, a number of problems can occur.

As we've already learnt, English stress is formed by a combination of extra breath energy, a lift in pitch and a lengthening of sound, which is placed on the strong syllables of a word that we wish to make prominent for the listener. If we don't want to commit fully to the meaning and emotion of the text (for a variety of reasons, including fear, nervousness, lack of understanding or insufficient preparation) then we will pull back on the breath energy, limit the lift in pitch and not lengthen the sound as much as is needed. This means that we barely stress at all, lightening the weight of the stresses across each phrase. Because stress helps create the intonation pattern, this ends up flattening the tune, effectively communicating nothing in particular to the listener.

The opposite can occur as well. In an attempt to sound interesting or in our eagerness to get the message across, we can over-stress. This means putting too much breath energy into each stressed syllable and lengthening the sounds too far. It creates a heavy, plodding effect that can work against the meaning and emotion of the text, again, communicating nothing much in particular.

Sometimes we use stress inappropriately, stressing syllables that would not normally be stressed in spontaneous speech. This makes us sound like we are speaking writing, rather than lifting the words off the page and bringing them to life. The most common example is 'a', as in '*there was **a** report on the news about it*' or '*we need to conduct **a** survey*'. Instead of using a neutral schwa (see Chapter 1), the full weight of the sound is used – '*ay*' – which devalues the word following it and holds up the rhythmic flow. Stressing '*a*' is regularly used by news presenters, who read from autoscript teleprompters, and, politicians, who have learnt a speech prepared by someone else and haven't yet made the words their own.

Another example is when readers or speakers of memorised text stress pronouns inappropriately. There are very few instances where pronouns are stressed in spontaneous speech (check out the exceptions in Chapter 1); however, speakers often emphasise them in the process of delivering text. For example: '*It doesn't suit **me***' instead of '*It doesn't **suit** me*'.

We've already learnt that the nucleus is key to the way in which we stress across a phrase (see Chapter 1). Sometimes, when we are reading aloud or performing text from memory, we place the nucleus on the wrong syllable for the context of the thought. This is an interpretative mistake on the part of the speaker/actor: context hasn't been taken into account. Take, for example, the phrase '*I know this man*'. If we've never heard about the man before (there was no prior mention of him) then perhaps the nucleus should occur on '*man*'. If we've already learnt something about the man in the preceding text then perhaps we need to place the nuclear stress on '*know*'. Context decides where the nucleus occurs in a phrase and has a marked effect on interpretation.

Other problems occur when we read or speak from memory dialogue, direct speech or text that has been written in the first person. In such instances we channel the voice of another person, which must include the idiosyncratic stress habits of their original accent-dialect. Is the character a native or non-native speaker of English? If the speaker is a native speaker of English, are they English, Scottish, Irish, Welsh, American, Canadian or Australasian? If the speaker is

American, are they from New York or Tennessee? If the speaker is English, are they from London or Yorkshire? Word and Connected Speech Stress will need to change accordingly.

SUMMING UP: THE PITFALLS

- Avoid lightening stress too much. Instead, think carefully about what you want to say and fully commit to that as you speak.

- Avoid over-stressing across a phrase. Instead, think carefully about what the specifics are that you want to convey and only use stress to make that distinct.

- Avoid stressing syllables that would normally be neutralised in the flow of spontaneous speech (e.g. 'a'). Instead, think carefully about what you want to say and focus on the key content in the phrase that needs to be stressed.

- Avoid stressing pronouns inappropriately. Instead, think carefully about what you want so say and focus on the key content in each phrase that needs to be stressed.

- Avoid placing the nuclear stress on syllables that distort the true meaning of the text. Instead, think carefully about what you want to say, paying particular attention to context.

- Avoid placing your own cultural and dialectical rhythm onto dialogue, direct speech or first person text (unless the character is very similar to you). Instead, research the way in which your character would use stress as part of their accent-dialect.

5. SPEAKING TEXT ALOUD: PITCHING AND TUNING

Our intonation patterns support meaning and intention. This is usually an unconscious, organic process in spontaneous speech but doesn't always follow through when we try to bring somebody else's words to life. For this reason, we need to be absolutely clear about what the author/character means and feels so that our intonation reinforces it. Of course, extra research should be undertaken if we speak in a different accent-dialect to that of the author/character (just as we discovered for stress). Pitch and tune can change dramatically, depending on where a character is from.

We've already learnt that if a speaker lightens their stress then the tune or intonation pattern tends to flatten. This creates a monotonous effect, divorcing the sound from the sense. Listeners will probably tune out. However, the opposite can occur as well, where a reader exaggerates their intonation pattern, wildly swinging it around. This is particularly true of many adults who come to read children's stories in an attempt to make the text sound 'interesting'. In such instances the speaker comes across as patronising and the sense is distorted.

Speakers often use a repetitive pattern of tunes when speaking text aloud, particularly if there are long passages of descriptive narrative. Instead of making these passages distinct and specific by varying their intonation to the demands of the description, speakers generalise the text with recurring tunes that become meaningless. The most common example is a series of falling tunes that start and finish on exactly the same note, despite differences in meaning.

Key changes can cause difficulties as well. Whenever there is a new point or a major thought change in the text that requires a key change, speakers often start on the same note as the previous point or thought change. This sounds a little bit like a newsreader or priest delivering a sermon (both tend to rely on a limited amount of tunes). Consequently, listeners often find it difficult to maintain attention, focusing on the tune rather than the words.

Whilst on the subject of key changes, parenthesis needs careful consideration in the delivery of written text. We learnt in Chapter 1 that we use a key change to mark parenthesis in our speech (where one thought is interrupted by the insertion of another thought before the speaker/writer returns to the original thought). In writing, this is usually marked by brackets, commas or dashes around the inserted thought. In speech, a key change occurs, indicating to the listener that the thought is an insertion. We often use a lower key for the inserted/parenthetical thought and then return to our original key afterwards.

However, often speakers fail to return to their original key, which can cause confusion for the listener.

SUMMING UP: THE PITFALLS

- Avoid placing your own cultural and dialectical rhythm onto dialogue, direct speech or first person text (unless the character is very similar to you). Instead, research the way in which your character would use intonation as part of their accent-dialect.

- Avoid lightening stress too much, which can flatten an intonation pattern into a monotone. Instead, think carefully about what you want to say and fully commit to that as you speak.

- Avoid exaggerating the range of your intonation patterns so that they become meaningless. Instead, stop trying so hard to be interesting and think carefully about what you need to get across.

- Avoid repeating the same tune over and over again. Instead, think carefully about what you want to say and practise (just as an exercise) starting each phrase on a new note.

- Avoid starting each key change for new points/major thought changes on the same note. Instead, think carefully about what you want to say and practise (just as an exercise) varying these notes.

- Take care with parenthesis so that key changes make sense of the text. As an exercise, treat each one like an aside (where a character moves out of role to speak to the audience and then returns back again). The key changes should automatically follow-through once you start 'moving' the text.

6. SPEAKING TEXT ALOUD: PACING

The pace of our speech varies, depending on the meaning and emotion we want to convey. Again, this is an unconscious, organic process in spontaneous speech but has to be recreated when we want to bring somebody else's words to life. If we are not truly connected to what we are speaking about then we tend to keep at a steady tempo that doesn't necessarily relate to the meaning and emotion within the text. In fact, many teachers/lecturers/directors ask actors to slow down or speed up overall (in keeping with their vision of the play/performance) without realising that variations need to occur within this speed.

Often, when a teacher/lecturer/director says 'act faster' (and, yes, I have heard those actual words used in rehearsal) actors pace up with an increase in volume and pitch. This combination isn't always appropriate and should only be used for extreme emotional moments.

We've already learnt that blurring is a natural rhythmic feature of spontaneous speech because word boundaries only exist in our minds (see Chapter 1). However, when we try to recreate rhythmic blurring for spoken text, problems can occur. In an attempt to sound 'natural', a speaker can over-blur so that general clarity is lost and listeners will struggle to recognise meaning. This is quite common when actors work on camera. On the other hand, in an attempt to maintain clarity, a speaker can over-articulate, losing all sense of blurring: in other words, over-pronouncing each sound, giving them their full isolated weight and so distorting the natural speech rhythm. This often occurs when teachers/lecturers/directors ask actors to 'watch their articulation'.

SUMMING UP: THE PITFALLS

- Avoid remaining at the same pace throughout. Instead, think about the words and images you want to get across and let them dictate variations in pace.

- Avoid playing the combination of fast pace, loud volume and high pitch key unless there are moments of absolute intensity in the text.

Instead (just as an exercise) practise finding a faster pace with a softer volume and a lower pitch key, or, a slower pace with a softer volume and a higher pitch key. Find out what sort of emotions and meanings these combinations convey.

- Avoid over-blurring so that distinct meaning is lost. Instead, work on articulation exercises away from the text. With enough practice, your muscles should maintain precision without you having to think about it in the moment and a clearer speech rhythm should be restored.

- Avoid over-articulating so that blurring (and therefore, rhythmic flow) is lost. Instead, practise articulation exercises away from the text so that you don't have to think about clarity in the moment of speaking. Then, simply go with the tempo and flow of the text, dictated by the meaning and emotion.

7. PRACTICAL WORK

I've spent a great deal of time discussing how speech rhythm and written rhythm operate theoretically: now it's time to introduce some exercises that will help your students arrive at a practical understanding. Their comprehension and confidence can only grow through a hands-on process with you as facilitator. An initial warm-up will ready them for the work to come and practical skill-based work with prose text will build their core knowledge. The reason why we will be using prose in this part of the book is so that your actors can explore the rhythmic values of written text without the overcomplication of character dialogue or direct speech (which will be explored in greater detail in Part Two). In this way they may only need to make minute adjustments to their own voices in order to bring the texts to life, staying within the operating structure of their own accent-dialect.

WARM-UP EXERCISES

Any exploration of text should begin with a warm-up so that your actors can be vocally free, open and flexible for the work to come. There is a detailed and specific chapter on warming up your voice in my book *Classic Voice: Working with Actors on Vocal Style*, which will help you to structure your own warm-ups. In the meantime, try introducing the following exercises. Make sure you teach them in the order they've been listed as each exercise feeds into the next.

A SHORT WARM-UP FOR GENERAL TEXT WORK

Releasing and Breathing

– Ask your actors to sit on the edge of a firm chair. They should give into their weight, through their bottom, without leaning back into the chair or collapsing their spine. Get them to focus on feeling their weight down and their spine lengthening up.

– Now ask them to place their hands on their lower abdomen and gently breathe in and out through the mouth, slowly deepening their intake so they can feel the muscles move beneath their hands (the lower the better). Coach them to start releasing their breath on a long 'fffff' sound, right to the end of their breath stream so they feel the muscles contract, ready for the next intake of breath. After a series of these breaths, move them onto a long 'sssss' sound, followed by a 'vvvvv' sound, then a 'zzzzz' sound. Keep coaching them to 'pour' the sound out of their body.

– Now ask your actors to raise one arm above them, feeling the stretch from the finger tips right down that side of the body. They should then place their other hand on the front of the ribcage they're stretching and move through the 'fffff', 'sssss', 'vvvvv' and 'zzzzz', focusing on the breath moving into that side of the body. When they allow their arm to flop down, one side of their body may feel more open. Get them to repeat the exercise on the other side.

– Now ask them to flop their upper body over onto their knees (so they're upside down), still gently breathing in and out through the mouth, slowly deepening their intake. Because their abdominal muscles will be all scrunched up, the breath should open up the muscles in the back. Coach them to *think/visualise* the breath there, moving into the 'fffff', 'sssss', 'vvvvv' and 'zzzzz'.

– Get them to roll up through the spine back into a sitting position on the edge of their chair (again, thinking their weight down and their spine lengthened up). They should now repeat the original exercise of releasing the 'fffff', 'sssss', 'vvvvv' and 'zzzzz' from their belly. You may find that their breathing is deeper, the sound is more freely released and it carries on for a longer period of time.

Resonating and Stretching the Range

— Whilst still sitting in the chair, ask your actors to gently pat their face and scalp so they become a little bit tingly.

— Now ask them to massage the face gently with their fingertips. Make sure they're very gentle around the sinus area. Humming on 'mmm' or 'ng' (the final sound in 'sing') might help them to open up their resonating spaces.

— Blowing through the lips like a horse will help bring resonant sound forward onto the mask of the face. There has to be a strong supported breath for the exercise to work (breath strength will motivate the lip movement). See if your actors can add vocalised sound to it. There may be someone in the group who has trouble with this (usually because of a weak breath stream). If so just ask them to try it in short spurts or blips. If this is still too difficult then ask them to reconnect back to their breath on an 'fffff' sound. Those that can make it work may find their faces feel 'itchy' afterwards, which is perfect.

— It's very important that you play with the range of your actors' voices in preparation for the work on intonation. Again, ask your actors to blow through their lips like a horse but, this time, starting at the top of their range and gliding through to the bottom. It's useful if they move their finger from a high position to a low position as they make the sound. Now get them to draw some imaginary wavy lines in the air with their finger and, again, let the sound follow the movement. If they are having difficulties creating or maintaining the blowing through the lips then ask them to try these exercises on a hum (lips gently together, back of the tongue dropped).

Articulating Word

— Your actors should still be sitting on the edge of their chair. Time for some text. Give each of them *one* of the following extracts. If you have a large group then use all four pieces but vary them around the room.

— Ask everybody to read through the words silently just to make sense of the meaning. Ask them to silently read through it again, but this time, as if they are reading it aloud in their heads (transferring it into the tempo in which they would speak it aloud).

— Now get them to mouth the words silently to themselves. Speaking is a physical activity and their muscles will need to know exactly what steps they will need to take (in the same way a dancer's body needs to know the steps of a dance). Encourage your actors to really use their lips and tongue, and, feel the length and weight of the words in their mouth.

– Ask them to vocalise the words aloud in their own space and time. As the noise level will increase and you need them to listen back to what they're saying, ask them to cup one hand a couple of centimetres away from their ear and cup the other hand a couple of centimetres away from their mouth so they can focus in on the words. Make sure they don't devoice into a breathy whisper – keep them on their voices.

– Now ask everybody to speak the text aloud but exaggerate the consonant sounds, over-exploring their shape, length and weight. Finally, ask them to speak the words of the text again, focusing on the meaning and forgetting about the previous exercise. They should retain some consonant clarity without having to think about it and an appropriate amount of blurring will occur.

TEXT-BASED EXERCISES

The following texts have been chosen because (a) they're thoroughly good reads, and (b) they provide good opportunities for exploring the elements within spoken/written rhythm. It's a good idea to start by handing out just one extract to each actor (as stipulated in the warm-up) but it would be useful for them to try out the exercises on all four pieces at some stage, given that there are different rhythmic demands in each.

If you are going to try these exercises out in a class/workshop situation then vary the four extracts around the room. Break the group down into smaller units (3-4 people) and let each small group work on the same extract. They can then play around with the exercises together, feeding in new ideas to each other as they work.

EXTRACT 1

Reason for inclusion: This extract contains a descriptive list. It's very easy to fall into a pattern of repeated rhythms rather than bring each image to life specifically.

Taken from the book Red Dog *by Louis de Bernières.*

Red Cat was the boss of all the cats in the Dampier.

He was a ginger tom, big, muscly and mean. He had green eyes and tatty ears, he had a slantways scar on his nose, he had a white bib on his chest, and a tail that was barred in lighter and darker shades. He had great big paws, and when he stretched them out, the claws would spring from their sheaths like curved swords. When he sat on your lap and purred, you could feel the vibration shaking the bones in your head. When you dangled a string in front of him to make him play, you made very sure that your fingers were out of his reach. When he caught a rat, you could hear the crunch of its bones as Red Cat munched it up. When he yowled and wauled at night to attract the lady cats who were the mothers of his kittens, it sounded as though a baby was being tortured to death. When he ate his dinner, he could, if he chose, wolf it almost as fast as Red Dog. Red Cat had never lost a fight.

If Red Cat saw a dog, his policy was to jump on its back, dig his claws in and ride it around the caravan park until it was too tired and terrified to run any more. Then Red Cat would jump off and swipe it across the nose, leaving four parallel scratches that trickled with blood. Then, when the dog rolled over and surrendered with its paws in the air, Red Cat would parade proudly away, the tip of his tale waving with self-satisfaction. More often than not, the dog would not come back to risk this treatment again.

Red Dog liked chasing cats, and had plenty of rake-marks on his snout to prove it. He was a cleverer dog than most, but like most dogs he had never really managed to learn that a dog always loses a fight with a cat, because eventually the cat will turn round and lash out. Red Dog was an optimist, and he sincerely believed that just because a cat runs away to begin with, then he must already be the winner. Anyway, it was such fun doing the chasing that, as far as he was concerned, it was worth getting scratched for it later.

When Red Dog explored the caravan park for the first time, he walked around the back of Nancy's allotment, and came face to face with Red Cat. Red Dog was overcome with excitement, and leaped forward to give chase.

He stopped a fraction of a second later, however, because Red Cat did not turn and run. He sat quite still, and opened his mouth and hissed. Red Dog was impressed by the pink tongue and the two rows of shiny white teeth.

He pounced again, but still Red Cat did not run. This time he flattened his ears and hissed again, even louder. Red Dog began to have doubts, but he couldn't resist having another try. Red Cat stood up, arched his back, flattened his ears and hissed, even more loudly. Red Dog sat back on his haunches, puzzled by this unusually valiant cat, but something made him have another try. Red Cat bushed up his tail, made the fur stand up on his back, flattened his ears, hissed, and hit out so quickly that Red Dog didn't even know what had happened until his nose began to sting and drip with blood.[16]

EXTRACT 2

Reason for inclusion: This extract contains a major key change and wide variation between intonation patterns from before the wave breaks to after the wave has broken. An interesting mix of short/long sentences and short/long paragraphs heightens the drama as well.

Taken from the novel Nation *by Terry Pratchett.*

The cloud was reaching up to the top of the sky, but there was something new down at sea level. It was a dark grey line, getting bigger. A wave? Well, he knew about waves. You attacked them before they attacked you. He'd learned how to play with them. Don't let them tumble you. Use them. Waves were easy.

But this one was not acting like the normal waves at the mouth of the reef. It seemed as though it was standing still.

He stared at it and realised what he was seeing. It looked as if it was standing still because it was a *big* wave a long way off, and it was moving very fast, dragging black night behind it.

Very fast, and not so far away now. Not a wave, either. It was too big. It was a mountain of water, with lightning dancing along the top, and it was rushing, and it was roaring, and it scooped up the canoe like a fly.

Soaring up into the towering, foaming curve of the wave, Mau thrust the paddle under the vines that held the outrigger and held on as –

– It rained. It was a heavy, muddy rain, full of ash and sadness. Mau awoke from dreams of roast pork and cheering men, and opened his eyes under a grey sky.

Then he was sick.

The canoe rocked gently in the swell while he added, in a small way, to what was already floating there – bits of wood, leaves, fish…

Cooked fish?

Mau paddled over to a large *bebe* fish, which he managed to drag aboard. It had been boiled, right enough, and it was a feast.

He needed a feast. He ached everywhere. One side of his head was sticky with, as it turned out, blood. At some point he must have hit it on the side of the canoe, which wasn't surprising. The ride through the wave was an ear-banging, chest-burning memory, the kind of dream you are happy to wake up from. All he'd been able to do was hold on.

There had been a tunnel in the water, like a moving cave of air in the roll of the giant wave, and then there had been a *storm* of surf as the canoe came out of the water like a dolphin. He would swear it had leaped in the air. And there had been singing! He'd heard it for just a few seconds, while the canoe raced down the back of the wave. It must have been a god, or maybe a demon…or maybe it was just what you hear in your head as you half fly and half drown, in a world where water and air are changing places every second.[17]

EXTRACT 3

Reason for inclusion: There are major changes to pace, pitch and intonation within this extract. Some long sentences with the occasional parenthesis help us to see the way in which Mr Fisher's inner thoughts flow.

Taken from the short story Fule's Gold *by Joanne Harris, published in* Jigs *and* Reels.

It had been a disappointing term at St. Oswald's. For most of the boys in 3F, creative writing was on a par with country dancing and food technology on the cosmic scale of things. And now, with Christmas around the corner and exams looming large, creativity in general was at its lowest ebb. Oh, he'd tried to engage their interest. But books just didn't seem to kindle the same enthusiasm as they had in the old days. Mr Fisher remembered a time – surely not so long ago – when books were golden, when imaginations soared, when the world was filled with stories which ran like gazelles and pounced like tigers and exploded like rockets, illuminating minds and hearts. He had seen it happen; had seen whole classes swept away in the fever. In those days, there were heroes; there were dragons and dinosaurs, there were space adventurers and soldiers of fortune and giant apes. In those days, thought Mr Fisher, we dreamed in colour, though films were in black and white, good always triumphed in the end, and only Americans spoke American.

Now everything was in black and white, and though Mr Fisher continued to teach with as much devotion to duty as he had forty years before, he was secretly aware that his voice had begun to lack conviction. To these boys, these sullen boys with their gelled hair and perfect teeth, everything was boring. Shakespeare was boring. Dickens was boring. There didn't seem to be a single story left in the world that they hadn't heard before. And over the years, though he had tried to stop it, a terrible lassitude had crept over Mr Fisher, who had once dreamed so fiercely of writing stories of his own; a terrible conviction. They had come to the end of the seam, he understood. There were no more stories to be written. The magic had run out.[18]

EXTRACT 4

Reason for inclusion: The sparsity of Carver's prose provides a challenge in itself. One thing happens, then another, then another. There is little explanatory detail which creates a short, sharp, choppy rhythmic style.

Taken from the short story The Bath *by Raymond Carver, published in* What We Talk About When We Talk About Love. *Carver fans will know that he rewrote this story in 1983, adding in a great deal more detail and changing its name to* A Small Good Thing.

Monday morning, the boy was walking to school. He was in the company of another boy, the two boys passing a bag of potato chips back and forth between them. The birthday boy was trying to trick the other boy into telling what he was going to give in the way of a present.

At an intersection, without looking, the birthday boy stepped off the curb, and was promptly knocked down by a car. He fell on his side, his head in the gutter, his legs in the road moving as if he were climbing a wall.

The other boy stood holding the potato chips. He was wondering if he should finish the rest or continue on to school.

The birthday boy did not cry. But neither did he wish to talk anymore. He would not answer when the other boy asked what it felt like to be hit by a car. The birthday boy got up and turned back for home, at which time the other boy waved good-bye and headed off for school.

The birthday boy told his mother what had happened. They sat together on the sofa. She held his hands in her lap. This is what she was doing when the boy pulled his hands away and lay down on his back.

Of course, the birthday party never happened. The birthday boy was in the hospital instead. The mother sat by the bed. She was waiting for the boy to wake up. The father hurried over from his office. He sat next to the mother. So now the both of them waited for the boy to wake up. They waited for hours, and then the father went home to take a bath.

The man drove home from the hospital. He drove the streets faster than he should. It had been a good life till now. There had been work, fatherhood, family. The man had been lucky and happy. But fear made him want a bath.

He pulled into the driveway. He sat in the car trying to make his legs work. The child had been hit by a car and he was in the hospital, but he was going to be all right.[19]

Make sure your students have warmed up prior to embarking on the following exercises and activities. They can be used on any of the extracts but it's a good idea for your students to try them out on just one extract before moving onto the next.

CATHERINE WEATE

EXERCISES AND ACTIVITIES

Phrasing and Pausing

– After your students have finished speaking the text for the first time (see 'A Short Warm-Up for General Text Work') ask them to speak it aloud again but, this time, concentrating on feeling the different weights and lengths of the clauses and sentences in their mouths. In this way, they will start to see (and hear) where the variations occur.

– Armed with this knowledge, they now need to focus on verbal word grouping: finding out where the sense-groups start and finish. Ask them to speak the text aloud again, slowly, sense-group by sense-group. They should break where it makes sense for the thought to break, not necessarily where there is punctuation (although this can be used for guidance).

– Now they need to speed up and find the natural flow of the text. This will help them to find out where the end of breath-groups occur (i.e. breathing where there is enough time in the meaningful flow of the text to breathe). Breath pauses can be marked, if necessary, with a pencilled slash between the words on the page. In this way, their bodies will get to know where they are headed and their breath rhythm should start to work in tandem with the text's rhythm.

– Pull out some difficult phrasing examples from each of the extracts for your students to focus on in particular. They should be particularly tricky for establishing breath rhythm. Here are some suggestions:

Extract 1
Red Cat bushed up his tail, made the fur stand up on his back, flattened his ears, hissed, and hit out so quickly that Red Dog didn't even know what had happened until his nose began to sting and drip with blood.

Extract 2
It must have been a god, or maybe a demon…or maybe it was just what you hear in your head as you half fly and half drown, in a world where water and air are changing places every second.

Extract 3
Mr Fisher remembered a time – surely not so long ago – when books were golden, when imaginations soared, when the world was filled with stories which ran like gazelles and pounced like tigers and exploded like rockets, illuminating minds and hearts.

Extract 4
The birthday boy was trying to trick the other boy into telling what he was going to give in the way of a present.

Stressing

– Pull out a clause or a series of clauses from each of the extracts. Ask your students to speak them aloud a number of times then mark where they believe the stresses occur, particularly the nucleus. Remind them that phrasing/pausing will help define where the nucleus occurs. Because this is an artificial exercise, be careful that they don't over-stress. A good antidote to this is to get them to try the clause(s) at different speeds as well as (semi-spontaneously) to a friend/partner. Once they've finished, ask them to place the clause(s) back into the text, speaking the whole extract aloud. Has the context changed the positioning of their original stressing? Here are some suggestions of sample clauses to use for this exercise:

> Extract 1
> *Red Cat stood up, arched his back, flattened his ears and hissed, even more loudly.*
>
> Extract 2
> *It looked as if it was standing still because it was a big wave a long way off, and it was moving very fast, dragging black night behind it.*
>
> Extract 3
> *For most of the boys in 3F, creative writing was on a par with country dancing and food technology on the cosmic scale of things.*
>
> Extract 4
> *At an intersection, without looking, the birthday boy stepped off the curb, and was promptly knocked down by a car.*

– Now ask your students to speak the whole text through again, giving a little more weight into the stresses (particularly the nuclear stresses). Then, ask them to forget the exercise and speak the text through for the sense. They should retain the sense of the stress without resorting to over-stressing.

Pitching and Tuning

– Ask your students to speak their extract again but this time exaggerating intonation, moving all over their pitch range and working against the meaning of the text. They should then forget the exercise and just speak the text for sense and emotion. This will help widen pitch ranges and make intonation patterns more flexible.

– It's also important that your students avoid repeating the same intonation pattern (over and over again, like a broken record) on each new phrase. One way of breaking this habit is to get them, as they read, to begin each breath-group on the same note as the previous breath-group finished on. This is particularly good for opening up intonation on lists in long descriptive passages. Those students who are working on Extract 1 should try it out on the first large paragraph that describes Red Cat.

Of course, this isn't the way intonation should be used (it needs to be much more dependent on the sense and emotion). For this reason, the exercise should be completed and then forgotten. But in the doing, patterns of repeated tunes will be broken and your students can then focus, more precisely, on communicating the text.

– Choose some phrases from the extracts and ask your students to speak them aloud a number of times, really listening to the intonation patterns they've used. If they have trouble, then ask them to record it. They should then try using the same intonation pattern on sounds (e.g. 'dededede' or 'lalalala') or numbers instead. This will open up their ears and secure the pattern for them. It's a particularly useful exercise for intonation on dramatic or emotional description.

> Extract 1
> *Red Dog was overcome with excitement, and leaped forward to give chase.*
>
> Extract 2
> *It was a mountain of water, with lightning dancing along the top…*
>
> Extract 3
> *Oh, he'd tried to engage their interest.*
>
> Extract 4
> *He fell on his side, his head in the gutter, his legs in the road moving as if he were climbing a wall.*

– Extract 2 has the largest and most dramatic key change (before and after the wave) but Extracts 1, 3 and 4 have minor key changes as well. Ask your students to find them and practise marking those changes. They should take the time to experiment, trying the key change on different notes in order to discover what works best for the sense and emotion. Then, they will need to think about combining this pitch change with pace and volume changes as well.

– Choose some examples of parenthesis from each of the text extracts and ask your students to experiment with their technical delivery (extract 3 has the most). Remember that they will need to change pitch, pace and volume for the inserted thought and then return to the original note, pace and volume when the main thought continues on. Here are some examples of parenthesis to use for this exercise. The inserted thoughts are marked in bold.

> Extract 1
> *When he ate his dinner, he could, **if he chose**, wolf it almost as fast as Red Dog.*
>
> Extract 2
> *One side of his head was sticky with, **as it turned out**, blood.*

Extract 3

*Mr Fisher remembered a time – **surely not so long ago** – when books were golden...*

Extract 4

*At an intersection, **without looking**, the birthday boy stepped off the curb, and was promptly knocked down by a car.*

Pacing

– There are a number of pace changes throughout these extracts. Your students will have found some of them already when focusing on key changes and parenthesis (see above). However, there are many more to be found and experimented with (lengthening and shortening syllables for the desired effect). Get them to practise them out of context before placing them back into the extract as a whole.

8. REVISITING THE BASICS

Here are some important points to remember from this chapter:

- Rhythm in writing is created through word/image choice, punctuation, sentence length and paragraph structure (i.e. the patterns on the page).

- Writing is usually more formal than speech, however, playwrights who create dialogue and novelists who include direct speech or write in first-person prose often use contractions, hesitations, fillers, elisions, assimilations and dialect on the written page to provide a degree of vocal realism.

- The rhythmic combination of phrasing, pausing, stressing, pitching, tuning and pacing are necessary to lift writing off the page for an audience. Actors need to focus on word/image and meaning/emotion without superimposing their own idiosyncratic speech rhythms onto the text. Practical exercises with a technical focus can be a useful way of drawing out textual rhythms and finding deeper levels of meaning.

NOTES

1. Stephen, P. (1994), *The Language Instinct*. London: Penguin Books, p. 264.

2. Wells, J.C. (2009), *English Intonation: An Introduction*. Cambridge: Cambridge University Press, p. 7.

3. Stephen, P. (1994), *The Language Instinct*. London: Penguin Books, p. 224.

4. Wertenbaker, T. (1988), *Our Country's Good*. London: Methuen, p. 53.

5. Chevalier, T. (2009), *Remarkable Creatures*. London: Harper Collins, p. 59.

6. Williams, T. (2004), *Talkin' Loud*. London: Oberon Books, p. 77.

7. Byatt, A.S. (2010), *The Children's Book*. London: Vintage, p. 245.

8. Ibid., p. 287.

9. Ibid., p. 605.

10. Carver, R. (1993), 'A Serious Talk', in *What We Talk About When We Talk About Love*. London: Harvill Press, p. 90.

11. Tsiolkas, C. (2008), *The Slap*. Crows Nest, N.S.W. : Allen and Unwin, p. 39.

12. Carey, P. (2001), *True History of the Kelly Gang*. London: Faber and Faber, p. 161.

13. Hosseini, K. (2003), *The Kite Runner*. London: Bloomsbury, p. 53.

14. Munro, A. (2005), 'Tricks', in *Runaway*. New York: Chatto and Windus, p. 239.

15. Pinter, H. (1986), *Betrayal*, in *Plays Four*. London: Faber and Faber, p. 198.

16. Bernieres, L. (2001), *Red Dog*. London: Secker and Warburg 2001, pp. 77-79.

17. Pratchett, T. (2009), *Nation* London: Corgi, p. 20.

18. Harris, J. (2004), 'Fule's Gold', in *Jigs and Reels*. London: Doubleday, pp. 41-42.

19. Carver, R. (1981), 'The Bath', in *What We Talk About When We Talk About Love*. London: Harvill Press, pp. 39-40.

SUGGESTED READING

Jones, D. ([1918] 1989), *An Outline of English Phonetics: Ninth Edition.* Cambridge: Cambridge University Press.

Marshall, L. (2008), *The Body Speaks.* London: Methuen Drama.

Pinker, S. (1994), *The Language Instinct.* London: Penguin Books.

Sharpe, E. & Haydn Rowles, J. (2007), *How to Do Accents.* London: Oberon Books.

Tannen, D. (2007), *Talking Voices: Repetition, Dialogue, and Imagery in Conversational Discourse.* Cambridge: Cambridge University Press.

Weate, C. (2009), *Classic Voice: Working with Actors on Vocal Style.* London: Oberon Books.

Wells, J.C. (2009), *English Intonation: An Introduction.* Cambridge: Cambridge University Press.

PART TWO:
REALISTIC DRAMA

CHAPTER 3: JOURNEYS, DEMANDS AND CHALLENGES

1. CONTEXT

Dramatic realism emerged in the mid-nineteenth century, where theatre sought to make sense of the world by placing the realities of human existence at its centre.

Belief in 'humanism' had become widespread amongst the European intelligentsia. Previously at the core of Renaissance thinking, humanism re-surfaced in the eighteenth century alongside an increase in scientific achievement. Humanists believed that human endeavour, rather than the machinations of a religious deity, was the dominant driving force in the world. This placed greater emphasis on individual responsibility: humans, it was argued, are capable of changing their circumstances, of forging their own fate, rather than relying on a god or gods to create happiness.

The movement was helped along by Darwin's theory of evolution, published in *On the Origin of Species* in 1859; Marx's argument for a stateless, classless society with a more equal distribution of wealth, published in *The Communist Manifesto* in 1848; and, later still, Freud, who placed human desires, needs and motivations at the centre of his psychoanalytical theory.

Playwrights emerged who were interested in exploring real people struggling through real lives in a contemporary setting. This was in direct contrast to the heightened romanticism that was evoked in previous plays. It was the private, everyday moments that came to the fore, rather than the public moments of the state. Ultimately, a focus on human behaviour led to the exploration of how an individual dealt with the threats, restrictions and opportunities placed on them by society as part of their everyday lives. The internal mechanisms of character, their relationship to others and their relationship to the world around them became, therefore, key elements in realist drama. This meant that audiences were watching plays with characters they recognised, settings that seemed familiar and issues that were relevant to their own lives.

2. REALISM vs. NATURALISM

Many theorists and practitioners use the terms 'realism' and 'naturalism' interchangeably. But what is the difference between them? And how does one define a realistic play as opposed to a naturalistic play?

(a) THE BROAD BRUSHSTROKES OF DRAMATIC REALISM

- *Humanistic.* Realist drama is based on the idea that humans can drive their own destiny rather than relying on a god or gods to determine their fate.

- *Socially motivated.* Realist drama often appears when the values of a society are being questioned so playwrights usually have a political viewpoint and show characters reacting with or against society: this tends to focus on class experience – nineteenth century realist drama leans towards middle-class experience, whilst twentieth-century realist drama inclines more towards working-class experience.

- *Content driven.* Realist playwrights create truthful, believable *content* in their stories but do not necessarily challenge the *form* in which these stories are presented so the conservative three-act play remains dominant, although there are exceptions: in three acts playwrights could establish character and setting, create complications and then build to a crisis or climax that might or might not be resolved.

- *Protagonist centric.* Content is usually centred around an individual whose predicament pinpoints the political viewpoint of the playwright: in twentieth-century realist drama the protagonist is often socially marginal so that the playwright can comment on class issues.

- **Current.** Stories and their characters exist in the period in which the playwright lives, providing audiences with recognisable features of their own lives, including up-to-date colloquial speech and everyday language.

- **Physically detailed.** Playwrights recreate realistic environments for their characters, simply removing the 'fourth wall' in a story so that the audience can be swept into the world of the play – ordinary rooms with the cluttered minutiae of everyday existence are commonplace and playwrights often include detailed stage directions so that actors can find their way around the stage.

- **Theatricalised.** Realist playwrights do not present a completed snapshot of life as we know it, they decide on certain elements of a story or a character's life that will best promote their own political agenda or particular ideology with an audience, thereby creating the theatrical illusion of reality.

(b) THE BROAD BRUSHSTROKES OF NATURALISM

- **Photographic snapshot.** Although realist drama creates a detailed physical environment, naturalistic drama goes one step further, providing intricate truthful detail to create a snapshot of life as we know it without compromise.

- **Environmentally overwhelming.** Realist drama usually shows characters reacting with or against their environment; in naturalistic drama the environment often overwhelms the people who live in it giving the impression of less social concern.

Barry Reckord, in the foreword to his 1963 play *Skyvers*, describes the artistic differences between realism and naturalism much more succinctly. His play follows five teenage boys in their last week of school. Every aspect of the world he creates is bleak – the education system, the school, the teachers and the students. The boys speak in colloquial London dialect, which widens the divide between them and the teachers (it's almost as if they are speaking completely different languages). Reckord's thoughts on artistically constructing a reality (or theatricalising reality) for his audience are enormously useful in the ongoing quest to define realism and naturalism.

> Although I have avoided any sort of artificially heightened language and kept within the range of cockney idiom, the language in this play is clearly invented. Schoolboys, on the whole, don't talk in the way I make them talk. Usually their talk is less interesting. But if the play sounds real it is because I've got down what these boys do in fact think and feel, although often they are too inarticulate to say it. This, to me, is the imaginative process – the whole business of writing…
>
> This is a very different thing from documentary or naturalism, which I would define as the capturing of surface reality. Writers always want to get away from the surface. They want to reflect the underbelly of feeling, and in the attempt always have to face the crucial question of speech. They all have to heighten speech, but how? Do they heighten within the common idiom, or do they go outside it, use phrases that people would never say, *artificially* heighten? This is in one form or another the underlying debate in recent drama. What is heightened speech? It is an old question, but absolutely crucial. For me, heightened speech is ordinary speech which is at the same time perceptive… The best word for this is realism, and realism should never be confused with naturalism. The distinction is useful. Naturalistic speech is ordinary speech which is commonplace. Realistic speech sounds like ordinary speech but it has to be invented to convey an area of experience which is not on the surface.[1]

3. THE RISE OF REALISM: PLAYS AND PLAYWRIGHTS

The rise of dramatic realism followed quite different routes through England, America and Australia, despite relatively similar beginnings. This section maps the journey of dramatic realism from the late nineteenth century to the mid-1960s.

(a) EARLY INFLUENCES

Europe spawned a range of realistic playwrights in the mid- to late nineteenth century, who significantly influenced the development of dramatic realism in the English-speaking world. In particular: the Norwegian, Henrik Ibsen (1828-1906) and the Russian, Anton Chekhov (1860-1904).

Henrik Ibsen was influenced by a nationalist trend in Norwegian art and literature that developed in the 1840s. His first play, *Catiline* (1849) was rejected by the theatrical establishment, who were more interested in imitations of popular Danish plays. However, by 1850, a permanent theatre was created in Bergen, and for the first time actors who were native speakers of Norwegian (rather than Danish) were employed. Ibsen worked as a stage instructor and resident author at the aptly named Norwegian Theatre, working closely with the artistic director. Here he wrote plays on Norwegian historical and literary themes although they weren't particularly successful. However, he gained a great deal of theatrical experience and, in 1857 he left Bergen to work at the Christiana Theatre. The next few years were difficult ones for him financially, the theatre was closed with bankruptcy and he received little other work or recognition. Self-imposed exile was the answer and for many years he spent much of his time in Italy and Germany. The first of his plays to receive some critical acclaim was *Brand* (1865). However, it is *Peer Gynt* (1867), *A Doll's House* (1879), *Ghosts* (1881), *An Enemy of the People* (1882), *The Wild Duck* (1884), *The Lady from the Sea* (1888), *Hedda Gabler* (1890), *The Master Builder* (1892), *Little Eyolf* (1894) and *John Gabriel Borkman* (1896) for which he is best remembered.

Ibsen's legacy, controversial at the time, was to question the moral framework of society through the commonplace worlds of ordinary middle-class people. For example, *A Doll's House* examines the dissatisfaction of women within the institution of marriage by focusing on the relationship between a lawyer and his wife, whilst *Ghosts* sheds light on traditional bourgeois taboos such as infidelity, illegitimacy, incest, venereal disease and euthanasia. *Ghosts*, in particular, was considered quite shocking and received damning reviews across Europe. Ibsen's response was to write *Enemy of the People*, where an individual stands alone on the moral high ground, despite the opinions of the collective group. A doctor discovers that a public bath, the sole draw for tourists to a town, is being polluted by the local tannery. He expects veneration for his discovery but instead is vilified by the local community and labelled 'an enemy of the people.'

> The majority is never right. Never, I tell you! That's one of those community lies that free thinking men have got to rebel against! Who form the majority – in any country? The wise or the fools? I think we'd all have to agree that the fools are in a terrifying, overwhelming majority all over the world![2]

Ibsen peppered his plays with real people in real worlds who faced real problems. He hoped that this would, inevitably, open the eyes of his audiences and provoke social change.

Anton Chekhov was a doctor, short story writer and playwright, most famously known for *Ivanov* (1887), *The Seagull* (1896), *Uncle Vanya* (1899), *The Three Sisters* (1901) and *The Cherry Orchard* (1904). He lived at a significant time in Russian history when the old aristocratic way of life was disappearing and a new technological age (with revolutionary murmurings) was in the process of being born: serfs were freed soon after his birth and the Bolshevik revolution occurred only thirteen years after his death. Consequently the characters he created tended to be stuck between an old and new world (sometimes tragically, often comically).

The Seagull helped launch the Moscow Art Theatre, which was founded by Constantin Stanislavski and Vladimir Nemirovich-Danchenko as a reaction against the more melodramatic theatrical styles in Russia at the time. The play was a runaway success and heralded a new type of naturalistic theatre.

Chekhov tends to be labelled more of a naturalist than a realist, for a number of reasons. First, he had a naturalistic eye for detail which helped him create highly specific and detailed environments for his characters. Secondly, rather than impose dramatic moments onto these environments, he simply allowed his characters to live their lives through them. This meant that they were often overwhelmed by the world surrounding them and frustratingly, unable to grow and move forward through it. Thirdly, therefore, unlike realism, social change wasn't an option as his characters couldn't be motivated into action. Chekhov didn't feel the need to explain, moralise or champion a cause; he just wanted to represent human life truthfully with all its significance and insignificance, its sense of expectation and despair.

(b) ENGLAND

The most popular forms of English theatre, in the first half of the nineteenth century, consisted of entertainments for the working classes, such as music hall burlesques, freak shows and visual spectacles (often involving performing animals). Drama was melodrama or adapted versions of Shakespeare, operating as vehicles for the star performers of the day. However, by the middle of the century the situation started to shift, for a variety of reasons: Queen Victoria became interested in theatre, providing an all -important air of respectability; the Theatres Act was passed, allowing legitimate drama to be performed at places other than Covent Garden and Drury Lane, as long as they first gained approval from the Lord Chamberlain; newspapers started to print more detailed critical reviews of theatre performances; and, railways increased, giving the suburban middle classes greater access to city theatres. Consequently, in the second half of the century the amount of London theatres tripled, new playwrights emerged (such as Tom Robertson, Henry Arthur Jones and Arthur Wing Pinero) and melodrama was replaced with gentility, sentimentality and conservative morality that appealed to the respectable middle-class family. An early proponent of realism within the confines of this world was **Tom Robertson**, actor, director and playwright. He aimed to reproduce the characters, settings and speech of the middle-class drawing-room set. His issue-based dramas, such as *Caste*, where class prejudice was raised (albeit in a melodramatic way), were also new to the English stage. However, what stunned audiences the most was the realistic dramatic business that Robertson instituted on stage, such as making and pouring a real cup of tea.

Into this middle-class theatrical idyll, stepped Ibsen, and the press exploded with moral outrage. His plays were translated for the English stage by the

Scottish drama critic, William Archer, and championed by an Irish critic, **George Bernard Shaw**. Shaw, in fact, gave a talk on Ibsen in 1890 to the Fabian Society (a socialist group who sought change through reform rather than revolution) of which he was a member. The following year, *Ghosts* received its first London performance and the press reacted in abject horror so Shaw turned his talk into a book: *The Quintessence of Ibsenism*. In it he discusses a review by Clement Scott of *The Daily Telegraph*:

> He accused Ibsen of dramatic impotence, ludicrous amateurishness, nastiness, vulgarity, egotism, coarseness, absurdity, uninteresting verbosity, and "suburbanity", declaring that he has taken ideas that would have inspired a great tragic poet, and vulgarized and debased them in dull, hateful, loathsome, horrible plays. This criticism, which occurs in a notice of the first performance of *Ghosts* in England, is to be found in *The Daily Telegraph* for the 14th March 1891, and is supplemented by a leading article which compares the play to an open drain, a loathsome sore unbandaged, a dirty act done publicly, or a lazar house with all its doors and windows open. Bestial, cynical, disgusting, poisonous, sickly, delirious, indecent, loathsome, fetid, literary carrion, crapulous stuff, clinical confessions: all these epithets are used in the article as descriptions of Ibsen's work. "Realism," said the writer, "is one thing; but the nostrils of the audience must not be visibly held before a play can be stamped as true to nature." [3]

Ibsen's work influenced Shaw enormously. Like Ibsen, he used his plays to highlight particular social problems, working to expose late nineteenth- and early twentieth-century society for its injustice, hypocrisy and prudery. He was particularly interested in equal rights for women and created female characters who eschewed traditional roles, uncovered double standards, celebrated their sexuality and/or fought their own causes. The most memorable include: Mrs Warren in *Mrs. Warren's Profession* (1893), Candida in *Candida* (1894), Lady Cicely Waynflete in *Captain Brassbound's Conversion* (1899), Barbara Undershaft in *Major Barbara* (1905), Lina Szczepanowska in *Misalliance* (1909), Hesione Hushabye in *Heartbreak House* (1917) and Joan in *Saint Joan* (1923).

Shaw used a variety of techniques to expose the ills of society. First, he inverted traditional morals through comedy so that audiences were made aware of a problem by either laughing at themselves or an element of society that was clearly (to him) ludicrous. Secondly, he used debate to argue a point: his characters would often sit around and talk for long periods of time, denying his audience the opportunity of seeing any action or visual spectacle and forcing them to engage with real arguments. *Getting Married, Misalliance* and *Heartbreak House* in particular, rely on lengthy debate to get their points across and it is through them that Shaw has been credited with inventing the 'play of ideas'. Thirdly, he used shock tactics, creating characters and stories that were not acceptable to the society of the time. In fact, the Lord Chamberlain refused to grant public licences to three of Shaw's plays so that they could only be seen in private performances held by the playwright himself. In particular, *Mrs Warren's Profession* was considered horribly immoral because Mrs Warren made the practical career choice of brothel madam and likened marriage to a form of prostitution.

Not all of Shaw's plays follow this formula consistently (he did occasionally deviate to undertake some experiments with dramatic form) but it is, ultimately, what he has become best known for. He even manages to satirise his style (and the reaction of the critics to it) in *Fanny's First Play* (1911). Fanny and her father invite a group of theatre critics to watch a performance of Fanny's play (presented anonymously) and comment on what they see. We are introduced to the critics before the play starts, watch the play with them and then hear their pronouncements at the end. It happens to be a 'play of ideas' and the critics all argue about who might have written it. Although Shaw is rejected his work is commented upon in the same way as it was in real theatre reviews of the period.

VAUGHAN: Well, at all events, you can't deny that the characters in this play were quite distinguishable from one another. That proves it's not by Shaw, because all Shaw's characters are himself: mere puppets stuck up to spout Shaw. It's only the actors that make them seem different.

BANNAL: There can be no doubt of that: everybody knows it. But Shaw doesn't write his plays as plays. All he wants to do is to insult everybody all round and set us talking about him.

TROTTER (*Wearily.*): And naturally, here we are all talking about him. For heaven's sake, let us change the subject.[4]

It seems that realism was a little ahead of its time: not particularly favoured by audiences and critics or, indeed, other playwrights. In the first half of the twentieth century, most audiences didn't want to go to the theatre to see the nitty-gritty of real life represented on stage: their world was being shattered by economic depression and war. Understandably, they wanted and needed escapism. So typical theatrical fare included: comedy of manners (following the formulas of eighteenth-century dramas), costume dramas (set in a specific period in history), light operetta and musicals (either home grown or imported from Broadway) or the country house play/drawing-room drama. The theatre critic, Kenneth Tynan, savaged the latter format mercilessly:

> Its setting is a country house in what used to be called Loamshire but is now, as a heroic tribute to realism, sometimes called Berkshire. Except when someone must sneeze, or be murdered, the sun invariably shines. The inhabitants belong to a social class derived partly from the playwright's vision of the leisured life he will lead after the play is a success – this being the only effort of imagination he is called upon to make. Joys and sorrows are giggles and whimpers: the crash of denunciation dwindles into 'Oh, stuff Mummy!' and 'Oh, really Daddy!'. And so grim is the continuity of these things that the foregoing paragraph might have been written at any time during the last thirty years.[5]

Theatrical experimentation did exist in the first half of the twentieth century but not in realism: new types of verse drama and groundbreaking absurdist drama appeared during this period (discussed in Part 3 of this book). If plays did explore social or state problems, they did so within the confines of a particular social set, such as dramas by J.B. Priestley and Terrence Rattigan. It wasn't until the mid-fifties that playwrights started to experiment with realism. The first of these was **John Osborne** with his play *Look Back in Anger* in 1956, which paved the way for what is now called 'New Wave' theatre.

Once again, dramatic realism became the focus at a time when questions were being raised about the state of society. Despite conservative political stability, the development of post-war affluence and a boom in consumer goods, society in the 1950s was divided along a number of lines: age versus youth, British culture versus American culture (American cinematic misfits such as James Dean and Marlon Brando 'spoke' to British youth), middle-class conservatism versus radical dissent (the Suez crisis protests and the nuclear disarmament campaign); and, black versus white (the Notting Hill race riots). Some of these divisions were products of the 1944 Education Act, which had given greater access to secondary education and, consequently, higher education. Therefore, youth in the 1950s were perhaps better educated and more politicised than their working class counterparts in previous generations. *Look Back in Anger* was born out of this. Jimmy Porter and his wife Alison live in a one-room apartment in the English Midlands. Jimmy is an intelligent but angry young man, who runs a market sweet stall. He grew up working class, educated himself and is now restless and frustrated with his life. His wife Alison comes from a privileged middle-class environment and Jimmy is constantly taunting her about it. The contempt Jimmy feels for Alison's family is often transferred onto Alison herself and it is then that the acerbic attacks become personal.

The play was performed for the first time by the English Stage Company, newly established in 1955 at the Royal Court Theatre with George Devine as artistic director and Tony Richardson as his assistant. Initially, the plan was to house an international programme there, with a particular focus on Brecht or the direction of plays in a Brechtian style. However, their priorities soon shifted towards a writers' theatre with the emphasis on encouraging, supporting and providing opportunities for new contemporary dramatists who otherwise would be required to compromise their artistic and political integrity in the commercial theatre world of the West End. *Look Back in Anger* was the third play of the season but their first experiment in this new writers' theatre.

The play itself was groundbreaking for a number of different reasons. First, the setting (squalid domesticity in all its grimy detail was on show, giving rise to the term 'kitchen-sink drama'); secondly, the characters and their raw emotions (such as the 'angry' post-war youth challenged by a world that didn't understand him); and, thirdly, the language (blunt vocabulary, contemporary rhythms and politicised rhetoric). However, the play still relied on a conservative three-act format with neatly arranged act-endings and character entrances, carefully orchestrated, if obvious, repetition (the positioning of both Alison and Helena at the ironing board, for example) and even the use of a stock-device – the loss of a child – to develop the action, heighten the emotional impact and enable reconciliation to occur between the two principal characters. The fact that the play's conventions were immediately readable meant that critical attention was more easily focused around the issues that it seemed to be raising.[6]

The reviews of the time were mixed but, whatever they thought of the play itself, critics still recognised its importance:

A first play by an exciting new English writer – 27-year-old John Osborne – burst on the London stage last night. It is intense, feverish, undisciplined. It is even crazy. But it is young, young, young. (John Barber, *Daily Express*)

His (Porter's) is genuinely the modern accent – one can hear it no doubt in every other Expresso bar, witty, relentless, pitiless and utterly without belief…don't miss this play. If you are young, it will speak for you. If you are middle-aged, it will tell you what the young are feeling. (T.C. Worsely, *New Statesman*)[7]

However, audiences weren't in a rush to see it and box office takings were poor. It didn't really take off until an eighteen-minute extract of the play was broadcast on the BBC and it reached a wider audience. Nowadays, *Look Back in Anger* feels quite dated as the issues it raises are less relevant and its shock value has been outstripped by theatre it later inspired.

But inspire new playwrights it did. **Arnold Wesker** was one of them, entering a playwriting competition organised by the *Observer* with *The Kitchen* (1957) set in a restaurant kitchen where thirty workers, such as chefs and waitresses, go about their daily chores. However, it was his trilogy of plays in 1958, consisting of *Chicken Soup with Barley*, *Roots* and *I'm Talking About Jerusalem,* that seem more closely linked to the dramatic realism of Osborne. These plays, like *Look Back in Anger*, are set in working-class domestic interiors with characters who react against the world in which they live.

Chicken Soup with Barley tells the story of the East End Jewish Kahn family from 1936 to 1956 against a volatile political environment and a growing disillusionment in communist ideology. In Act One the characters are drawn into the battle of Cable Street when Oswald Moseley's fascists march through the Jewish East End community but by Act Three the Soviet invasion of Hungary provides a backdrop to their disenchantment and failure to survive as a family. *Roots* picks up the story of Beatie Bryant, the girlfriend of Ronnie Kahn (the son in *Chicken Soup*) who visits her family's Norfolk farming community, where she enters into a process of self-discovery and finds her own voice. *I'm Talking About Jerusalem* traces the story of Ada Kahn (the daughter in *Chicken Soup*) and her husband, Dave, who move to Norfolk to live a more simple life off the land but their experiment fails and they are forced to return to the city. In this way, Wesker shows how the post-war government missed the opportunity to create a new 'Jerusalem'.

Wesker drew heavily on his own background for his writing. Like the Kahn's he was born into a family of working-class Jewish immigrants in the East End of London. He'd spent time as a furniture maker, lived on the land in Norfolk and completed National Service in the RAF. He drew on this latter experience in *Chips With Everything* (1962) following the experiences of a group of Air Force conscripts during basic training in the 1950s. There is more visual action in this play than many other realist plays of the period as we watch physically awkward men turned into physically competent militants. However, the main focus centres around a class struggle: conflict occurs when recruits from different parts of society are thrown into a hierarchical world that demands social conformity.

Another playwright inspired by the new realist movement of the 1950s was **Shelagh Delaney**. Of working-class origins, Delaney produced her landmark play *A Taste of Honey* (1958) at only eighteen years of age. Set in Salford, Lancashire, where she grew up, *A Taste of Honey* tells the story of a seventeen-year-old working-class girl called Jo. Jo's relationships with her mother (the sexually promiscuous Helen who deserts her), Jimmy (the black sailor with whom she has a brief affair and becomes pregnant) and Geoffrey (her homosexual friend who becomes her only 'family') allow

Delaney to explore issues of gender, sexual orientation, class and race. However, it also provided an opportunity to explore the language and rhythms of the northern working classes.

A Taste of Honey was first performed by Joan Littlewood's Theatre Workshop at Theatre Royal Stratford East (a theatre group committed to radical socialism and keen to perform to working-class audiences although their usual preference was for non-realistic staging) and was later transferred to London's West End. Her second play *The Lion in Love* was completed two years later but she didn't write another play for almost twenty years. The writer Jeanette Winterson has commented that her reviews 'read like a depressing essay in sexism'[8] and suggests that Delaney was not given the support that other playwrights received from the British theatrical establishment during this period in order to develop her craft and continue writing for the theatre.

It was only natural that this new type of social realism gravitated towards the big screen, where its gritty realism could be explored in greater detail. In the late 1950s, Tony Richardson (director at the Royal Court) and John Osborne set up **Woodfall Films** in order to create the film version of *Look Back in Anger*. Financing was finally secured from America when Richard Burton was cast as Jimmy Porter. Woodfall then produced a series of films set in the industrial north of England: collaborating with Shelagh Delaney on the film version of *A Taste of Honey* (1961) and the fiction writer, Alan Sillitoe, on *Saturday Night and Sunday Morning* (1960) and *The Loneliness of the Long Distance Runner* (1962). Vic Films also focused on the northern working-class experience with *A Kind of Loving* (1962) and *Billy Liar* (1963). Most of these films depict characters living in bleak and melancholy conditions, using the vocabulary and speech rhythms of the north: a new experience for audiences at the time.

Television wasn't to be left out and in 1960 **Granada Television** took the risk of producing thirteen episodes of *Coronation Street*, set in a fictional northern town, using local northern actors speaking in northern dialect. Few thought it would last the run, yet its enduring appeal assured its place on English television where it has been running for over fifty years.

In the 1960s another groundbreaking playwright emerged from the Royal Court writers' group: **Edward Bond**. Born into a north London working-class family, Bond lived through the London bombings as a child, which helped shape his views on terror and violence. He left school early and educated himself whilst working in factories. After national service in the British Army he submitted plays to the Royal Court and was invited to join their writers' group, which included other notable playwrights such as Arnold Wesker and John Arden. In his first two plays – *The Pope's Wedding* (1962) and *Saved* (1965) – association with the Royal Court helped Bond develop a realistic style, bordering on naturalistic. His characters were overwhelmed by their environments with little chance of transformation or escape.

The Pope's Wedding was staged at one of the Court's Sunday night writers' evenings and explores tensions in a declining rural community where boredom festers into aggression. *Saved* was presented in a private members' club at the Royal Court to bypass the Lord Chamberlain's office who would not licence it for public performance. Set in a bleak South London, blighted by economic depression, the characters have nothing to do and nowhere to go and eventually drift into violence. Shocked audiences often shouted out loud during performances, critics described it as 'obscene' and 'sadistic', organisations were set up to try and withdraw it from the stage. The scene that caused the most offence involved a baby being stoned to death in its pram by a group of boys. Given the uproar it caused, the authorities felt they had no choice but to act and members of the Royal Court management were arrested on a technicality. Although the Royal Court lost its case in court, the event did spark debate about censorship, eventually closing the Lord Chamberlain's office in September 1968. Bond's *Early Morning* (1967) was the last complete play in England to be banned before the censor's departure.

However, *Saved* wasn't just trying to shock audiences out of their complacencies. The theatre critic, Michael Billington sums up its significance neatly:

> *Saved* was a landmark play in many ways. It proved that the kind
> of violence accepted without demur in classical drama could

be applied to a contemporary issue. It showed that inarticulate characters were as worthy of dramatic attention as anyone else. It also exposed the absurdity of theatrical censorship and helped to promote its demise.[9]

And although Bond uses *Saved* to comment on violence as a product of social inequality and deprivation, it isn't all gloom and doom. The play's title provides the clue. Salvation is possible: change society and you can change the human spirit.

(c) AMERICA

Realism was already stylistically established in the late nineteenth-century American novel, with writers such as Henry James and Mark Twain, however, American theatre lagged behind. Audiences flocked to: popular entertainments (including minstrel shows, vaudeville shows, circuses, burlesques and extravaganzas); adaptations from French, English and German melodrama (such as *The Hunchback, Richelieu*); English comedies from the eighteenth century (such as *The School for Scandal* and *She Stoops to Conquer*); Irish plays (such as *The Shaughraun* and *The Colleen Bawn*); and, Shakespeare (starring famous classical American actors).

Home-grown material was harder to find. This was partially because it was cheaper for theatre managers to pirate European productions than buy a play from an American dramatist, and, partially because it was thought that audiences preferred more 'sophisticated' fare from Europe. American playwrights did exist but many had to work as theatre managers in order to stage their own material. Changes to the International Copyright Law in 1891 however, meant that European material became expensive so theatre managers were forced to reconsider local material. The type of plays presented can be divided into six categories:

- The one-character vehicle (written for a star actor's portrayal of a specific character: for example, Joe Jefferson who played Rip Van Winkle for fifty years).

- The play based on American history, legend or literature (for example, *The Legend of Sleepy Hollow* or *Uncle Tom's Cabin*).

- The melodrama (popular for its use of stock characters, familiar plots and extravagant staging).

- The local-colour play (a comedy or melodrama set in a specific American locale – usually urban – with American characters: for example, *Poor of New York* by Dion Boucicault and *Under the Gaslight* by Augustin Daly).

- The Western play (a comedy or melodrama with a Western flavour: for example, *Davy Crockett* by Frank Hitchcock).

- The modern-life play (commenting on American social conditions but with a melodramatic flavour: for example, *Divorce* and *Pique* both by Augustin Daly and *The Banker's Daughter* by Bronson Howard).

The local-colour play and the modern-life play provided American audiences with their first glimpses of realistic subject matter. However, nearly all plays of the period were visually staged with realistic detail: some effects were quite spectacular and included full size railroad trains and ice floes on stage. The producer/director/playwright, **David Belasco**, was a particular master at these effects and his most famous examples include detailed meals with real food cooked on stage, an operational sawmill and simulated rain. On one occasion he took apart a room in a real boarding house (even cutting away the walls) and then reassembled it on stage. Henry James found this realistic detail extreme and suggested that Americans would soon see 'Romeo drink real poison and Medea murder a fresh pair of babes every night.'[10]

Henry James, **Mark Twain** and **William Dean Howells** (authors, critics and realists) recognised that theatre in the late nineteenth century had developed the raw materials of realism but wanted to see plays that were realistic in subject matter, plot and character as well. For this reason they all tried writing their own plays in the genre, none of which were particularly successful. However, a turning point in the movement came when Ibsen's plays were staged for the first time in America, and, when a local playwright, James A. Herne, wrote *Margaret Fleming*.

Needless to say, Ibsen was received in a similar manner in America as he had been in England. Some critics, such as Howells, were excited by his plays, others, such as William Winter, were morally outraged. Winter, in fact, likened Ibsen to a disease that infected the theatre. However, it is **James A. Herne** who is now credited with initiating home-grown realism in the American theatre. His early plays (some of them devised in collaboration with David Belasco) included stock plots and characters of the period but *Margaret Fleming* was different. Here his focus shifted to social determinism and the sexual double standards that existed for men and women in the society of the time, which scandalised audiences in Boston where it was first staged. Despite some melodramatic moments, Herne created characters with emotional depth and a world more real than had previously been seen in an American play. As the new century dawned, Ibsen's and Herne's work inspired other playwrights and characters started to discuss social problems much more openly, settings became more realistic, plots less predictable, characters more psychologically complex and dialogue started to capture more of the idiosyncratic rhythms of everyday American speech.

In 1915, a group of amateurs, led by George Cram Cook, set up the **Provincetown Players**, staging plays in a small theatre on a wharf in Provincetown, Massachusetts. Their objective was to create a community of artists who would collectively create and perform new American plays, taking risks with emerging playwrights, unknown actors and untried designers. The careers of Susan Glaspell (Cook's wife) and **Eugene O'Neill** were successfully launched through their experimental processes. The wharf itself provided the group with a particularly vivid setting. Although described as a theatre, in reality it was nothing more than a rickety fishing shack suspended over the sea. When O'Neill's play *Bound East for Cardiff* (set on a sailing ship in a storm) was first performed, the elements surrounding the theatre provided a realistic framework for the story being presented on stage. Large windows and skylights continually reminded the audience of the elements surrounding them. Rain could be heard on the roof and, when the tide was in, the sea could be felt, spraying up through gaps and knotholes in the floorboards. However, in late 1916, the group moved to New York City in order to provide an alternative to the superficial material being presented on Broadway. They survived there until 1929, becoming an economic casualty of the Great Depression.

Eugene O'Neill was the son of the popular actor, James O'Neill, who specialised in performing romantic melodrama. O'Neill, who often accompanied his father on tour, voiced his dislike of the genre, despite the fact that he later included melodramatic elements into some of his realist plays (defending himself by saying 'in moments of great stress life copies melodrama'[11]). His influences were firmly grounded in European realism from seeing American productions of Ibsen and Shaw. The early plays were essentially realistic, such as *Anna Christie* (1920) but were followed by an expressionistic period, where he experimented with anti-realistic devices (such as masks, choruses and audience asides) to heighten or distort the behaviour of his characters. In his later years, O'Neill returned to social realism in plays such as *The Iceman Cometh* (1939) and *Long Day's Journey Into Night* (1941), which effectively combined detailed worlds and complex characters to create the illusion of real life on stage.

His settings were full of meticulous detail, more naturalistic than realistic. Whilst working on *Long Day's Journey Into Night,* he created an entire floor plan of the Tyrone house, including windows, doors and furniture in rooms that would never be seen on stage. Characters evolved in much the same way, through detailed mapping of their psychological conflicts. As far back as 1922 he was quoted in an interview as saying:

> Sure I'll write about happiness if I can happen to meet up with that luxury, and find it sufficiently dramatic and in harmony with any deep rhythm in life…I don't love life because it's pretty. Prettiness is only clothes deep. I am a truer lover than that. I love it naked. There is beauty to me in its ugliness.[12]

O'Neill received the Nobel Prize for literature in 1936 and Pulitzer Prizes for four of his plays: *Beyond the Horizon, Anna Christie, Strange Interlude* and *Long Day's Journey Into Night*. Despite the awards he had his detractors, who openly made fun of him. He was criticised for the length of his plays (theatres were often forced to schedule dinner breaks for audiences), for characters who made speeches rather than engaging in dialogue and for his distrust of American directors and actors. He expressed this distrust to his friend, the critic and film producer Kenneth Macgowan, whilst contemplating the staging of *The Iceman Cometh*.

> I don't write this as a piece of playwrighting. *They do it. They have to.* Each of them! In just that way! It is tragically, pitifully important to them to do this! They *must* tell these lies as a first step in taking up life again… If our American acting and directing cannot hold this scene up without skimping it, then to hell with our theatre![13]

O'Neill's interest in character motivation was fuelled by Freudian psychology. Freud had visited America and given a series of lectures in 1909 and a number of his publications were translated and published in America around the same time. By the 1920s Freudian psychoanalysis had become a widely accepted theory and O'Neill drew on it when creating character: revealing the inner depths of the human psyche and the external conditions such as family and society that helped to shape it. But he wasn't alone: other playwrights of the 1920s and 1930s were similarly influenced by Freud and the experience of the individual character became the primary focus in many plays of the period. However, audiences were also seeking escapism from economic depression and two world wars so, like England, there were also plenty of comedies, musicals and costume dramas playing to packed houses.

Realistic regional dramas started to appear during this period where characters were formed and conflict was created out of specific rural environments. **Owen Davis**'s play *Icebound*, set in Maine, won a Pulitzer Prize in 1923. **Paul Green** focused on life in North Carolina: *In Abraham's Bosom* was produced by the Provincetown Players and depicted the African American experience in the South, winning a Pulitzer Prize in 1927. **DuBose** and **Dorothy Heyward**'s play *Porgy* eventually evolved into the opera *Porgy and Bess* with music by George Gershwin. Novels set in regional locations were also adapted for the stage, such as Edith Wharton's *Ethan Frome* in 1936 and John Steinbeck's *Of Mice and Men* in 1937. Another type of realism of the period was urban drama, inspired by city life during the Great Depression. Working-class dramas such as **Elmer Rice**'s *Street Scene* (1929), which won a Pulitzer Prize, and **Sidney Kingsley**'s *Dead End* (1936) were both set in outdoor city locations.

Lillian Hellman's dramas were considered gritty and controversial. Her first play, *The Children's Hour* (1934), tells the story of two teachers in charge of a private school for girls who are falsely accused of having a lesbian relationship by a vindictive student. It draws together themes of victimisation, powerlessness and the importance of individual responsibility. Although classified as realism, it does have melodramatic moments, particularly at the end when one of the teachers, ashamed that she might indeed have had sexual feelings for her friend, shoots herself. The play received a long run and an enthusiastic reception on Broadway although its subject matter was considered a little too shocking for a Pulitzer Prize (the theatre critics of the time were so outraged they consequently formed the New York Drama Critics' Circle). However, outside of New York, the reaction was different. Boston and Chicago banned it and, in England, the Lord Chamberlain's office refused to grant it a licence.

Another Hellman success was *The Little Foxes* (1939), which focuses on a Southern family and their corrupt business dealings. This too has melodramatic overtones with revenge, blackmail and murder at its core. In 1946 Hellman produced a prequel to *The Little Foxes*, called *Another Part of the Forest*, which explores the early lives of her original characters, focusing on how events and environment influence their later actions.

However, it was **Clifford Odets** who became known as one of the leading proponents of theatre that dealt with social protest in the 1930s. He started his working life as an actor and was an instrumental member of the Group Theatre in New York, a collective set up by Harold Clurman, Cheryl Crawford and Lee Strasberg in 1931 to create a permanent ensemble committed to performing drama that dealt with political and social issues. Odets' early plays championed the voice of the working classes and he drew inspiration from human perseverance during the economic deprivation of the Great Depression. His most realistic early plays include: *Awake and Sing* (1935) following the story of a Jewish family in New York, *Till the Day I Die* (1935) focusing on the communist resistance against the Nazi party and *Golden Boy* (1937) about the rise of a prize fighter and his struggle between compromising his ideals and what he truly loved in order to gain fame and financial success.

The Great Depression also helped shape the works of **Tennessee Williams** and **Arthur Miller**. They both started writing during the Thirties, a period of massive social change, they both questioned the validity of the American dream and both created isolated individuals fighting for survival within a difficult and confusing world (such as Williams' Blanche DuBois in *A Streetcar Named Desire* and Miller's Willy Loman in *Death of a Salesman*).

Tennessee Williams was born in Mississippi and set many of his plays in the American South. Influenced by Chekhov's *The Cherry Orchard*, he saw that Southern elegance, beauty and civility could not survive in the modern world. His realism was often romantic (with fading beauty, youthful death, redeeming love) and usually poetic (with lyrical, metaphorical, allusive and ambivalent language) but it still packed a punch. It had been shaped by the American cinema (watching films in his youth instead of going to the theatre) and a strongly developed sense of social justice (working on protest plays for a political theatre group in St Louis). 'My interest in social problems is as great as my interest in the theatre…I try to write all my plays so that they carry some social message along with the story.'[14]

His first play to be seen on Broadway was *The Glass Menagerie* (1955), which was well received and ran for 561 performances. His second great success was *A Streetcar Named Desire* (1947), which won a Pulitzer Prize. *Cat on a Hot Tin Roof* (1955) also won a Pulitzer Prize and, controversially, brought Williams' sexuality into the limelight through the character of Brick and questions surrounding the relationship he had with his dead friend Skipper. Despite the contentious material, it was made into a film by MGM in 1958 and was nominated for a number of Academy Awards (although the script was toned down and the homosexual references were muted).

Arthur Miller's concept of dramatic reality was entirely different. If Williams had been influenced by a Chekhovian world, Miller was more interested in the social concerns of Ibsen and Shaw. His plays are crowded with working men and women, who spend their lives trying to survive change but usually failing. He warned against the dangers of capitalism and a corrupted establishment that thrived at the expense of the ordinary individual. He also believed that a collective voice could be far more powerful than an individual one but that the individual must still fight for the good of common man. He voiced his concerns in a conservative post-war world and was, therefore, considered a political activist.

However, this didn't stop his plays from receiving critical approval and box office success. His first major hit was *All My Sons* (1947), which is realistic in content and form and focused on the issue of individual social responsibility. Joe Keller is a small manufacturer who has committed a crime – producing defective aeroplane parts causing the death of twenty-seven aviators during the war – but successfully avoided blame (a little like Bernick in Ibsen's *Pillars of Society*). However, he is forced to confront the issue when his son Chris questions his actions.

Although many of Miller's works present socially real characters, he also experimented with dramatic form (like O'Neill and Williams) producing both epic and expressionistic plays.

Rather than focus on the large social issues of his day, **William Inge** explored the experience of small-town life in America through plays such as *Come Back, Little Sheba* (1950), *Picnic* (1953), *Bus Stop* (1955) and *The Dark at the Top of the Stairs* (1957). The media of the 1950s celebrated small-town America as an ideal: Inge focused on the darker side. His characters were ordinary, empty, lonely, suffocated and frustrated. Many of them wanted to escape their small-town existence but were trapped by their circumstances, their relationships and their aspirations, and, were ultimately forced into making unhappy compromises. Christopher Bigsby in *Modern American Drama* says: 'His was the realist's urge to tell the small truths which accumulate into a larger truth. So, small-town America becomes an image of life itself…'[15]

Born and raised in Independence, Kansas, Inge was considered one of the major new playwrights of the post-war era, alongside Tennessee Williams and Arthur Miller. When *Come Back Little Sheba* was staged, The New York Drama Critics' Circle called him the most promising new playwright of 1950. In 1953 he won a Pulitzer Prize, the New York Drama Critics' Circle Award and the Donaldson Award for *Picnic*. His plays of the 1950s all achieved considerable critical acclaim and substantial box office success, however, unlike his two fellow post-war playwrights, he became unfashionable in the 1960s and his later plays weren't nearly as successful. Inge eventually took his own life in 1973, depressed that he wasn't able to write anymore.

Lorraine Hansberry's *A Raisin in the Sun* was produced on Broadway in 1959. It was a season of firsts: never before had an African American woman staged a play on Broadway let alone won a New York Drama Critics' Circle Award. *A Raisin in the Sun* also launched the careers of a number of black actors and was the first Broadway play to be directed by a black director. In the past, access to the theatre for African Americans had either been prohibited or severely discouraged although there had been a few playwrights who had broken through the barriers to stage their works, such as Langston Hughes, Theodore Ward and Louis Peterson. However, Lorraine Hansberry achieved something more: she brought a socially realistic play about black civil rights to the frontline of American theatre.

Inspired by her family's legal battle against racially segregated housing laws, *A Raisin in the Sun* tells the story of an African American family who receive some insurance money and decide to move to the suburbs in order to escape the life that they will surely face in an inner-city black ghetto. Their choice of a white neighbourhood brings them into conflict with the racist residents who do not want them there. The title of the play comes from a line in Langston Hughes' poem *Harlem*.

Hansberry created a realistic plot with believable characters and wasn't interested in experimenting with dramatic form. However, her version of reality not only defined the African American experience of her time but also looked forward to a more positive future. In a magazine interview she stated: 'The realistic playwright states not only what is, but what can and should be'.[16] Her next play, *The Sign in Sidney Brustein's Window* was less well received and, during its run in 1964, she lost her battle with cancer.

Edward Albee was raised in luxury but struggled to find his place in the world, trying his hand at a variety of jobs as well as writing poetry and novels (unsuccessfully) in his spare time. It wasn't until he was in his thirties that Thornton Wilder suggested he should try writing drama. Albee's plays of social realism, such as *The Zoo Story, Who's Afraid of Virginia Woolf* and

A Delicate Balance are generally thought to be his strongest works. In them he explores the desolate depths of the human psyche through complex moral debate. However, his greatest achievement was in creating plays rich in linguistic inventiveness. They are wordy and static (mostly talk and not much action) but their imaginative word games drew audiences in.

In *Who's Afraid of Virginia Woolf,* George (an Associate Professor in History) and his wife Martha (the daughter of the president of the college) invite over Nick (the new young Biology Professor) and his wife, Honey, for late night drinks after a party. George and Martha engage in relentless drinking and vicious verbal competitions, mostly directed towards each other but sometimes towards their guests. The play opened on Broadway in 1963, winning both a Tony Award and the New York Drama Critics' Circle Award for Best Play. It was also selected by the Pulitzer Prize jury of 1963 but the prize's trustees objected to the play's sexual content and so, in the end, it was decided that no prize would be awarded that year. However, Albee was later vindicated with Pulitzer Prizes for *A Delicate Balance* (1966) and *Seascape* (1975).

Realism rose to the forefront of American theatre much more rapidly than in English theatre for a variety of reasons. First and foremost, Americans were much more interested in the psyche of the inner self, partially fuelled by Freud and partially fuelled by the individual self-interest that was needed to pursue the great American dream. Secondly, born out of this mentality, American actor training became committed, quite early on, to exploring the depths of psychological believability, and this tradition became increasingly difficult to break. And thirdly, the early development of American cinema played its part. Many American playwrights combined their careers with screenwriting in Hollywood. In addition, many realist plays were given the big screen treatment, such as those by Eugene O'Neill, Lillian Hellman, Clifford Odets, Tennessee Williams, Arthur Miller, William Inge, Lorraine Hansberry and Edward Albee. Therefore, in turn, cinematic realism inspired whole new generations of theatre dramatists.

(d) AUSTRALIA

The rise of dramatic realism in Australia was some time in coming. In the late nineteenth/early twentieth century, local playwrights trying to find their own style, form and subject matter were thwarted by the dominance of European and American theatrical fare produced by commercial and repertory theatre companies.

The commercial theatre was run by large companies such as J.C. Williamson's (commonly known as 'The Firm'). They focused on producing popular entertainments that would bring them the greatest financial gain. Most of their programmes were imported from England and America and included melodramas, operas, musical comedies, music hall burlesques, vaudeville shows and pantomimes. Occasionally they produced a serious English or American drama but brought out star actors from the original foreign productions in order to secure good box offices. Productions of local plays were rarer.

The repertory theatre was created to produce dramas that the commercial theatre ignored. They focused primarily on imported drama from Europe and America, including melodramas, farces and drawing-room comedies. A few repertory companies presented plays by European and American realists or popular works by local playwrights but they were atypical. Most repertory theatre productions started life on a conservative London West End stage. The smaller repertory companies in each major city (the Little Theatres) were usually amateur with, initially, poor production values and inexperienced actors.

Local playwrights, therefore, found it difficult to get their works staged and not all their texts have survived. However, it is clear that melodrama was the dominant type of drama used by local playwrights in the late nineteenth/early twentieth century theatre, albeit melodrama set in an Australian locale with Australian characters. Understandably, the common theme was searching for identity within a strange land, whether that be in a bush or outback drama, a gold-rush drama, a convict or transportation drama or a city drama.

The most commonly produced early Australian play was the bush or outback drama, where the central protagonist was not a human being but the land. Dramatic events were drawn out of the forces of nature, such as flood, drought and fire. Character became insignificant in comparison so dramatists tended to create stock character types: hardy pioneers trying to tame the land, loyal homestead wives, dangerous bushrangers and the stereotypical 'blackfella'.

Despite the melodramatic plots and stock characters, playwrights and producers tried to create realistic stage settings. Verandas with a homestead garden and a backcloth of painted scenes from the outback were common. Indoor settings were usually within a bush hut with rough timber furniture and windows through which could be seen more painted scenes of the outback. Rain, pounding on the roof when the drought broke, was customary. Animals were used as well. In 1903, *The Breaking of the Drought* by Arthur Shirley had a live emu wandering across the stage and real crows flew down from above. In 1907, *The Squatter's Daughter* by Bert Bailey and Edmund Duggan had a full flock of sheep on stage as well as laughing kookaburras.

One of the most famous local dramas of the period started life as a series of stories by **Arthur Hoey Davis** (otherwise known as **Steele Rudd**). In 1895 his story *Starting the Selection* was published in a newspaper, where a character called Dad Rudd sets up a small farm near Emu Creek. Rudd turned this story into a book called *On Our Selection*. Nine sequels followed. Their success was due in part to the characters who became household names, the familiarity of the struggle with the land and the broad humour which Australians recognised as their own. In 1912, Bert Bailey and Edmund Duggan adapted *On Our Selection* into a melodrama for the stage. It was a commercial success which led to numerous copies by other playwrights, and, later on, radio and film versions.

Yet this was all still a long way off from a realistic representation of Australian life. Even the commercial staging of Ibsen's *The Doll's House* in 1890 didn't particularly inspire local playwrights. The moralists were outraged of course, but there were also some favourable reviews. 'The Sydney *Bulletin* thought it marked "an epoch in Sydney stage history," and (in the inevitable clamour) that Norah's morals were as proper material for the drama as Lady Macbeth's, Camille's, and Flora Tosca's.'[17] However, Ibsen had very little to do with the white Australian search for identity that was inherent in the local plays of the period. It wasn't until the 1920s that melodramatic plots started to wane and playwrights tried to be more authentic.

The strongest voice for authenticity was that of **Louis Esson**. Born in Edinburgh in 1878, Esson moved to Melbourne with his widowed mother and siblings at the age of three. A trip to Europe as a young adult introduced him to Dublin's Abbey Theatre, the Irish playwright J.M. Synge and the poet and playwright W.B. Yeats, both of whom urged him to create a national drama. Yeats told Esson to 'Keep within your own borders!' and 'If you want to do anything you must regard your own country as the centre of the universe.'[18] Also, 'that in Australia he had the people and the land and that his job was to try to get the right relationship between them.'[19]

Esson's plays explore the themes of working-class urban and bush life. However, his first full-length play *The Time is Not Yet Ripe* (1912) was a political society comedy in the spirit of George Bernard Shaw. His most successful plays were the bush dramas, including the short play *The Drovers* (1923) and full-length play *Mother and Son* (1923). His urban plays focused on a variety of inner-city Melbourne characters, such as the short plays *The Woman Tamer* (1910) and *The Sacred Place* (1912), and the full-length play, *The Bride of Gospel Place* (1926). Despite struggling to find a style of his own, Esson's dramas were a turning point.

Esson also fought hard to create a national theatre and, with **Stewart Macky** and **Vance Palmer**, founded the **Pioneer Players** in 1922. They set up shop in a dreary ex-Temperance Hall in Melbourne and all three founders wrote plays that were performed there, alongside other Australian plays of the period. Unfortunately it wasn't a success: the production values were poor, the actors were unskilled and audiences scarce. It closed in 1926. The final production was *The Bride of Gospel Place* and Esson's comments about one of its performances in a letter to Vance Palmer are telling:

> On the whole we did very well. It was a fairly smooth performance with less prompting than usual, and by good luck we had a satisfactory audience… It was a slow start as usual, not a laugh coming till page 5. We had only two breaks, Joe going out for a plate and not returning, but Frank as Smithy covered it up cleverly, and even Rowe didn't notice it. The second was that the curtain in Act III fell on the screen.[20]

Katharine Susannah Prichard, from Western Australia, had some of her plays performed by the Pioneer Players. She often used the theatre to try out new ideas for her short stories and novels. *Brumby Innes* (1927) is considered her most important drama although it was written for the 1927 *Triad* playwriting competition after the Pioneer Players had folded. Part of the competition prize included having the play staged by 'The Firm' (J.C. Williamson's), however its subject matter was considered far too controversial. *Brumby Innes* waited 45 years for its first production and was finally premiered by the Australian Performing Group and the Nindethana Company (an indigenous company) at the Pram Factory, Melbourne, in 1972.

Brumby Innes confronted taboos such as the white assault on indigenous communities and the volatile nature of relationships between outback men and women. The owner of an outback station, Brumby Innes, maintains his dominance in a difficult environment through brutality and violence. His actions are often shocking (he rapes both black and white women) but he is still presented as an attractive and desirable man. Prichard spent time researching indigenous language and dance from the north-west of Australia, moving aboriginal characters away from the stereotyped and generic 'blackfella'. It was a landmark moment for home-grown dramatic realism and it wasn't even staged.

From the late 1920s to the 1950s, the bush or outback drama turned into the station drama. The original pioneers in bush huts were replaced by settlers with established homesteads so family sagas were common. They struggled against the climate, natural disaster, the banks and children who were trying to escape to the city. Thwarted love stories (where daughters fell for dangerous young men rather than the neighbouring squatter's son) and thrillers (where isolated homesteads were threatened by ghosts or dangerous strangers) were familiar plots to audiences of the period. There were also country town dramas which focused on threats to whole communities such as the harsh environment, city politicians or an outsider who had entered the community.

Military dramas drawn from Australian experiences in the First and Second World Wars appeared as well, born out of national pride in local heroism. There were similarities between these plays and the themes developed in the earlier outback dramas. First of all, there was the concept of Australian mateship and loyalty, which survived all disasters and made sacrifice tolerable. Secondly, there was the significance of the suffering, whether it be that of the outback settlers against natural disaster, or, that of expendable Australian soldiers led to needless slaughter by the British.

Betty Roland's *A Touch of Silk* (1928) was one of the early station dramas and included aspects of the military theme by focusing on the story of an ex-soldier from the First World War. Jim has brought home a French war bride, Jeanne, (his very own 'touch of silk') to the family farm in rural outback Australia. However, he finds himself torn between the European cosmopolitan values of his wife and the Australian outback values of his mother. When Jeanne purchases some silk underwear from a travelling salesman (her 'touch of silk') she not only endangers the family's precarious financial situation but also her marriage. Jim fatally injures the salesman and Jeanne finds herself confessing to an affair that she didn't have in order to justify Jim's violence in the local community.

Roland (christened Mary Isobel Maclean) was a 25-year-old housewife when she wrote *A Touch of Silk*. She boldly took the play to the Melbourne Repertory Theatre, where it was recognised as a landmark piece and, consequently, was staged in the same year. However, despite some good reviews, it wasn't considered commercial enough for the big companies so it was soon relegated to occasional performances by amateur repertory groups. In 1955, when theatrical realism became fashionable in Australia, Roland re-wrote *A Touch of Silk* in order to soften some of the melodramatic elements.

Economic depression in Australia during the 1920s and 1930s gave birth to new movements in social and political theatre, much of it realistic in orientation. The New Theatre Movement was organised around the New Theatre League in Sydney, set up in 1936, the New Theatre Club in Melbourne and the Unity Theatre in Brisbane, both set up in 1937. Political revues and left-wing political satire emphasised the class struggle and encouraged social change.

Dymphna Cusack, **George Landen Dann**, **Mona Brand** and **Oriel Gray** were four prominent left-wing playwrights of the 1930s and 1940s associated with the New Theatre Movement (alongside Betty Roland and Katharine Susannah Prichard). **Dymphna Cusack** was concerned with the conflicting role of women in middle-class society although she did tend to over-sentimentalise her subject matter. *Red Sky at Morning* (1942) set in an isolated inn in New South Wales in 1812 (and made into a film in 1944 starring Peter Finch) was pure melodrama. However, *Morning Sacrifice* (1942), set in the staffroom of a girls' school, is less romantic, focusing on society's attitude towards female sexuality. In *Comets Soon Pass* (1943) a group of characters are trapped by flood waters and have to wait for rescue, providing an opportunity to explore the conflict between social and individual responsibility.

George Landen Dann also dealt with gender politics although his primary focus became Australian race relations, drawn from direct experience of aboriginal communities during his travels around the Queensland outback. Controversy surrounded his work because he stood against the assimilation policies that had been promoted by the government and accepted by the society of his time. His play *In Beauty It Is Finished* won a playwriting competition in 1931, the prize being a production of the play at the Brisbane Repertory Theatre. However, when it leaked out that the story included a relationship between a white prostitute and mixed-race man, it was denounced by the press and Dann was forced to make changes to the text. His best-known play was *Fountains Beyond* (1942) focusing on race relations in a predominantly white middle-class town. When the white community try to close an aboriginal settlement, a visiting female author from England takes up the black cause with the local aboriginal leader,

Vic. However, their activism fails and the community is given notice to leave land that they have lived on for generations.

Oriel Gray's *Burst of Summer* (1959) was similar to Dann's *Fountains Beyond* in that it dealt with small town prejudice of the aboriginal community. The story is based on the true-life experience of a young aboriginal, Ngarla Kunoth, who was chosen to play the title role in the film *Jedda* (1955). After the movie had been released, she was returned to her original life and was forced to confront the prejudices of the community who had once championed her.

Mona Brand also wrote about racial politics but with a wider world view. *Here Under Heaven* (1948) is essentially a station drama but focuses on the difficulties faced by a Chinese war bride. *Strangers in the Land* (1952) is a political statement about British imperialism in Malaya, and, *No Strings Attached* (1958) about American CIA interference in an imaginary South-East Asian country (written after time spent in Hanoi as a teacher). The only reason her plays are published in Australia is because of their success in Russia and China.

Although many of these playwrights did not see their works staged in the theatre, some were successfully presented on radio. Radio drama operated in a weekly repertory format with professional production values, professional actors and a wide listening audience. This was often the only way in which playwrights could develop their craft. Plays were presented in repertory with the same actors broadcasting a new play each week. Betty Roland's *A Touch of Silk* received at least fifteen airings across regional stations between the 1930s and 1950s.

The Australian New Wave in theatre was launched with **Ray Lawler**'s *Summer of the Seventeenth Doll* (1955), a year before Osborne's *Look Back in Anger* and the English New Wave. *Summer of the Seventeenth Doll* was joint winner of the Playwrights Advisory Board play competition of 1955, alongside Oriel Gray's period play *The Torrents*. However, it was *The Doll* (as it is colloquially known) that was chosen by the brand-new Australian Elizabethan Trust to kick-start its mission of promoting Australian plays and Australian theatre. Consequently, the trustees gave financial support to the Union Theatre Repertory Company in Melbourne for its staging, so that it became one of the first Australian plays to receive professional assistance outside of the commercial theatre.

The Doll is set in a contemporary urban living room in the Melbourne suburb of Carlton and is peopled with working-class Australians who speak in instantly recognisable voices. For seventeen years, Roo and Barney, sugarcane cutters in Queensland, have travelled south to Melbourne for their 'off' season fun with barmaids, Olive and Nancy. Each year they bring a fairground kewpie doll as a present. However, the seventeenth year is different. Nancy has married so Olive has tried to replace her with another barmaid, Pearl. Far from the idyllic time expected by all, this seventeenth summer is fraught with tension, partially because of difficulties up north, where Roo was shown up by a younger, stronger man and left the cane fields early and partially because of the missing Nancy. Roo, Barney and Olive all desperately try to recreate the glamour and fun of earlier times but their youth can't be recaptured.

The Doll transferred to Sydney in 1956 and then went on a thirteen week tour. The critic, Lindsay Browne in the *Sydney Morning Herald* said:

> This fine play, untransplantably Australian in all its accents, gave Australian theatregoers the chance to feel as American audiences must have felt when O'Neill first began to assert American vitality and independence in drama, or the Irish must have felt when Synge gave them *The Playboy of the Western World*. This was real and exciting Australiana, with Australian spirit springing from the deep heart of the characters, and never merely pretending that Australianism is a few well-placed bonzers, too-rights, strike-me-luckies and good-Os...[21]

In April 1957, after a week in Nottingham and another week in Edinburgh, *The Doll* opened at the New Theatre in London, co-produced by Sir Laurence Olivier, again receiving excellent reviews. Kenneth Tynan described it as

> ...a play about working people who were neither "grim" nor "funny", neither sentimentalised nor patronised, neither used to point a social moral nor derided as quaint and improbable clowns. Instead they were presented as human beings in their own right, exulting in universal pleasures and nagged by universal

griefs. They were poor only in passing…The play that pulled off the feat is *Summer of the Seventeenth Doll*, and if Ray Lawler, its Australian author, is aware of the magnitude of the achievement, I shall be the most astonished critic in London, for I am sure revolution was not in his mind when he wrote it. He was merely born with something that most English playwrights acquire only after a struggle and express only with the utmost embarrassment – respect for ordinary people.[22]

After seven months in London and winning the 1957 Evening Standard Award for the best new play, *The Doll* transferred to New York, where it was less successful with American audiences. Critics found the language and accents difficult to follow and the characters too commonplace so its impact was muted. The run only lasted five weeks.

In 1959, *Summer of the Seventeenth Doll* was made into the film *Season of Passion* by the US company Hecht-Hill-Lancaster for United Artists. The casting, complete with American accents, missed the point of the play, with Ernest Borgnine (Roo), John Mills (Barney), Ann Baxter (Olive) and Angela Lansbury (Pearl). The setting was changed to Sydney so that lovely shots of the harbour and bridge could be included, again missing the point. The ending was also changed, resolving the situation into a happy one. Needless to say it didn't do well with critics or the box office.

In the mid-1970s, Lawler wrote two new plays with the same characters but covering the period prior to *Summer of the Seventeenth Doll*. *Kid Stakes* (set in the first summer) and *Other Times* (set in the ninth winter) introduce us to Nancy and explore the other characters in more detail. All three plays have become known as *The Doll Trilogy*.

Understandably, the success of *The Doll* inspired other playwrights to explore realistic suburban themes, which became known as 'backyard dramas'. **Richard Beynon**'s *The Shifting Heart* (1956) and **Alan Seymour**'s *The One Day of the Year* (1960) were the two most famous examples of the period. *The Shifting Heart* was actually set in a backyard – that of a family of Italian immigrants attempting to assimilate into a Melbourne suburb. Post-war immigration policy had changed the face of inner-city communities and xenophobia had risen to the surface of Australian society. *The Shifting*

Heart focused on the difficulties faced by immigrants and their children who were ostensibly living between two worlds. Kenneth Tynan described the play as 'a pungent piece of Australiana'[23] when it received the share of third prize in the London *Observer* playwriting competition of 1956.

In the 1950s Australia was gaining confidence as a nation (economically and culturally) so it was only natural that playwriting reflected this. *One Day of the Year* exposes the hypocrisy of Anzac Day (the national holiday that honours Australian and New Zealand troops who fought at Gallipoli in the First World War) through the eyes of a father-son relationship. The issue of youth vs. age in 1950s England was just as strong in Australia and the gender gap provides Seymour with the opportunity of airing differing views of Australian patriotism. The play was rejected by the Adelaide Festival of 1960 in order to avoid offence to returned servicemen and wasn't performed until 1961 by an amateur theatre group.

After the initial rush of excitement, 'backyard realism' fizzled out and an anti-realistic period in Australian theatre rose to the surface, evident in the plays of Patrick White and Dorothy Hewett. However, **Dorothy Hewett**'s *This Old Man Comes Rolling Home* (1957), about the struggles of a family living in one of the poorest and most deprived suburbs of inner-city Sydney, was crafted in the social realist tradition. Although Hewett had written it in 1957 (inspired by other backyard dramas of the period) it didn't appear on the stage until 1967 and was then considered 'out-of-date' and 'old -fashioned' by the critics. It wasn't until the late 1960s and early 1970s that a new 'New Wave' emerged in Australian drama through the playwrights: **Jack Hibberd**, **John Romeril**, **Alexander Buzo** and **David Williamson**.

4. THE RISE OF REALISTIC ACTING

Dramatic realism requires actors to focus on recreating a real human being within the constraints of their particular world. It is a representation of real life on stage with all the myriad of experiences and emotions that this entails. Therefore, as dramatic realism developed, actors were required to change their way of working. Previously, they focused on superficial techniques where voice and body demonstrated clichéd stock emotions in order to convey melodramatic plots. These techniques were clearly unsuitable for realistic plays and the focus soon shifted to the human character and how its inner psyche, within the circumstances of a play, could be portrayed truthfully. Unsurprisingly, new acting methodologies were developed to support this shift in thinking.

In nineteenth-century Russia, the company at the Moscow Art Theatre recognised that, if Chekhov's texts were to be brought to life on the stage, different rehearsal techniques were required. So Constantin Stanislavski, one of the theatre's founders, created a practical and scientific system (for a scientific age) whereby actors could develop more appropriate skills. His notes and books were eventually translated and his system spread across the English-speaking world.

In 1930s America, the Group Theatre founders (Harold Clurman, Cheryl Crawford and Lee Strasberg) adapted Stanislavski's system into The Method so that their permanent ensemble could focus on a more truthful embodiment of the characters they were presenting in plays of social and political protest. Whereas Stanislavski had focused on building character through a system of technical rehearsal exercises, The Method encouraged a full psychological immersion in character. Many actors who worked in the Group Theatre and trained at its successor, the Actors Studio, moved into cinema acting so that The Method became firmly established as a way of working in Hollywood films of the period.

In 1950s England, producers, directors and actors were heavily influenced by realistic performances in Hollywood films. Stanislavski and The Method were discussed in theatre circles but, rather than develop its own methodology, British theatre simply looked for new types of actors to embody the characters of New Wave theatre, cinema and television. Actors who came from a working-class background were popular with the Royal Court, the Theatre Royal Stratford East, Woodfall Films, Vic Films and Granada Television, who were able to draw on their experiences as well as their regional dialects in plays, cinema and television of the period. Casting mistakes were still made (note Richard Burton's cut-glass upper-class accent as Jimmy Porter in the film version of *Look Back in Anger*) but it did allow a whole new and different generation of actors to emerge.

5. VOCAL DEMANDS

The vocal demands of dramatic realism lie within the language of the text. Realistic playwrights use language to:

- Supply situational/environmental information about a character (for example, their class and background)

- Provide clues about a character's internal thoughts and emotions

- Create relationship (or a lack of relationship) between characters

- Cultivate a particular social/political viewpoint

The way in which playwrights do this is through:

- Vocabulary (the individual words a character uses)

- Rhythm (the way in which a character combines these words to form particular patterns)

- Sharing Rhythms (the way in which characters exchange dialogue)

Analysis of the linguistic features within a realistic text will help actors understand a character and provide them with important information about creating vocal characterisation, including their speech rhythms and vocal mannerisms. This prevents actors from artificially imposing their own ideas about vocal truthfulness onto the text and forces them to work with the playwright's intentions.

However, it is important to note that realistic characters, like human beings, often hide their true emotions, despite the words they use. Therefore, a character's vocabulary can conceal intention just as effectively as expose it. We don't always express our true feelings, saying one thing when we mean another. Texts usually provide us with tiny linguistic clues to indicate otherwise. Sometimes the smallest verbal hesitation can be meaningful. Sometimes a wall of words, a barrage of rhetoric or a sequence of overblown romanticism indicates concealment of some kind.

Equally important to remember is that realistic drama reflects the period in which it was written. Earlier in this chapter I mentioned that one of the features of realism is that it is 'current'. Because language (including slang, colloquialisms, dialect) evolves over time, often a play that was once considered contemporary and modern is now thought of as old-fashioned and anachronistic. Here is an example from Barry Reckord's 1963 play *Skyvers*, written in colloquial London dialect of the period.

This extract is dialogue taken from the play Skyvers by Barry Reckord. The story follows the lives of five teenage boys in their last week at a London school.

BROOK: Colley, let 'im 'ave 'is bloody match and let's go up to Soho tonight.

CRAGGE: Tonight's the match. You can go up to Soho any night.

COLMAN: *(To CRAGGE.)* It was a rotten swiz we paid twelve and six for that time. Why don't we try for a quid.

BROOK: How about it, Craggsie?

COLMAN: *(To CRAGGE.)* After the match.

CRAGGE: D'you think paying twice as much means they strip right down to the niff.

COLMAN: 'E can't afford a quid. His dad's hard up.

BROOK: Dunno about his dad. He's as tight as a crab's arse and that is watertight.

CRAGGE: Look, we've seen it once. You won't see no more in Soho for a quid than you see for three and six in the flicks. The only difference is in Soho you'll get coppers asking 'ow old you are.

BROOK: You teether. *(To COLMAN.)* Let's push.[24]

Here is another period piece from Louis Esson's *The Woman Tamed*, written in 1910. It is an early attempt to write in Australian dialect of the period.

This extract is dialogue taken from the one-act play The Woman Tamed *by Louis Esson. Set in inner-city Melbourne in 1910, we meet the underworld characters of Katie and Chopsey Ryan.*

KATIE: *(Scornfully.)* W'y dont yer git work! You aint no decent thief.

CHOPSEY: *(Stung.)* You know too much, do'nt yer?

KATIE: Fat lot you ever done! I aint seen yer dive on no red lot. I ain't seen yer stoush no rozzer. I aint even 'erd abowt yer in ther 'Erald for snow-droppin'. Ow now. Not you! You pl'y ther organ.

CHOPSEY: D'yer think I tell wimmen my bis?

KATIE: Y'aint got none. Yer cud'nt git er job roastin' peanuts. Yer cudn't orf side in er 4d. fish joint.

CHOPSEY: Yer carnt kid me. I know wot wimmin is.

KATIE: Yer w'z proud ter git on with me.

CHOPSEY: Gorblime, proud! I cud 'ave 'ad Fishy Liz.

KATIE: Fishy Liz! Ken she keep er bloke?

CHOPSEY: Y'aint ther only silver fish in ther pond.

KATIE: You're orl tork.[25]

This means that most of the realistic drama previously discussed are period pieces and need to be treated accordingly. Yes, it is important for an actor to find the vocal truth of a character but it should be the vocal truth of a particular snapshot in time. London actors who come to play a character in *Skyvers* may draw on some of their own dialectical understanding of contemporary London speech but will still need to capture the vocal rhythms of London in 1963 as expressed in Reckord's representation of that on the written page.

Given the focus on character and relationship and the way in which they are communicated through the language of realistic texts, the following three chapters will discuss and provide practical work for:

CATHERINE WEATE

- **Creating Vocal Characterisation**

- **Dealing with Dialogue / Revealing Relationships**

- **Capturing the Colloquial**

The final chapter in Part Two:

- **Voicing the Verbatim** focuses on Verbatim Theatre from England in the late twentieth/early twenty-first century. Factual (usually politicised) events are recreated using the verbatim speech from real-life interviews, first-hand testimonies and documented public inquiries. It requires a workshop all of its own to deal with the naturalistic rhythms inherent in the writing.

CHAPTER 4: CREATING VOCAL CHARACTERISATION

Each human voice possesses its own distinct features, recognisable to those who are familiar with the speaker's sound and particular style of communication. Friends, family and familiar acquaintances do not always need an introduction when they telephone us: we know who they are because of their vocal/speech features. Of course these features can vary enormously, depending on the context and situation in which communication takes place, yet despite this they usually remain identifiably familiar.

Working on a character's voice, therefore, is all about recreating these features i.e. developing an idiosyncratic *sound quality* and capturing individual *speech rhythms* peculiar to that character. These can then be applied to different contexts, situations and relationships in order to find range and variation (otherwise the character will become one-dimensional). The starting point for this journey must be the play itself: an actor needs to research the text practically, analysing the character's vocabulary and the way in which their words are (rhythmically) patterned on the page within particular contexts and situations. In this way, a character's voice can be brought to life as the playwright intended.

1. VOCAB RESEARCH

As we learnt in Chapter 2: 'Rhythm in Writing', writers choose their words carefully in order to create particular images, ideas, thoughts and emotions in the minds and hearts of readers. This is no less true for realistic playwrights: the difference being that their words are spoken through the physical/vocal embodiment of character in order to affect the minds and hearts of the audience. Therefore, the words a playwright has chosen to use provide us with a vast amount of information about character. A character's vocabulary places them in a particular country, culture, environment, class, educational background, profession, community and/or period in time. Just as importantly, they provide us with information about a character's inner life and emotional state. Here are a few linguistic features that actors should look for when starting their vocal research:

- Colloquialisms (the words we use in informal everyday conversations, usually drawn from a geographical region and part of our accent/ dialect)

- Slang (the words we use in informal everyday conversation that are non-standard and often considered vulgar by standard speakers)

- Expletives (the words we use to curse or swear, often obscene or profane and usually used in surprise or anger or to strengthen a point, idea or argument in conversation)

- Jargon (the words we use that bind us to a particular type of work, profession, interest or hobby)

- Clichés (the words, phrases and sayings we use so often that they become commonplace and trite, losing the impact of their original meaning)

- Rhetoric (the ornate words we use to persuade or convince, particularly in the context of speaking publicly)

- Lyricisms (the ornate and often musical words we use to express emotion)

- Trivia (the words we use that express unimportant information)

- Irrelevances (the words we use that aren't important to and often unrelated to the matter being discussed)

Once these elements have been recognised, they need to be questioned: *why* has the character used these particular words? For example, many of Chekhov's characters use irrelevances and trivia in their vocabulary. They try to communicate directly but often find it impossible, repressing their vocal energy. The Southern American heroines in Tennessee Williams' plays also use language as a mask. Blanche from *A Streetcar Named Desire* remains allusive by blending ornate lyrical imagery with archaic, antiquated language as well as French vocabulary directed towards those who don't understand it.

Wesker's *Chips with Everything* employs differences in vocabulary to distinguish class background. The working-class recruits use informal vocabulary, such as colloquialisms and slang, whilst the non-working-class recruits and officers use more formal and eloquent vocabulary (Dickey: 'Good old Cannibal! He uttered a syllable of many dimensions. The circumlocircle of his mouth has moved. Direct yourself to the bar, old son, and purchase for us some brown liquid'[26]). *Chips with Everything* also includes military jargon, binding the characters together in mutual experience, despite their differences in background.

Jimmy Porter in Osborne's *Look Back in Anger* uses a blend of rhetoric and lyrical imagery in his angry tirades. 'No one can raise themselves out of their delicious sloth.'[27], 'Behold the Lady Pusillanimous'[28], 'She has the passion of a python. She just devours me whole every time, as if I were some over-large rabbit.'[29] He uses this language as a weapon in psychological warfare against Alison.

The critic Michael Billington uses the phrase 'linguistic impoverishment'[30] to describe Edward Bond's *Saved*. The characters' vocabulary places them in a distinct environment and class: it is colloquial, spare and brutal.

2. RHYTHMIC RESEARCH

Chapter 2: 'Rhythm in Writing' discussed how rhythm is created by writers through word/image choice, punctuation, sentence length and paragraph structure (i.e. the patterns on the page). Realistic playwrights do the same although it is word/image choice, punctuation, sentence and speech length that will ultimately determine the vocal rhythms of character. Also, playwrights may use contractions, hesitations, fillers, elisions, assimilations and attempt to reproduce the sounds of a particular dialect on the written page. Here are a few rhythmic features of realistic text that actors should look for when starting their vocal research:

- Frequent use of a particular sound that reinforces the image, thought or emotion the character is trying to convey

- Frequent use of short vowels creating a staccato and/or sharper speech

- Frequent use of long vowels and/or words of more than one syllable creating a smoother flowing speech

- Frequent use of verbs and active words that pace up the text

- Frequent use of passive words that slow the tempo down

- Broken (disfluent) speech with lots of punctuation to indicate hesitations and incomplete thoughts

- Broken (disfluent speech) with fillers (sort of, like, kind of, you know, you see etc.)

- Fluent speech with less punctuation breaking it up

- Length of phrases, sentences and speeches

- Repeated words and/or phrases

- Grammatical errors

- Word contractions (such as 'can't' for 'cannot') that create informal speech and allow the words to flow

- Phonetical representation of dialect on the written page, including assimilations, elisions, word contractions and blurring as part of a particular accent

Again, once these elements have been recognised, they need to be questioned: *why* has the character created these particular rhythmic patterns? Take for example, repetition, which is an essential element of human communication. All human beings repeat words and phrases but the reasons why we do this vary enormously. Chekhov uses the rhythmic device of the repeated phrase to great effect. Sometimes a character repeats to try and convince themselves of a particular argument/point/idea: sometimes it is there as a device to reveal inner frustration, locking the character into a cycle in which they are unable to communicate. Jimmy Porter in Osborne's *Look Back in Anger* uses rhythmic repetitions for particular effect in his psychological games with Alison: 'Well she can talk can't she? You can talk, can't you?'.[31]

And why, as human beings, do we vary the length of our phrases and sentences? In Edward Bond's *Saved*, each speech is composed of extremely short phrases, no more than a few sentences long. This creates a sharp, disconcerting staccato effect and contributes to the emotional weight of situation. We feel Pam's trauma with: 'No 'ome. No friends. Baby dead. Gone. Fred gone.'[32]

In other plays, we hear characters deliver quite lengthy speeches with longer, more complex phrases and sentences. Speech-making is often a device used by playwrights to provide characters with opportunities to air their inner thoughts (either to other characters or to themselves in a soliloquy). However, we as human beings often do deliver speeches when we have something important to say or want to 'hold the floor' in a particular situation: This is almost always with others: we rarely soliloquise at length to ourselves. When focusing on characters who speak at length, the key is to chart/note the rhythmic features and/or changes that occur throughout the speech and question them accordingly. Characters who deliver lengthy speeches are usually quite articulate or they find their articulacy in the process of speaking. Jimmy Porter in Osborne's *Look Back in Anger* delivers articulate tirades but he often loses his way and they end with a whimper rather than a revolutionary call to arms. On the other hand, Beattie Bryant in Wesker's *Roots*, finds her articulacy in her final speech: 'D'you hear that? D'you hear it? Did you listen to me? I'm talking. Jennie, Frankie, Mother – I'm not quoting no more.'[33]

Some realistic playwrights attempt to write dialogue in a phonetical approximation of the characters' accent/dialect, using spelling that more-or-less resembles the characters' pronunciation. Sometimes this can be difficult to decipher, sometimes it can be helpful, providing guidelines as to how the characters operate rhythmically. Other realistic playwrights focus on the rhythm of an accent without including dialectical spelling. Character dialogue, in Clifford Odets' play *Awake and Sing!*, captures the speech rhythms of a particular community, culture and environment. Speak the text aloud and you can feel and hear the rhythm of a New York Jewish accent of the period. Bessie Berger: 'I could die from shame. A year already he runs around with her. He brought her once for supper. Believe me, she didn't come again, no!'[34]

3. APPLYING THE RESEARCH

Once an actor has researched the text they need to start applying this knowledge in practical exercises and activities. Without practical application, character development becomes an academic activity and will not necessarily translate into performance. The actor's mind may understand the character but their body (and voice) will not. A summary of the process is:

1. Understand (so the actor doesn't superimpose a superficial voice onto the text or rely on their own idiosyncratic speech rhythms)

2. Apply (so that the actor's body and voice 'understands' as well)

Practical application requires working on both the sound quality of the character's voice and the speech rhythms inherent in their words/dialogue.

Working on sound quality is a physical process. In real life, the quality of our sound is affected by what our body is doing. Therefore, this process needs to be recreated in the development of character. The actor needs to take what they already know about the character from their research and develop their character's physicality. This will create certain tensions in the body and affect the way in which breath flows. In turn, restriction of the breath will affect the resonance or quality of the sound, perhaps creating something a little more nasal or something lighter and headier. It's important not to overcomplicate this process with technical terms as this will overcomplicate the creative process and, ultimately, prevent the actor from creating a fully dimensional human voice. They will cling to one particular sound or one particular way of working so that the audience will be distracted by their voice and have difficulty in listening to what the character is actually talking about. Once the overall sound quality has been established then the actor must practise using it in different situational contexts, both inside and outside of the play, in order to ensure that it is adaptable to reality. An actor I recently worked with came up with a wonderful sound for the character he was rehearsing but only realised how caricatured it was when he came to applying it to different contexts. Try as he may, he couldn't make it work on quieter, more sinister scenes, only the ones that were loud, noisy and over-the-top. In cases such as these, the vocal choices need adjustment and/or softening.

When focusing on a character's speech rhythms, it is important that the actor understands and practises the character's accent away from the text **before** starting this process (because of the way in which human speech rhythm is bound up with accent). Chapter 6: 'Capturing Colloquialism' provides useful detail on how to go about this.

Once the actor is clear about accent, they can focus on lifting the character's specific speech rhythms off the page, based on their previous research of the text. Practical exercises and activities will help them to find the rhythmic flow of the text and bring it to life for an audience. For more detail on this process, take a look at the workshop plan within this chapter (see pages 128-35).

4. TEXT SAMPLES

We will be working on Chekhov's *Ivanov*, in a version by Tom Stoppard in the workshop plan for this chapter. There are two reasons why I've chosen scenes from this text:

1. Because it is a translated text in a standard form of written English, your actors will be able to focus on the characters' vocal features without necessarily changing their own accents. The aim will be to establish status rather than region.

2. Because Tom Stoppard is a contemporary playwright in his own right, the translation has a feel for the rhythms of contemporary speech. As discussed in my previous book *Classic Voice*, every translated text has two voices within it, that of the playwright and that of the translator. Translated versions of the same text can feel very different, so choosing a translation suitable for purpose is essential.

Text Sample 1: Creating Vocal Characterisation

The following text has been taken from Act Three of Anton Chekhov's *Ivanov*, in a version by Tom Stoppard. The original text was written in 1887 but Tom Stoppard's text was first presented by the Donmar Warehouse at the Wyndham's Theatre, London, in September 2008, directed by Michael Grandage.

The story so far:

Ivanov is in an emotional crisis. Described as 'the wrong side of forty' and losing the ideals of his youth, he doesn't know how he can go on living. Despite being a landowner, he has significant debt and has fallen out of love with his wife at a time when she really needs him (her death from tuberculosis is imminent). He tries to escape from his problems by visiting neighbouring landowners every night only to become obsessed with their young daughter. His sense of guilt and self-loathing is apparent through every physical and vocal nuance as he speaks his thoughts aloud to himself.

IVANOV: *(Aside.)* Oh God, how I despise myself! I hate the sound of my voice, my footsteps, hate my hands, these clothes, my very thoughts… It's ridiculous, isn't it? – It's infuriating. Hardly a year ago I was a fit man, cheerful, always on the go…I was good with my hands, I could talk to bring tears to the eyes, even of some loutish peasant. I could weep myself when I saw suffering – and get angry when I saw wickedness. I knew inspiration, knew the charm and poetry of quiet nights when I'd work at my desk till dawn, or let my mind go wandering. I had faith, I looked at the future as trustfully as I'd look into my mother's eyes…and now, oh god, I'm so tired, I believe in nothing, idling away the nights. My brain, my hands, my feet won't do what I tell them. The estate is going to ruin, the woods fall to the axe. *(Weeps.)* My land looks back at me like an abandoned child. I'm not hoping for anything, I'm not sorry for anything, and I dread every new day. And then there's Anna. I've watched her fading away, worn away by her feelings of guilt, and still – God knows – never a glance or a word of reproach! And now I've fallen out of love. How? Why? What for? I just don't understand it. And here she is, dying in pain, and here am I, running away from her pale face, her sunken chest, her pleading eyes, like a complete coward. It's beyond shame.

    (Pause.)

And now Sasha – a mere child…feeling sorry for me and thinking she's in love with me – and suddenly I'm intoxicated, I forget everything, like someone carried away by a piece of Beethoven or something, shouting about happiness and a new life, and next moment I have about as much belief in this happy new life as I have in fairies. What is wrong with me?! What is this edge I'm pushing myself over? Why am I so helpless? What's happening to my nerves? If my sick wife says a word out of place, or a servant annoys me, or a book goes missing, I explode, I'm horrible to everyone, I don't recognise myself any more.

    (Pause.)

I simply don't know what's going on with me. I might just as well put a bullet in my head!

Ivanov by Anton Chekhov in a version by Tom Stoppard. Published by Faber and Faber.[35]

Text Sample 2: Creating Vocal Characterisation

The following text has been taken from Act Three of Anton Chekhov's *Ivanov*, in a version by Tom Stoppard. See Text Sample 1 for production history.

The story so far:

Sasha is twenty, beautiful and the daughter of wealthy landowners. Her life appears trouble-free, apart from the fact she has fallen in love with one of her neighbours, Ivanov. Ivanov is in an emotional crisis. Described as 'the wrong side of forty' and losing the ideals of his youth, he doesn't know how he can go on living. Despite being a landowner, he has significant debt and has fallen out of love with his wife at a time when she really needs him (her death from tuberculosis is imminent). He is full of guilt and self-loathing. Here, Sasha explains why she loves him.

SASHA: There's a lot that men don't understand. Every girl is drawn to a man who needs her, because what we're looking for is love that gives us something to do. Not passive love. Do you see? Active love. Men put their work first, love has to take second place – a chat, a walk in the garden, some pleasant times, a few tears on her grave, and that's about it. But for us, love is the reason for living. Loving you means dreaming of curing you of your unhappiness, of following you to the ends of the earth. Where you go, there I'll go – to the mountaintop or into the abyss. I'd love more than anything to spend all night doing your paperwork for you, or to walk by your side for miles and miles. Once, about three years ago, at harvest time, you showed up all covered in dust and sunburnt, you were exhausted, and you asked for a drink of water. I brought you a glass, but you were stretched out on the sofa, dead to the world. You slept the whole day and I stood by the door keeping watch so that no one came in. I felt so happy. The more you do for love, the more love you feel.

Ivanov by Anton Chekhov in a version by Tom Stoppard. Published by Faber and Faber.[36]

5. WORKSHOP PLAN

There are two ways in which to approach realistic text in a vocal workshop:

1. Ask participants to read the play beforehand (so they understand character and situation), and, to speak the text sample aloud a number of times (so that its rhythms become familiar to the brain and mouth). This means they will be able to focus on the workshop exercises and activities in greater depth.

2. Don't ask the participants to prepare anything before the workshop: simply give them the sample text on the day in order to experiment with the language and its rhythms without knowledge of character and situation. Sometimes this opens participants up to the text without prejudice. Of course they will need to go back and read the text and do in-depth research after the workshop, otherwise the process will become empty and superficial.

The following workshop asks participants to prepare beforehand but there is no reason why you can't change the format to suit your needs.

WORKSHOP PLAN: CREATING VOCAL CHARACTERISATION

Objectives

- To explore the vocal demands of realistic text, using the speech of a specific individual character

- To experiment with different sound qualities for this character, based on knowledge of the text

- To discover the shifts and nuances of this character's speech rhythm, based on the rhythmic features within the text

- To apply what has been learnt about vocal characterisation to different contexts and situations, adjusting where necessary, in order to create a believable human being.

Materials

You will need:

– Separate copies of the *Ivanov* extracts, as provided in the previous 'Text Sample' boxes, for each member of the workshop group (dependant on their gender)

– Large sheets of paper and felt-tip pens for brainstorming ideas.

Actor Preparation

Before the workshop, ask your actors to:

– Read the play from which their chosen extract has been taken (so they understand the character and his/her energy, drive and motivation)

– Speak the text excerpt aloud *at least* ten times (so that its rhythms become familiar to the brain and mouth) without memorising it (otherwise a particular rhythm will become fixed and almost immovable).

Activities and Exercises

1. Brainstorming

Ask your actors to form small groups (each group member must have completed their preparatory homework on the SAME text excerpt). Then ask them to note down points about the vocabulary and rhythm within the excerpt, using the large sheets of paper and pens you have provided

– Vocabulary they should look for (as listed on page 121): colloquialisms, slang, expletives, jargon, clichés, rhetoric, lyricisms, trivia and irrelevances

– Rhythmic features they should look for (as listed on pages 122-3): frequent use of particular sounds, frequent use of short or long vowels, frequent use of verbs and active words, frequent use of passive words, broken speech, fillers, different phrase lengths, repeated words and/or phrases, grammatical errors, word contractions and written dialect.

When they have completed these notes they need to discuss, as a group, *why* they think the character has used these particular words and rhythmic features, plus, *what* they tell us about the character within this moment in time.

Each group can then share their findings with the whole group.

2. Warming up

(a) Grounding, Centring, Aligning

Ask your actors to ground, centre and align their bodies. Here are some simple directions you can give them:

– Stomp firmly with your feet into the ground

– Balance your weight between both feet

– Balance your weight between your toes and heels

– Release your weight down through the feet

– Unlock your knees

– Lengthen up through the spine (touch a point at the crown of the head and feel the body lengthen up towards this point, without losing the weight in your feet)

– Focus on a point just below the horizon so that the back of your neck is long

– Shake out your body and repeat the whole process.

(b) Breathing and Resonating

Ask your actors to centre their breath, build resonant vibration and focus their sound. Here are some simple directions you can give them:

– Imagine a clear plastic tube running from your lips to your belly. Focus on the breath running freely and silently up and down this tube, without obstruction

– Keep this image but start taking these silent breaths in and out through the mouth, deepening and lengthening them each time

– Now on the outgoing breath, 'pour' out a long, easy 'fffff' sound, right to the end of the breath stream so that you can feel the muscles contract, ready for the next intake of breath. On the next breath try 'sssss', then 'vvvvv' and then 'zzzzz'

– Keep this same breath rhythm but switch to a hum ('mmmmm') on the outgoing breath. Make sure the lips are placed lightly together and the back of the tongue is dropped. Concentrate on building vibration on the lips

– Now think the hum ('mmmmm') onto the cheekbones. Place your fingertips there so that you can feel the vibration. Repeat with the bridge of the nose, temples, top of the head and chest

– Shake out your body and then ground, centre and align once again

– Warm up the face by patting it and massaging it with the fingertips. Do some chewing (with the mouth open) and sneering (lifting the upper lip muscles). Vibrate the lips like a horse ('bwwww') up and down through your range

– Shake out your body once again then repeat the whole warm-up process from the beginning. The vibrations on the lips, cheekbones, bridge of the nose, temples, top of the head and chest should be stronger now

– Focus on a point just under your horizon so that the back of the neck is aligned. Send some 'fffffs', 'vvvvvs', 'sssss', 'zzzzzs' and 'mmmmms' to this point without losing alignment. Make sure that the in-breath is still centred down to the belly

– Now walk towards that point with one of these sounds. Turn and find a new point, breathe in to the belly and, using a different sound, walk to that point. Keep repeating this process until you have used all of the sounds we've worked on

– Shake out your body.

(c) Articulating

Ask your actors to be precise, crisp and muscular with their consonant placement. They should be able to maintain precision whilst using different rhythms. Here are some simple exercises that will help:

– Be firm and muscular with the lip consonants / p / and / b /. Try / ppp ppp ppp pah / and / bbb bbb bbb bah / in different rhythmic combinations (e.g. / ppp **ppp** ppp **pah** / or / pp**p** ppp pp**p** **pah** /)

– Be crisp and muscular with the tongue tip placement for / t / and / d / (tongue tip to the upper gum ridge). Try / ttt ttt ttt tah / and / ddd ddd ddd dah / in different rhythmic combinations (e.g. / ttt ttt **ttt tah** / or / ttt **ttt** ttt **tah** /)

– Be clear and muscular with the back of the tongue placement for / k / and / g /. Try / kkk kkk kkk kah / and / ggg ggg ggg gah / in different rhythmic combinations (e.g. / **kkk** kkk **kkk kah** / or / kkk kkk kkk **kah** /).

3. Creating Vocal Characterisation

These exercises draw on the research completed in the brainstorming session and the physical/vocal work undertaken in the warm-up so please make sure they've been covered before moving on (tempting as it may be to simply 'cut to the chase').

(a) Forming a Photographic Still

Ask your actors to create a photographic still of their character, taken just moments before the start of the text excerpt. Try using these directions:

– Start in a grounded, centred and aligned position (see warm-up). Take what you know about the character from your research and adjust into a stance that is appropriate for the moment before the text excerpt. Create a frozen still life photograph. Make specific decisions about each part of your body. Experiment with:

Feet placement (How far apart are the feet? What angle are they in relation to one another? Why?)

Weight distribution (Where does the weight sit? Forwards, backwards, on both feet or just one? Why?)

Pelvic placement (Is the pelvis centred, tilted or twisted within this weight distribution? Why?)

Upper body placement (Is the upper body centred over this weight distribution or is the character leaning backwards or forwards? Why?)

Arm placement (At what level are the arms and hands held? Why?)

Spinal length (Is the spine lengthened, sunk or curved? Why?)

Head placement (Is the head centred over the weight distribution or tilted or twisted in any way? Why?)

Eye line (How has the head placement affected the character's line of sight? Where are you looking? Why?).

(b) Breathing Life into the Photographic Still

Although your actors have created a photographic still life of their character, they need to become a living human being. Let them breathe. Try using these directions:

– Think about how the character's physical stance affects the breath journey through the body. If your weight distribution is off-centre, your spine is twisted or you are holding more upper body tension than usual, feel how much harder you have to work to get the breath down to the belly and back up through that open tube (from the warm-up). If you can barely breathe at all then ever-so-slightly readjust your physicality so that you can. The actor behind the character must be able to find a centred breath.

(c) Finding Voice in the Photographic Still

Now that your actors can breathe in their physicality, they need to start experimenting with the sound of their character's voice. Try using these directions:

– Once your character is breathing in their physicality, take a short line from the text extract and try it out loud a number of times. Allow the decisions you have made about the character's physicality to inform the way in which you make sound. If you are weighted physically then the sound will probably be heavy and resonant too. If you have your head up in the clouds then the sound may be lighter. Start adjusting the sound to match your physicality

– Keep repeating the line. Now think about where the sound vibration is coming from specifically, based on the work you did in the warm-up (the chest, cheekbones, bridge of the nose, temples or top of the head). Go back and hum ('mmmmm') from this point and strengthen the vibration (without pushing it). Try the line again a number of times

– Human beings don't just speak on the one pitch so let's find the range of your character's voice. Go back to the hum ('mmmmm') and move up and down a few notes either way but make sure the sound is still vibrating. Now try the line again

– Now speak the whole text extract, maintaining the physical stance of your character and the breath flow through the body. Don't worry if you have trouble maintaining the sound quality: adjustments are a natural part of the process. In fact, try not to cling too heavily to your decisions. They should only be a starting point or frame of reference. Allow the character's sound to grow out of them.

(d) Moving the Character: Finding the Rhythm

Your actors need to be able to move in their physicality in order to discover their physical rhythm and, ultimately, their vocal rhythm. Ask them to start moving around the space in their character's physicality. Here are some questions to throw at them whilst they are walking. There is no need for responses; they just need to absorb them and make a mental, internal note of the answers, adjusting their actions if appropriate.

– Where is the weight distribution as you move?

– Which part of the body leads and what is left behind?

– Do you prefer moving directly to a destination or indirectly (with the journey broken)?

– What is your pace/speed preference?

– How does this affect your breath energy?

Now ask them to add in sound as they move. Each out breath should release a new sound. Coach them to move through 'fffff', 'vvvvv', 'sssss', 'zzzzz' and, finally, the hum ('mmmmm')

– How does your breath energy affect the volume of the sound in the space?

– Does your character enjoy making these sounds/listening to the sound of their own voice in the space? How does this information affect the sound?

They should now speak the text extract as they move. Coach them to feel the speech rhythm through their bodies as they walk (placing their feet down on particularly strong beats, finding fluidity when speech flows, slowing down or speeding up as required, stopping on long pauses). There should be a change of direction each time there is an abrupt change or sharp shift in the speech rhythm. Keep them repeating the text so that they are clear about the rhythm. Add in one final question (which may change what they are doing):

– Does your character enjoy speaking (and relish what they are saying)? Or are they disconnected/fearful/shy of the words they are bringing into the space?

Finally, ask your actors to stop moving and go back to the photographic snapshot of their physicality and speak the whole text extract again. This isn't necessarily the way it should be performed but you need to make sure that the rhythm has become part of your actors' bodies, without them having to remember it.

If there are any particular issues that need addressing regarding the rhythm then take some of the exercises for phrasing and pausing, stressing, pitching and tuning, and, pacing from Chapter Two.

(e) Contextualising the vocal characterisation

Your actors now need to apply what they've learnt about their character's voice and rhythmic speech patterns to different situations. As we learnt in Chapter 1, human beings adjust their voice/speech depending on the context in which they are speaking, the importance/familiarity/emotional relationship with the information they are communicating and the relationship with whom they are speaking it to. To test this out, either set up improvised scenes between characters or use scenes from different parts of the play. In either scenario, ask your actors to reconnect back to their physicality and try some sound work before launching into the scene. They may need to adjust some of the decisions they have made in order to meet the demands of different situations and contexts. This is absolutely normal.

3. Debriefing

Allow some time for a group debriefing session. Use the following questions as a starting point for the discussion:

– What did the initial brainstorming research tell you about the character?

– Can you describe the sound quality you developed for the character?

– Can you describe the rhythm of your character's speech?

– When you applied the process from the solo text excerpt to different scenes, did your voice/speech change in any way?

– Can you describe these changes?

6. REVISITING THE BASICS

Here are some important points to remember from this chapter:

- Creating a character's voice for a realistic play means recreating the distinct vocal/speech features of a specific human voice.

- The starting point for this journey must be the play itself: an actor needs to practically research the text, analysing the character's vocabulary and the way in which their words are (rhythmically) patterned on the page.

- This research/knowledge then needs to be applied to practical exercises and activities. Practical application requires working on both the *sound quality* of the character's voice and the *speech rhythms* inherent in their words/dialogue.

- Sound quality and speech rhythm can vary enormously, depending on the situation in which communication takes place. Therefore, they need to be applied to different contexts and relationships in order to find range and variation.

CHAPTER 5: DEALING WITH DIALOGUE / REVEALING RELATIONSHIPS

1. SPOKEN DIALOGUE

Spoken dialogue is a two-way exchange. Sounds obvious but it's surprising how many actors work on character in isolation. From a vocal perspective it's imperative to focus on how a character interacts with other characters. This is because we don't just choose our vocabulary in isolation; we play off each other's words and rhythms, revealing not only ourselves but our relationship with others.

Human beings speak in markedly different ways depending on the relationship between speakers (e.g. personal or professional, open or closed, intimate or distant), and where the conversation is situated (e.g. public or private, familiar or unfamiliar). Vocabulary, rhythm and tone colour will automatically adapt to these relationships and contexts. *At the same time*, participants will adjust to each other's vocabulary, rhythm and tone colour. For example: if we speak to a friend or a lover in a public arena where we don't want to reveal our relationship, our conversation may seem cold and distant; however, familiarity and intimacy will be revealed through the way in which we (unconsciously) shadow each other's words and rhythms. Unpacking these shared words and rhythms in realistic drama will, therefore, bring us closer to understanding a character.

(a) RHYTHMIC SYNCHRONY

We often physically and vocally mirror the people with whom we interact. This is called rhythmic synchrony. I'm sure you've noticed moments in conversation when your arms or legs are crossed in exactly the same way as the other speaker/listener, or, when you've repeated words they've just used, or, accidentally (and embarrassingly) copied their accent when responding to something they have said. Physical and vocal mirroring is a normal part of human interaction. Why do we do it? Simply put, it is our unconscious desire to participate and be accepted by the speaker into the conversation/ interaction. It can even occur when we dislike a speaker. We may reject what they're saying but mirroring suggests that we still want to be part of the argument. Mirroring will be absent only if we (truly) do not wish to take part in a conversation.

(b) ALLO-REPETITION

Vocally, rhythmic synchrony occurs when we repeat elements of what the speaker has just uttered. This is also called *allo-repetition* or the repetition of others (as opposed to *self-repetition* when we repeat ourselves). Allo-repetition can involve:

- Repeating or echoing back the exact words of the speaker in the exact same rhythmic pattern

- Repeating or echoing back only some of the words/part of the phrase the speaker has used

- Repeating or echoing back only one of the words the speaker has used

- Repeating the exact words of the speaker but changing a question into a statement or a statement into a question (Speaker 1: You know about it? Speaker 2: You know about it)

- Repeating or echoing back the words of the speaker but changing the person or tense (Speaker 1: You know about it? Speaker 2: I know about it)

- Repeating or echoing back the thoughts put forward by the speaker but paraphrasing their words

- Echoing back the rhythmic pattern of the speaker but using different words

- Repeating the words of others who aren't present (usually when we are recounting what somebody has said to us): in this case we can either use their exact words or a paraphrased version

Allo-repetition is important for a number of reasons. First and foremost, it is about our need to participate in the conversation. Secondly, it helps us bond with the speaker, thereby strengthening relationship. Thirdly, it's a useful way of showing that we are listening by ratifying the speaker's words. Fourthly, it can aid comprehension if we repeat the speaker's words back to them for confirmation. Fifthly, it generates interesting conversation. Far from being boring, it creates a poetical pattern that helps maintain the involvement of both participants. Sixthly, psychoanalysts like Freud have found that human beings take pleasure in imitation – we actually enjoy repeating the words and rhythms of others. Finally, from the linguist, Deborah Tannen:

> Finding a way into a conversation is like joining a line of dancers. It is not enough to know where other dancers have been; one must also know where they are headed: To bring one's feet into coordination with theirs, one must grasp the pattern in order to foresee where their feet will come down next.[37]

(c) REDUNDANCY

Allo-repetition and self-repetition are also part of another linguistic group called Redundancy. This is when we use words, phrases and sounds that are superfluous to the meaning we are trying to communicate. In addition to repetition, redundancy includes:

- Filler words and phrases (that do not contribute to the core information we are speaking about) e.g. 'well', 'anyway', 'you know', 'like', 'I mean'

- Encouragement words, phrases and sounds (that are only used to persuade the speaker to continue) e.g. 'go on', 'really?', 'so?', 'and then?', 'oh?'

- Agreement signals (that are only used to indicate concurrence with the speaker) e.g. grunts and mumbles

Importantly, redundancy aids fluency in conversation, giving the speaker an opportunity to think about what they might say next without resorting to silence, and, giving the listener time to absorb what has been said so that new information is spread out over more time and the conversation is less dense.

(d) INTERRUPTED, OVERLAPPED AND UNFINISHED SPEECH

Redundancy also helps prevent interruptions. Leaving silences is risky, opening up opportunities for other participants in the conversation to dive in. We find it easier to repeat or add a filler word or sound before we move off onto something new.

Interruption disrupts the two-way exchange, violating the turn-taking rule that we learn as children (one person speaks and the other person waits for them to finish before speaking themselves). Despite this, it is a normal part of everyday conversation. Interruptions occur because a participant is over-enthusiastic or they want to stop a speaker from airing unwanted information or they need to take the floor to push their own point forward.

Overlapped speech is even more common: it's extremely rare for a conversation not to include some overlapping. Essentially, this is when a participant starts speaking before the other participant has finished. Even though overlapping also infringes the turn-taking rule, it usually occurs for positive reasons. It's all about listeners showing interest in the conversation and starting to speak earlier than their 'turn'.

However, we don't always complete our speech, leaving unfinished phrases hanging in the air. This is because either we: lose what we're about to say next; become too emotional about the subject matter; aren't sure of how the listener will react to our words so change our minds about finishing what we were going to say; or, have been given agreement signals by the listener that they understand so there is no need to go on.

2. WRITTEN DIALOGUE

In realistic drama, dialogue usually looks/sounds like normal, everyday conversation. The majority of actors and audiences recognise it as such. However, it isn't: written dialogue is only an *adapted version* of everyday conversation, giving us the illusion of reality. Many playwrights strip away redundancy, overlapping and unfinished phrases, in order to expose meaning more acutely. In these plays, characters are bound by the turn-taking rule (one person speaks and then another and so on). However, in the last few decades it has become fashionable to include more of the spoken features of everyday conversation in written dialogue. Apart from sounding 'real' (if the actors can make it work) it has the added bonus of helping the audience to comprehend the material, giving them time to take in information, just as if they were participating in a real conversation.

However, most realistic playwrights use allo-repetition deliberately to bind characters together in a mutual exchange, reveal relationship, create a rhythmically interesting scene and drive the drama forward. Non-realistic playwrights often enhance or increase rhythmic repetition to create a particular dramatic effect (but more about that in Part Three of this book).

In one of the following text samples, Blanche and Stella in Tennessee Williams' *A Streetcar Named Desire* are diametrically opposed. Despite their disagreement they are constantly repeating each other's words and phrases. They have a synchronicity all of their own, derived from the shared intimacy of sisterhood. Repetition also helps them drive their conversation forward into a mini-climax.

Lack of repetition between characters often tells us that either one or both characters involved in the exchange do not want to participate. Bolette and Lyngstrand in Ibsen's *The Lady From the Sea* text sample are diametrically opposed as well but their lack of synchronicity is telling. The only rhythms that are shared between them are the beats that build discomfort.

Therefore, in order to come to a greater understanding of the relationship between characters, actors must look for and question the spoken rhythmic features in written dialogue, and, apply this knowledge in practical exercise.

3. TEXT SAMPLES

The following scenes reveal three very different relationships. In Text Sample 1, Bolette and Lyngstrand illustrate male/female courtship going wrong. In Text Sample 2, Blanche and Stella show female sisterhood in opposition. In Text Sample 3, we are invited into the intimacy of male/female friendship with Cliff and Alison.

Text Sample 1: Dealing with Dialogue / Revealing Relationships

The following text has been taken from Act Three of Henrik Ibsen's *The Lady From the Sea*, in a version by Pam Gems. The original text was written in 1888 but Pam Gems' text was first performed at the Almeida Theatre in London in May 2003, directed by Trevor Nunn.

The story so far:

Bolette is the daughter of Doctor Wangel. Her mother is dead and Wangel has remarried. His second wife, Ellida, is the 'Lady of the Sea' of the title. She grew up in a lighthouse and is obsessed with all things watery. Her ethereal nature is unable to cope with the household so practical-minded Bolette has taken over. Lyngstrand is a sculptor who is dying of consumption. Bolette understands and knows this but is still outraged by his insensitivity towards women.

The conservatory, the garden in view. BOLETTE sits on the sofa, embroidering. LYNGSTRAND sits at the round table.

LYNGSTRAND: That looks very complicated, the edging.

BOLETTE: Not really, not so long as you keep count of the stitches.

LYNGSTRAND: Is it your own design?

BOLETTE: No, no, I need something to copy.

LYNGSTRAND: So it's not really an art.

BOLETTE: More of a handicraft.

LYNGSTRAND: You might, perhaps, become more artistic.

BOLETTE: I don't have the talent.

LYNGSTRAND: But if you were influenced, say, by an artist…

BOLETTE: You mean I could learn from him?

LYNGSTRAND: It could happen. By degrees.

BOLETTE: That would be a wonder.

LYNGSTRAND: Miss Wangel – have you ever – I mean, did it ever occur to you – have you ever thought about marriage?

BOLETTE: I beg your pardon?

LYNGSTRAND: I have.

BOLETTE: Oh?

LYNGSTRAND: Yes. I think about it a lot. A woman could be transformed –

BOLETTE: Transformed?

LYNGSTRAND: – by her husband's influence.

BOLETTE: Why would she want that?

LYNGSTRAND: In order to…so that she…

BOLETTE: Could share his interests, you mean?

LYNGSTRAND: Exactly.

BOLETTE: And acquire his abilities.

LYNGSTRAND: Absolutely. It could happen. Gradually. In a happy marriage.

BOLETTE: What about the other way round?

LYNGSTRAND: I'm sorry?

BOLLETE: He might get to grow like her.

LYNGSTRAND: Oh, no!

BOLETTE: Why not?

LYNGSTRAND: A man has his work, his vocation. It gives him a higher purpose in life, a calling.

BOLETTE: And that's true of all men? Every single one?

LYNGSTRAND: Well, artists in particular.

BOLETTE: You think they should marry? That an artist should be married?

LYNGSTRAND: Oh, yes. If there is someone he really loves.

BOLETTE: He shouldn't just live for his art?

LYNGSTRAND: Of course. But he can still get married.

BOLETTE: What about her?

LYNGSTRAND: Who?

BOLETTE: The woman, the wife. What is she to live for?

LYNGSTRAND: Him! She'll live for his art, then she'll be happy too. Believe me, Miss Wangel, there's the honour of being the wife of an artist – she can help him, inspire him, make his life easier by looking after him, seeing that he's comfortable. What a wonderful destiny for a woman!

BOLETTE: Do you know…I don't think I've ever heard such a barrel of conceit in all my life.

The Lady From the Sea by Henrik Ibsen in a version by Pam Gems. Published by Oberon Books.[38]

We understand Bolette's lack of regard for Lyngstrand at the outset of this scene. Her repeated negativity blocks his seemingly innocuous questions ('Not really, not so long as you keep count of the stitches' and 'No, no, I need something to copy').

When Lyngstrand attempts to understand her, there is rhythmic allo-repetition ('So it's not really an art' / 'More of a handicraft'). A series of quick, short lines follow, creating a speedy exchange. Then Lyngstrand misunderstands Bolette's 'That would be a wonder' and questions her about marriage. However, he is clearly uneasy, using unfinished phrases, redundancies and a complete rhythmic change.

Bolette is taken aback by the mention of marriage and, instead of responding, poses a series of questions. Her 'Transformed?' is not just allo-repetition but an interruption: she is clearly horrified by the word. Lyngstrand is suitably thrown and cannot finish his phrase, which Bolette – cool, calm, collected and (dangerously) in control – does for him.

Lyngstrand uses short, sharp (rather uncomfortable) sentences to elaborate his point ('Absolutely. It could happen. Gradually. In a happy marriage.'). When Bolette asks her next question ('What about the other way round?'), Lyngstrand is thrown ('I'm sorry?'). He finally finds fluency by spouting a theory ('A man has his work, his vocation. It gives him a higher purpose in life, a calling'). He even paraphrases to ensure that she has understood ('work'/'vocation' and 'higher purpose in life'/'a calling').

Bolette tries to goad him with further questions ('And that's true of all men? Every single one?'), self-repeating for extra emphasis. Lyngstrand's redundant 'Well' (in 'Well, artists in particular') indicates his discomfort: he realises the conversation is not moving in the direction he anticipated.

Bolette responds again with a double self-repeated question for extra emphasis ('You think they should marry? That an artist should be married?'). She continues to ask questions, driving him forward and into his final speech. She tries to emphasise the woman's concerns with 'The woman, the wife.' Instead Lyngstrand focuses on 'him' – repeating the word ad nauseam – indicating where his focus lies. This also creates a poetical rhythm ('she can help him, inspire him, make his life easier by looking after him'). Only his final announcement links back to her 'woman' but, of course, not in the way she intended ('What a wonderful destiny for a woman!'). An initial redundancy leads into Bolette's final and brutal outburst: she needs to speak plainly as anything less would be misunderstood again.

Text Sample 2: Dealing with Dialogue / Revealing Relationships

The following text has been taken from Scene Four of Tennessee Williams' *A Streetcar Named Desire*, published by Penguin. It was first performed in December 1947 at the Ethel Barrymore Theatre in New York and was directed by Elia Kazan.

The story so far:

Blanche DuBois, having fallen on hard times, arrives to stay with her sister, Stella, in New Orleans. She has delusions of grandeur from her southern background but the family plantation is long gone. She is still attractive but hides a drinking habit and a past of illicit lovers in seedy hotels. Once a teacher, she even seduced a seventeen-year-old student.

Her sister, Stella, is married to Stanley Kowalski, who sells car parts for a living. He has a violent temper and controls his wife sexually and emotionally. However, Stella is in love with him and reveals during the course of the play that she is pregnant. They live in a small apartment in a working-class neighbourhood, where the local streetcar is called 'Desire'. Blanche is like a fish-out-of-water and clashes with Stanley, her polar opposite. She is the old-world southern belle and he, the new-world worker from an immigrant background. Blanche doesn't understand how her sister could have married a man lacking in refinement.

Stanley holds a poker game at the apartment for a few of his friends. Blanche attempts to hold court and attracts the attentions of one of the poker players, Mitch.

Stanley, drunk, loses his temper. When Stella speaks up, he hits her, so the sisters escape to a neighbour's apartment for safety. However, Stanley isn't ready to let Stella go and drunkenly calls for her. Stella cannot resist him and returns. The next morning, Blanche is horrified to discover that Stella has forgotten Stanley's brutal violence towards her after a night of passion. She tries to convince Stella to leave him.

STELLA: I wish you'd just let things go, at least for a – while…

BLANCHE: Stella, I can't live with him! You can, he's your husband. But how could I stay here with him, after last night, with just those curtains between us?

STELLA: Blanche, you saw him at his worst last night.

BLANCHE: On the contrary, I saw him at his best! What such a man has to offer is animal force and he gave a wonderful exhibition of that! But the only way to live with such a man is to – go to bed with him! And that's your job – not mine!

STELLA: After you've rested a little, you'll see it's going to work out. You don't have to worry about anything while you're here. I mean – expenses…

BLANCHE: I have to plan for us both, to get us both – out!

STELLA: You take it for granted that I am in something that I want to get out of.

BLANCHE: I take it for granted that you still have sufficient memory of Belle Reve to find this place and these poker players impossible to live with.

STELLA: Well, you're taking entirely too much for granted.

BLANCHE: I can't believe you're in earnest.

STELLA: No?

BLANCHE: I understand how it happened – a little. You saw him in uniform, an officer, not here but –

STELLA: I'm not sure it would have made any difference where I saw him.

BLANCHE: Now don't say it was one of those mysterious electric things between people! If you do I'll laugh in your face.

STELLA: I am not going to say anything more at all about it!

BLANCHE: All right, then, don't!

STELLA: But there are things that happen between a man and a woman in the dark – that sort of make everything else seem – unimportant. (*Pause.*)

BLANCHE: What you are talking about is brutal desire – just – Desire! – the name of that rattle-trap street-car that bangs through the Quarter, up one old narrow street and down another…

STELLA: Haven't you ever ridden on that street-car?

BLANCHE: It brought me here. – Where I'm not wanted and where I'm ashamed to be...

STELLA: Then don't you think your superior attitude is a bit out of place?

BLANCHE: I am not being or feeling at all superior, Stella. Believe me I'm not! It's just this. This is how I look at it. A man like that is someone to go out with – once – twice – three times when the devil is in you. But live with! Have a child by?

STELLA: I have told you I love him.

BLANCHE: Then I *tremble* for you! I just – *tremble* for you...

STELLA: I can't help your trembling if you insist on trembling!

  (There is a pause.)

BLANCHE: May I – speak – *plainly*?

STELLA: Yes, do. Go ahead. As plainly as you want to.

  (Outside a train approaches. They are silent till the noise subsides.
  They are both in the bedroom.

  Under cover of the train's noise STANLEY enters from outside. He stands
  unseen by the women, holding some packages in his arms, and overhears
  their following conversation. He wears an undershirt and grease-stained
  seersucker pants.)

BLANCHE: Well – if you'll forgive me – he's *common*!

STELLA: Why, yes, I suppose he is.

A Streetcar Named Desire by Tennessee Williams. Published by Penguin.[39]

This scene is packed with allo-repetition because 1) the relationship between Blanche and Stella is intimate, known and familiar, and 2) both of them want to engage in the conversation: in fact, they *need* to engage in the argument. Constant repetition also helps create a poetical, seductive rhythm that drives us through to 'common' and Stella's afterthought of 'Why, yes, I suppose he is.'

Here are some examples:

  – last night (Blanche) / last night (Stella)

  – You saw him at his worst (Stella) / I saw him at his best (Blanche)

  – to get us both – out! (Blanche) / to get out of (Stella)

– You take it for granted (Stella) / I take it for granted (Blanche) / you're taking entirely too much for granted (Stella)

– You saw him… (Blanche) / …I saw him (Stella)

– Now don't say… (Blanche) / I am not going to say… (Stella)

– street-car (Blanche) / street-car (Stella)

– superior (Stella) / superior (Blanche)

– Then I *tremble* for you! I just – *tremble* for you… (Blanche) / I can't help your trembling if you insist on trembling! (Stella)

– May I – speak – *plainly*? (Blanche) / Yes, do. Go ahead. As plainly as you want to. (Stella)

Text Sample 3: Dealing with Dialogue / Revealing Relationship

The following text has been taken from Act 1 of John Osborne's *Look Back in Anger*, published by Penguin. It was first performed in May 1956 by the English Stage Company at the Royal Court Theatre in London and was directed by Tony Richardson.

The story so far:

Jimmy Porter and his wife Alison live in a one-room apartment in the English Midlands. Jimmy is an intelligent but angry young man, who runs a market sweet stall. He grew up working class, educated himself and is now restless and frustrated with his life. His wife Alison comes from a privileged middle-class environment and Jimmy is constantly taunting her about it. The contempt Jimmy feels for Alison's family is often transferred onto Alison herself and it is then that the acerbic attacks become personal. Their Welsh friend, Cliff, who lives in the bedroom across the hall, tries to keep the peace but comes under fire from Jimmy because of it. When Jimmy and Cliff indulge in some physical horseplay it soon turns rough and Cliff is pushed into Alison's ironing board, causing her to burn her arm. Jimmy leaves to sit in the next room with his trumpet, while Cliff is left to deal with the fallout. The scene reveals a tender friendship between Alison and Cliff, drawn together by their inability to deal with Jimmy. Alison reveals to him that she is pregnant and seeks his advice.

CLIFF: Here we are then. Let's have your arm.

> *(He kneels down beside her, and she holds out her arm.)*

> I've put it under the tap. It's quite soft. I'll do it ever so gently.

> *(Very carefully, he rubs the soap over the burn.)*

All right? *(She nods.)* You're a brave girl.

ALISON: I don't feel very brave. *(Tears harshening her voice.)* I really don't, Cliff. I don't think I can take much more. *(Turns her head away.)* I think I feel rather sick.

CLIFF: All over now. *(Puts the soap down.)* Would you like me to get you something?

(She shakes her head. He sits on the arm of the chair, and puts his arm around her. She leans her head back on to him.)

Don't upset yourself, lovely.

(He massages the back of her neck, and she lets her head fall forward.)

ALISON: Where is he?

CLIFF: In my room.

ALISON: What's he doing?

CLIFF: Lying on the bed. Reading, I think. *(Stroking her neck.)* That better?

(She leans back, and closes her eyes again.)

ALISON: Bless you.

(He kisses the top of her head.)

CLIFF: I don't think I'd have the courage to live on my own again – in spite of everything. I'm pretty rough, and pretty ordinary really, and I'd seem worse on my own. And you get fond of people too, worse luck.

ALISON: I don't think I want anything more to do with love. Any more. I can't take it on.

CLIFF: You're too young to start giving up. Too young, and too lovely. Perhaps I'd better put a bandage on that – do you think so?

ALISON: There's some on my dressing table.

(CLIFF crosses to the dressing table R.)

I keep looking back, as far as I remember, and I can't think what it was to feel young, really young. Jimmy said the same thing to me the other day. I pretended not to be listening – because I knew that would hurt him, I suppose. And – of course – he got savage, like tonight. But I knew just what he meant. I suppose it would have been so easy to say "Yes, darling, I know just what you mean. I know what you're feeling." *(Shrugs.)* It's those easy things that seem to be so impossible with us.

(CLIFF stands down R., holding the bandage, his back to her.)

CLIFF: I'm wondering how much longer I can go on watching you two tearing the insides out of each other. It looks pretty ugly sometimes.

ALISON: You wouldn't seriously think of leaving us, would you?

CLIFF: I suppose not. *(Crosses to her.)*

ALISON: I think I'm frightened. If only I knew what was going to happen.

CLIFF: *(Kneeling on the arm of the chair.)* Give it here. *(She holds out her arm.)* Yell out if I hurt you. *(He bandages it for her.)*

ALISON: *(Staring at her outstretched arm.)* Cliff –

CLIFF: Um? *(Slight pause.)* What is it, lovely?

ALISON: Nothing.

CLIFF: I said: what is it?

ALISON: You see – *(Hesitates.)* I'm pregnant.

CLIFF: *(After a few moments.)* I'll need some scissors.

ALISON: They're over there.

CLIFF: *(Crossing to the dressing table.)* That is something, isn't it? When did you find this out?

ALISON: Few days ago. It was a bit of a shock.

CLIFF: Yes, I dare say.

ALISON: After three years of married life, I have to get caught out now.

CLIFF: None of us infallible, I suppose. *(Crosses to her.)* Must say I'm surprised though.

ALISON: It's always been out of the question. What with – this place, and no money, and oh – everything. He's resented it, I know. What can you do?

CLIFF: You haven't told him yet.

ALISON: Not yet.

CLIFF: What are you going to do?

ALISON: I've no idea.

CLIFF: *(Having cut her bandage, he starts tying it.)* That too tight?

ALISON: Fine, thank you.

(She rises, goes to the ironing board, folds it up, and leans it against the food cupboard R.)

CLIFF: Is it… Is it…?

ALISON: Too late to avert the situation? *(Places the iron on the rack of the stove.)* I'm not certain yet. Maybe not. If not, there won't be any problem, will there?

CLIFF: And if it is too late?

(Her face is turned away from him. She simply shakes her head.)

Why don't you tell him now?

(She kneels down to pick up the clothes on the floor, and folds them up.)

After all, he does love you. You don't need me to tell you that.

ALISON: Can't you see? He'll suspect my motives at once. He never stops telling himself that I know how vulnerable he is. Tonight it might be all right – we'd make love. But later, we'd both lie awake, watching for the light to come through that little window, and dreading it. In the morning, he'd feel hoaxed, as if I were trying to kill him in the worst way of all. He'd watch me growing bigger every day, and I wouldn't dare to look at him.

CLIFF: You may have to face it, lovely.

Look Back in Anger by John Osborne. Published by Faber and Faber.[40]

Although there is allo-repetition in this scene, it is balanced out with self-repetition. It may appear as an intimate scene between friends but self-interest drives Cliff and Alison forward. Here are some examples of their repetitions:

You're a brave girl (Cliff) / I don't feel very brave. (Alison)

I don't feel very brave. I really don't, Cliff. I don't think I can take much more. I think I feel rather sick. (Alison)

I don't think I'd have the courage to live on my own again...I'd seem worse on my own. (Cliff)

I don't think... (Cliff) / I don't think... (Alison)

You're too young to start giving up. Too young, and too lovely. (Cliff)

You're too young to start giving up. Too young, and too lovely. (Cliff) / I can't think what it was to feel young. (Alison)

'Yes, darling, I know just what you mean. I know what you're feeling.' (Alison)

What is it, lovely?... I said: what is it? (Cliff)

Is it... Is it...? (Cliff)

Too late to avert the situation? (Alison) / And if it is too late? (Cliff)

Why don't you tell him now?... You don't need me to tell you that. (Cliff) / He never stops telling himself… (Alison)

The allo-repetition is less obvious once Alison has announced she is pregnant. In fact, once this announcement is made the characters lose their connection. Initially, Cliff does not respond to her announcement, instead he pauses before announcing 'I'll need some scissors'. This gives him time to take in the information before addressing it: clearly his life will be changing as well.

4. WORKSHOP PLAN

For actors, simply knowing about rhythmic synchrony and allo-repetition are enlightening and change the way in which they approach the text and develop character. There are two ways in which you can handle this workshop:

1. Ask participants to read the play beforehand (so they understand character and situation), and, undertake some of the work on building vocal characterisation from the previous chapter (so they have a starting point to enter the scene). This means they will be able to cover the workshop exercises and activities in depth.

2. Don't ask the participants to prepare anything before the workshop: simply give them the sample text on the day in order to experiment with word, rhythm and relationship. This may open up text, character and relationship for them before they start on their own personal research.

However, in both instances, it is important for them to undertake detailed accent preparation prior to the workshop (if their own accents differ to those of the text you are intending to work with). This is because human speech rhythm is bound up in accent and sloppy accents can superficialise character, situation and environment. If you are unsure of how to go about this type of work then take a look at Chapter 6: 'Capturing Colloquialism'.

The following workshop asks participants to prepare beforehand but there is no reason why you can't change the format to suit your needs.

WORKSHOP PLAN: DEALING WITH DIALOGUE / REVEALING RELATIONSHIP

Objectives

* To explore the vocal demands of realistic text through a duologue(s)

* To experiment with the spoken rhythmic features in duologues that help establish character, situation and relationship

* To discover how the spoken rhythmic features draw out the relationship between the characters.

Materials

You will need:

– Separate copies of the text extracts, as provided in the previous 'Text Sample' boxes, for each member of the workshop group.

– Highlighting pens

– Large sheets of paper and felt-tip pens.

Actor Preparation

Before the workshop, ask your actors to:

– Read the play from which their chosen extract has been taken (so they understand character and situation)

– Analyse and practise the accent of the character in their chosen extract (if it is different from their own accent)

– Undertake some of the work on building vocal characterisation from the previous chapter (so they have a starting point to enter the scene).

Activities and Exercises

1. Warming up

Divide the group into pairs (with the same people working together who will be rehearsing the text sample duologue). Set warm-up exercises that require partnership so that mutual patterns in breath, sound, word and rhythm can be explored (as well as warming up the voice). Here are some simple directions you can give them:

(a) Grounding, Centring, Aligning and Breathing

– Face each other. Place your feet a little further apart than hip width. Stomp firmly with your feet into the ground. Find a rhythm that you both feel comfortable following (without talking about it). Let your breath fall into this rhythm

– Stop stamping and feel your weight fall down through your feet, without collapsing your spine. Allow your breath a few moments to settle then release a long 'fffff' sound to your partner. Don't push it – just let it float over to them

– Either hold hands, grasp arms or stand back to back. No need to release any sound: just focus in on your partner's silent breath rhythm/pattern. You will find that your breathing patterns will start to synchronise. Don't change what you're doing consciously, just let it happen naturally. Once you feel this, start to release 'fffff' sounds again. They should fall into a similar synchronicity.

(b) Resonating and Articulating

– Face each other once again for some facial mirroring. One person should start 'pulling' some strange positions with their face (don't forget the lips and tongue). The other person must follow these actions. The lead can change at any time. After a few minutes, try adding sound that matches the facial images you are creating (although try not to overdo the volume). Your facial muscles, lips and tongue should end up feeling 'warm'

– Gently pat all over the front of your body with the flats of your hands and release a hum at the same time. Get your body warm and tingly. Ask your partner to do the same thing all over your back (right down to your feet and up again) whilst you hum. They should finish by placing the flats of their hands on your upper back and feel for the sound vibration. Swap over

– Slowly speak the following consonant sounds in time together / p / / b / / t / / d / / k / / g /. Aim for firm lips on the / p / and / b /. Aim for tongue tip precision with / t / and / d /. Aim for back of the tongue muscularity with / k / and / g /. Now start to increase the speed (still speaking in time together). Even with pace you should retain a sense of the individual sounds (e.g. the difference between / p / and / b /) and the precision/muscularity within them. Unconsciously, you will have chosen a particular rhythm in which to do this. Once it is mastered, change it completely and start again. Try a number of different rhythmic patterns with your partner and increase in speed each time.

2. Finding Rhythmic Synchrony

Generate a discussion with your actors about rhythmic synchrony. Ask them to contribute physical and vocal moments when they have found themselves mirroring another person in conversation.

Set up some role plays of familiar domestic scenes with vaguely similar relationships/content to the text samples your actors will be working on later (e.g. two sisters having an argument about one of their partners). After each role play, discuss the physical and vocal mirroring that was apparent with the whole group. Ask your actors to repeat their role plays but change the period/culture in which the role plays were situated to that of the text samples (hopefully they have already completed research on these elements). A final discussion should focus on how the physical and vocal mirroring differed between the two sets of role plays.

3. Analysing the Text

Ask your actors to remain in their pairings and read through the text out loud a couple of times (no other instructions). Then get them to highlight all the self-repetition, allo-repetition, redundancies, interruptions, overlapping and unfinished phrases, using the highlighter pens you have provided. Make sure that each feature is highlighted in a different colour (e.g. blue for all self-repetitions, green for all allo-repetitions etc.).

When they have completed these notes they need to discuss with their partner, *why* they think their character has used these particular words and rhythmic features, plus, *what* they tell us about the relationship between characters within this moment in time. This should (naturally and organically) lead them to answering the following questions:

– *What is the scene about?*

– *What do they want from each other?*

They then need to transfer the self-repetitions and allo-repetitions onto a large piece of paper with felt-tip pens and hang the paper on the wall where it can be easily seen by both actors.

4. Applying Analysis to Performance

Ask your actors to play their scenes again but this time, the only words they may use are the self-repetitions and allo-repetitions listed on the wall. Make sure they read off the wall and not off the page. They should still play 'what their character wants' as decided upon in the previous exercise but can only use the words listed on the wall. This will be a little harder if your actors are using the text sample from *The Lady from the Sea* but it is still an interesting exercise (albeit a little sparser). Generate a discussion to see if anything new occurred to them during the exercise about their characters' relationship.

Now ask them to speak the full text sample but, this time, perform a *mutually agreed physical action* when a self-repetition or allo-repetition occurs. If they want, they can also agree a separate action for each time a redundancy occurs. Ask them to try this through a number of times so that they become physically and vocally fluent. Then ask them to repeat the scene without the actions, allowing the pace and rhythm to be dictated by the pace and rhythm of the writing. Generate a discussion on what the exercise added to their performance.

> ### 3. Debriefing
>
> Allow some time for a group debriefing session (unless they have already answered the following questions during the course of the workshop).
>
> – How did the self-repetitions, allo-repetitions, redundancies, interruptions, overlapped speech, unfinished phrases and line length contribute to the rhythm of the text excerpt?
>
> – Consequently, what did this tell you about the relationship between your characters?

5. REVISITING THE BASICS

Here are some important points to remember from this chapter:

- We don't just choose our vocabulary in isolation; we play off each other's words and rhythms, revealing not only ourselves but our relationship with others.

- Rhythmic synchrony is when we physically and vocally mirror the people with whom we interact. Allo-repetition is vocal rhythmic synchrony, when we repeat elements of what the speaker has just uttered.

- In realistic drama, written dialogue is an adapted version of everyday conversation, giving us the illusion of reality. Many playwrights choose to use features of spoken conversation such as repetition, redundancy, interruptions, overlapped speech and unfinished phrases to help create this illusion.

- Analysing and experimenting with shared words and rhythms in realistic drama (as well as other features of spoken conversation) will bring us closer to understanding character and relationship.

CHAPTER 6: CAPTURING THE COLLOQUIAL

We all use informal colloquialisms in our everyday conversations. They are drawn from:

- the geographical region in which we live and/or were brought up as children

- the generation of people with whom we relate to the most

- the community or class of people with whom we spend the most time

Colloquialisms, therefore, create a connection between speakers from the same region, generation and/or community: we are automatically identifiable and, therefore, more easily included in conversation because of them.

In contemporary society, these boundaries aren't always precise. Immigration, travel, global media and social networking bring us into contact with new people and, therefore, new linguistic trends, widening our colloquial output. When we move to a different region, we practise new colloquialisms (often unconsciously) in order to become accepted more readily. However, we may also choose to retain some of our old colloquialisms (again, often unconsciously) in order to maintain our previous cultural identity. Colloquialisms, therefore, help *create* identity.

For this reason, playwrights of dramatic realism will often include colloquialisms in their texts to form character, bind characters together and create an easily identifiable world for the play. It is the actor's job to speak these colloquialisms as if they are familiar: they must find a rhythm and energy that is realistic and truthful for that particular character, in that particular moment and for that particular world.

In order to find the rhythm and energy of colloquialisms, actors must undertake practical work on the words themselves, as outlined in the workshop plan for this chapter. Prior to embarking on this process, however, some preparation is needed. Researching a regional accent helps actors engage with the sound patterns in colloquial words. Researching the colloquial words within the text helps to clarify and contextualise meaning for the actor.

1. ACCENT RESEARCH

Be cautious of actors who say they are good at accents. Usually this means they are good at mimicry. Mimics may convey an accent successfully but they will also bring a stereotyped character with it. This stereotyped character will prevent the mimic from using the accent with another character: they will be stuck in the rhythmic patterns of what they know how to do. For this reason, actors need to break down the accent into building blocks that can be built up again *with* the character they wish to portray. Never expect an actor to just 'do' an accent: the process requires time and in-depth analysis/practice.

It is important to state at the outset that this is not a book about accents. The following process shows how an actor can *approach* working on an accent.

(a) SOURCE MATERIAL

The starting point should be with original source material. This means finding recordings of native speakers of the accent you wish to research, preferably of the same gender/age as the character and from the same period as the play text. Sometimes this isn't easy but try to find as many that are as close to your requirements as possible. Never use recordings of actors trying to do the accent (like all human beings they are subject to mistakes) only native speakers.

You can always make your own source material by recording native speakers (if you know people who would be appropriate). Draw up a word list that they can read, which covers different types of vowel and consonant sounds, and then ask them to speak (at length) about something personal to them (such as a story from where they grew up). Personal memories often help us to revert (more fully) to our original rhythms, particularly if we are not currently living in our original accent region. Even better, try to record two people from the same region in conversation because (as we learnt in Chapter Five) rhythms are *shared* in dialogue.

Ask your actors to listen to these recordings a number of times so that their ears become familiar with the sounds, rhythms and energies of the native speaker before they commence further analysis. Occasionally, during the process, they will be asked to mimic sounds, words, phrases from these recordings but only as a starting point (not for the creation of character).

(b) POINTS OF TENSION AND SOUND PLACEMENT

We all tense certain muscles in the face and mouth when we speak in order to create the particular positions/shapes needed to form the sounds in our accent. This means that speakers from different regions will tense different sets of facial/oral muscles. Sometimes you can even tell where a person is from by the way in which they 'hold' their face when they're silent. These are known as the *points of tension* in an accent. In turn these tensions affect where the resonant sound comes from. This is commonly referred to as the *sound placement*.

Some Yorkshire speakers tighten their lower jaw and pull their lip edges slightly down. Although there is still an open space within the mouth, it feels as though it is placed at the back (because there isn't much space at the front – with the tight jaw/lips – for the sound to get out).

In a General American accent there is a sense of widening across the face. This means that with limited space the tongue is held quite high in the mouth, sending sound up through the hard palate to the nasal cavities. Therefore, the sound placement seems nasal.

Ask your actors to try a couple of the native speaker's phrases aloud. They should try and feel which parts of their face/mouth tense in order to recreate the sound. They might also like to try describing where the sound is coming from because of these tensions.

(c) RHYTHM

In Chapter 1 we learnt that speech rhythm is created by a combination of phrasing, pausing, stressing, pitching, tuning and pacing. Therefore, your actors need to listen for **regularly recurring patterns** of these elements in order to pinpoint the rhythm of an accent. Having a number of different recordings to hand will ensure they don't end up researching the individual, idiosyncratic patterns of one particular speaker.

Some useful questions might be: Is there a noticeable stress pattern? Do the vowels or the consonants hold the most weight? Is there a regularly recurring tune with similar notes across each phrase? If so, what is its shape? For example, Dublin accents tend to use long, almost sung vowels, drive through to the end of each phrase, and, use a tune that starts high, moves across the top of the phrase and ends on a lower note.

For most people, the tune (intonation) is the most obvious pattern. Ask your actors to listen again to the source material and see if they can identify a recurring tune. They can try and translate this into sounds or numbers (e.g. de, de, de, de, de or 1, 2, 3, 4, 5). For musical actors, singing the pattern can be useful: they can then hear/feel whether the tune has a major or minor quality. The tune of some accents is decidedly major (Received Pronunciation, General American) whilst others are decidedly minor (General Australian, Liverpool).

(d) VOWELS AND CONSONANTS

It's important for actors to stop thinking about spelling and start thinking about individual sounds: English spelling is not phonetic, often bearing no relation to the sound being made (unlike some other languages, such as Italian, where the spelling dictates pronunciation). The International Phonetics Alphabet (IPA) is a useful way of writing down sounds but if your actors have never learnt phonetics or once learnt it at drama school and have now forgotten the symbols, no matter. It's perfectly fine for them to devise their own symbols to document their findings, such as 'oo' for the vowel sound in 'blue', or, 'zh' for the medial consonant in 'treasure', as long as the focus is on individual sounds. There is a useful word list, originally devised by J.C. Wells and re-published in *How To Do Accents* by Edda Sharpe and Jan Hadyn Rowles that your actors can use as a checklist when they're picking out individual sounds in their original source material.[41]

Understanding the way in which vowels and consonants are created in the mouth is also important. Vowels are formed by the lips and the tongue shaping the breath stream (modifying the space within the mouth). Consonants are formed by the lips and the tongue coming into contact with, either each other, or another speech organ (obstructing or narrowing the space within the mouth).

Therefore, your actors need to focus in on vowel shape and consonant positioning in the mouths of their original sources. Of course they won't be able to see them but they will be able to listen, try out sounds/words/phrases and realise the shapes/positions for themselves. Comparing their own formation of a sound to that of their original sources is a useful starting point.

A vowel example might be: if your actor speaks a modern version of Received Pronunciation they may have a certain degree of lip rounding in 'oh' sounds, however this isn't present in many London accents.

A consonant example might be: a modern RP actor will probably place the tip of their tongue against the upper gum ridge to create the consonant sound 't', however in an Indian English accent the tip of the tongue has to curl backwards and flick off the front of the mouth roof.

(e) PRACTICE SENTENCES

Before trying out the accent with character and text, your actors need to spend time practising on sentences that include a variety of sounds in a range of combinations. You can either devise your own or pick out some from the original source recordings. Intensive sentence practice will make the new mouth shapes/positions familiar and comfortable. Revisiting the practice sentences throughout the rehearsal process will help your actors maintain and sustain the accent.

(f) THE PLAY TEXT

The next step is to test it out on the text. These are the elements that may weaken or 'throw' the accent:

– The idiosyncratic speech rhythms of their character

– The sharing of rhythms between characters

– Unfamiliar colloquialisms that are part of the accent region

– Meaning and emotion

In other words, your actors will be attempting to take their practical research and apply it to character and situation. If they attempt to do everything at once then the accent will slip and probably disappear altogether. They must practise it like a technical exercise, learning the shapes and positions for new words (over and over again) and then practising the individual words in phrases (over and over again) which will also help them find the new rhythmic pattern. In this way, the accent will become comfortable and flexible: they won't be thrown when focusing on character, situation and moment.

2. COLLOQUIAL RESEARCH

When working on realistic text it's important that your actors get to grips with all the informal words that originate from a specific geographical region, generation and/or community. This includes colloquialisms and any colloquial subsets, such as slang and expletives. Broadly speaking, colloquialisms are the words we use in everyday informal conversations (not for formalised written communication). Slang is even more informal and usually considered vulgar by standard speakers. Expletives are the words we use to curse or swear and are often obscene or profane.

If colloquialisms, slang and expletives help create cultural and situational identity for characters, actors need to use them as if they are part of their own identity. The character is comfortable speaking them so the actor must be comfortable with them as well. For this to happen they need to be crystal clear about meaning and then apply this knowledge to practical exercise in the rehearsal room.

(a) SEARCHING THE TEXT

The first step in the research process is for your actors to actively look for colloquialisms, slang and expletives in the text they are working on. The text samples further on in this chapter, taken from, *Peaches* by Nick Grosso (set in North London) and *Essex Girls* by Rebecca Prichard (set in Essex), are packed full of colloquialisms, slang and expletives. Here are some examples:

PETE: She looked *fresh*.

JOHNNY: Sweet like a puppy.

FRANK: Yeah – she's a real-life fucking diamond.

JOHNNY: Did you say hello?

PETE: Nah. I was driving.

JOHNNY: You fool. You fucked up – you shoulda pulled over.

FRANK: Yeah, you fucked up. You bad fool.

KELLY: I'm gonna piss meself in a minute. (*To the toilet.*) Caarrm – on.

HAYLEY: Me 'n' all (*To the toilet.*) 'Urry up. You goin' toilet or building it?

DIANE: (*To the toilet.*) You laying an egg or what?

HAYLEY: (*to DIANE and KELLY, rhetorically.*) 'Ooz in there?

DIANE: That April's a right snob.

HAYLEY: She's got summink coming to her.

KELLY: She's all right, I swear – she just don't wear the right clothes, that's all.

Given the amount of colloquialisms, slang and expletives present in these texts, it's almost impossible to get to grips with the characters without focusing on them. Underlining or drawing up lists may sound very basic but can be a surprisingly helpful part of the analytic process.

(b) PINPOINTING MEANING

Once your actors have drawn up their lists or underlined their text, they need to clarify the meaning of each word/phrase they've included. Again this sounds obvious but it's surprising how muddy we can be about colloquialisms when asked to explain them. We may *think* we know the meaning of a commonly used word or phrase but can we explain it to someone coming from outside of the region, generation or community?

Here are some words from the sample texts that may need further analysis by your actors:

Peaches by Nick Grosso

fresh
peach
real-life fucking diamond
shades
Safe
private dick

Essex Girls by Rebecca Prichard

piss meself
You laying an egg
In one ear
right snob
a swot

It's important to remember that colloquialisms, slang and expletives are constantly changing and evolving. What is linguistically fashionable one minute for a particular generation of people from a particular geographical region may not be the next. These texts were written in the mid-1990s so they're already out of date. Therefore, pinpointing the meaning of a colloquial word/phrase might require historical research as well.

When your actors are clear about meaning they must engage with context: why is the character using these particular words or phrases at this particular moment in time? Take a look at the following sequence taken from the *Peaches* text sample:

JOHNNY: Where was this?

PETE: At a bus stop.

JOHNNY: *What bus stop/*

PETE: I don't know – a bus stop – they all look the fucking same.

JOHNNY: Pete – where the fuck was this bus stop?

FRANK: Yeah, where the fuck was this fucking bus stop?

There are a number of reasons why Johnny, Pete and Frank use expletives in this exchange: to express extra annoyance, to emphasise a point/question, to create a pleasing rhythmic effect, to mirror one another (and thereby bond with each other) and, finally, to competitively top one another (who can fit the most expletives into the one sentence?).

(c) PRACTISING IN THE ACCENT

Your actors now need to practise speaking the colloquialisms, slang and expletives in the accent (away from the text). Their mouths must be able to handle tricky combinations of sounds. Also, they must know and practise the most commonly used stress in words of more than one syllable, the most commonly used stress across a colloquial phrase and how the tune/intonation pattern operates. Familiarity resides in how easily and smoothly your actors can handle the vowel shapes, the consonant positions and any unfamiliar rhythms.

The most difficult to handle are the expletives. This is partially because each geographical region has its own particular rhythmic energy for swearing that can be difficult to tap into. For example, most swearing in the South-East of England makes use of consonant energy (with extra bite in the consonants). However, Australian speakers use the vowels to energise their expletives. This tiny rhythmic shift makes all the difference for speakers working across these accents. In addition, some actors aren't comfortable swearing and find it difficult connecting to expletives. In such cases, extra practice is required so that rhythm, energy and drive are easy and familiar.

3. TEXT SAMPLES

We will be working on extracts from *Peaches* by Nick Grosso and *Essex Girls* by Rebecca Prichard in the workshop plan for this chapter. Neither text is necessarily categorised as Dramatic Realism but they have elements of dramatically realistic dialogue, particularly abundant in colloquialisms, slang and expletives.

Text Sample 1: Capturing the Colloquial

The following text has been taken from *Peaches* by Nick Grosso, which was performed as part of the Royal Court Young Writers' Festival at the Royal Court Theatre Upstairs in November 1994. It is published in *Coming On Strong (New Writing from the Royal Court Theatre)* by Faber and Faber.

The story so far:

This play explores the sex-obsessed lives of a group of young men who've just left college. Their concerns aren't about jobs, money or getting on in life, only with 'peaches' – good-looking girls – and how to meet them. This scene takes place in a North London flat. It starts with Pete ironing a shirt, Frank lying on the sofa and Johnny standing around.

PETE: I saw Milly yesterday.

   (FRANK and JOHNNY look at PETE..)

JOHNNY: Milly!

FRANK: Where?

PETE: At the bus stop.

JOHNNY: I love Milly.

FRANK: I love her too.

JOHNNY: Pity she don't love you.

FRANK: She loves me alright – she just don't know it.

PETE: She looked *fresh*.

JOHNNY: Sweet like a puppy.

FRANK: Yeah – she's a real-life fucking diamond.

JOHNNY: Did you say hello?

PETE: Nah. I was driving.

JOHNNY: You fool. You fucked up – you shoulda pulled over.

FRANK: Yeah, you fucked up. You bad fool.

JOHNNY: Did she see you?

PETE: Nah, I was wearing my shades.

JOHNNY: That's it – you fucked up…what was she doing?

PETE: Standing.

JOHNNY: With who?

PETE: On her own.

    (FRANK and JOHNNY glance at each other.)

BOTH: *Safe.*

JOHNNY: Where was this?

PETE: At a bus stop.

JOHNNY: *What bus stop/*

PETE: I don't know – a bus stop – they all look the fucking same.

JOHNNY: Pete – where the fuck was this bus stop?

FRANK: Yeah, where the fuck was this fucking bus stop?

PETE: How should I know?

    (FRANK and JOHNNY laugh.)

    Top of Highgate Road.

JOHNNY: Highgate Road!

FRANK: That means she's back at her dad's.

JOHNNY: Has she finished college?

FRANK: She's finished college, she's back at her dad's, she's fresh like a peach, and it's all happening.

JOHNNY: What time was this?

PETE: How should I know?

JOHNNY: Just tell me what fucking time it was!

PETE: I'm sorry – I didn't keep a time-check.

FRANK: You'll never make a private dick.

JOHNNY: Yeah – not like Philip Marlowe.

PETE: What's got into you two…?

JOHNNY: Was it morning? Afternoon? Evening? What?

PETE: It was in the morning.

JOHNNY: Like half-past eight?

PETE: Yeah, around that.

FRANK: Shit. That's early.

JOHNNY: I don't care, I'm gonna be there.

FRANK: What dya mean?

JOHNNY: The way I see it, she's got a job up west – Channel 4 most likely – and she gets the bus every day from the top of Highgate Hill. She's back in town, she's unattached – and I'm gonna party.

FRANK: Fuck it – I'm joining you.

PETE: Yeah! Me too!

FRANK: So she's working at Channel 4?

JOHNNY: Yeah. She's in charge of the peaches.

(Pause.)

PETE: I saw her last week too as it goes.

(FRANK and JOHNNY look at PETE.)

JOHNNY: What!

FRANK: Where?

PETE: Sainsbury's.

JOHNNY: You saw Milly Foster at Sainsbury's? You kept that quiet!

FRANK: Yeah – you kept that fucking quiet.

Peaches by Nick Grosso. Published by Faber and Faber in *Coming On Strong (New Writing from the Royal Court Theatre)*.[42]

Text Sample 2: Capturing the Colloquial

The following text has been taken from *Essex Girls* by Rebecca Prichard, which was performed as part of the Royal Court Young Writers' Festival at the Royal Court Theatre Upstairs in November 1994. It is published in *Coming On Strong (New Writing from the Royal Court Theatre)* by Faber and Faber.

The story so far:

Act One of *Essex Girls* focuses on three girls in the school toilets. There is an 'out of order' sign on one of the cubicle doors. Another toilet has a tampon in it so the girls are reluctant to use it. A third cubicle is locked so the girls assume someone is in there. Whilst waiting for it to become free they discuss boys, parties, families, school and their dreams for the future.

KELLY: I'm gonna piss meself in a minute. (*To the toilet.*) Caarrm – on.

HAYLEY: Me 'n' all (*To the toilet.*) 'Urry up. You goin' toilet or building it?

DIANE: (*To the toilet.*) You laying an egg or what?

HAYLEY: (*To DIANE and KELLY, rhetorically.*) 'Ooz in there? (*To KELLY.*) You goin' Typing?

KELLY: Dunno. (*To DIANE.*) Are you?

DIANE: Doubt it.

KELLY: So boring.

DIANE: You know, last time I saw Mrs Levitt I was sitting on the floor near the pipes. She comes up to me and goes, 'If you can't learn the attitude of a lady you'll never be a secretary.' I goes, 'I don't wanna be a secretary.'

KELLY: What did she say?

DIANE: She's deaf, in't she.

HAYLEY: In one ear. That April wants to be a journalist for magazines. She went to see her head of house about it.

DIANE: What did he say?

HAYLEY: He goes that it's very competitive or something.

DIANE: I ain't going to see them 'bout what I want to do. They'd say I should be a slave or something.

DIANE: That April's a right snob.

HAYLEY: She's got summink coming to her.

KELLY: She's all right, I swear — she just don't wear the right clothes, that's all. If she dressed like a swot all her life and worn National Healths, Mr Rainhill'd of given her all the info.

DIANE: We're all gonna get called in soon to talk about jobs.

HAYLEY: Are we?

DIANE: Yeah, we gonna get interviewed.

KELLY: I already had my interview. Iss borin'. I felt like they was all laughin' at me.

DIANE: Why?

KELLY: When 'e asked me about my future, I felt like 'e was being sarcastic.

HAYLEY: What did you say ya wanted to be?

KELLY: It was on his wall. A therapist.

DIANE: A what rapist?

KELLY: Therr-rapist.

HAYLEY: You ain't a therapist.

KELLY: Might b…

DIANE: That ain't a job, anyway. It's a hobby.

KELLY: It ain't a hobby.

HAYLEY: What is it, then?

DIANE: What else did he say?

KELLY: Same as usual. Work hard.

DIANE: That all?

KELLY: He said, 'I wanna see a change in you, Kelly. You've still got time. You can change.'

DIANE: Him? On about change? 'E don't even change his underwear, 'e don't even change his mind, let alone anything else.

KELLY: My sister done all right. She ain't got her exams.

DIANE: They don't know what they're on about.

HAYLEY: Oi, Diane, who are you going party with Friday night?

DIANE: Dunno. Might ask Paul Davies. (*Beat.*) Joke. Who you going with, Kell?

KELLY: Dunno yet. Dunno what I'm gonna wear either.

DIANE: I'm wearing (*She mimes lightly as she shows KELLY.*) me culottes, me…me wrap-over top and me…me black boots.

HAYLEY: (*Interrupting.*) Phobia arksed me if I wanna go with him.

KELLY: Who?

HAYLEY: You know that guy, Phobia.

DIANE: I don't know anyone called Phobia…

KELLY: (*Seriously.*) That's a girl's name, innit?

HAYLEY: Nah, it's a state of mind.

Essex Girls by Rebecca Prichard. Published by Faber and Faber in *Coming On Strong* (*New Writing from the Royal Court Theatre*). [43]

4. WORKSHOP PLAN

This workshop won't succeed if your actors haven't researched play, character and accent beforehand. Without this knowledge they will only be able to connect to the words in a superficial, one-dimensional manner. Do spend some time researching the accent with them, as described earlier in this chapter.

Workshop Plan: Capturing the Colloquial

Objectives

- To explore the informal words (such as colloquialisms, slang and expletives) that create character and situational identity in realistic dialogue

- To experiment with the rhythm and energy of colloquialisms within realistic dialogue

- To become familiar/comfortable/at ease with using colloquialisms, slang and expletives in realistic dialogue.

Materials

You will need:

– Separate copies of the text extracts, as provided in the previous 'Text Sample' boxes, for each member of the workshop group

– Large sheets of paper and felt-tip pens.

Actor Preparation

Before the workshop, ask your actors to:

– Read the play from which their chosen extract has been taken (so they understand the character and his/her energy, drive and motivation)

– Undertake accent research relevant to the play/character they will be working on (as outlined earlier in this chapter)

– Undertake colloquial research relevant to the text sample they will be working on (as outlined earlier in this chapter).

Activities and Exercises

Your actors should already know where the colloquialisms, slang and expletives occur in their chosen text (and have practised them in the accent). Get them to transfer them to a blank sheet of paper in a long list, before they commence the warm-up.

---

1. Warming up

(a) *Releasing, Grounding, Centring, Aligning, Breathing, Resonating*

– Ask your actors to lie down on the floor and stretch their bodies whilst yawning

– Now ask them to move into a semi-supine position, which means lying on their back, bending their knees and placing their feet flat on the floor. They may wish to use a small book under their head for comfort and spinal alignment. Get them to experiment with the placement of their feet (perhaps closer towards their buttocks) so that they feel more of their back touching the floor (without pushing down). Now coach them to give in to gravity and release their weight into the floor, particularly around the lower back. Help them to think their way up the spine, lengthening along the floor as they do so. When they reach the neck, ask them to move their head, gently, from side to side to release tension and then bring it back to centre

– They should now place their hands on their lower abdomen and allow their shoulders to ease out across the floor. Air should be floating in and out gently through the mouth. Ask them to start deepening their intake so they can feel the muscles move beneath their hands (the lower the better). Coach them to start releasing their breath on a long 'fffff' sound, right to the end of their breath stream so they feel the muscles contract, ready for the next intake of breath. After a series of these breaths, move them onto a long sssss sound, followed by a 'vvvvv' sound, then a 'zzzzz' sound. Keep coaching them to 'pour' the sound out of their body

– Now ask them to blow through their lips like a horse, vibrating the lips into a 'bwwwww', right to the end of their breath stream. Once their faces start to get itchy, ask them to add voiced sound, to increase their resonant vibration. Also, they should try moving from a top note down to a lower note and then vice versa.

2. Working on Word

– Ask your actors to stay in semi-supine but pick up their sheet of paper with the list of colloquialisms from the text. They should already be clear about the meaning for each of them

– Give them time to breathe into the centre of the body (just like the warm-up), thinking about the word/phrase as they do so, then releasing it out vocally into the space above them. Encourage them to try each one a number of times, exploring its weight, length, energy and overall rhythmic value (in the accent)

– Allow time for your actors to get slowly to their feet (through a spinal roll is best). They then need to ground, centre and align themselves (see the warm-up for Chapter 4 on pages 130-132)

– Ask them to face another actor in the group, choose one of the words or phrases on their list and explain its meaning. Vocalising the definition will force them to

---

pinpoint meaning more precisely. The other actor may ask questions if they don't understand. Then both actors should try vocalising the word/phrase a number of times to each other. They can then swap over and repeat the process with a word/ phrase from the other actor's list

– Ask each actor to find a new partner and repeat the process with a different word/ phrase and different person. They can keep doing this until their lists have been completed

– Now ask your actors to get into their text extract pairs/groups. Ask them to run through the text aloud but each time colloquialisms, slang or expletives occur, they should give their partner(s) a friendly shove on the shoulder, slap on the back, high five or just a bit of a jostle (depending on meaning and context). Ask them to repeat the exercise without the physical contact. The colloquial words should retain the physical energy and start to drive the text forward in a rhythm all of its own.

3. Debriefing

Allow some time for a group debriefing session.

– What have you learnt about character, relationship and situation in the text excerpt after working on colloquial words?

– In the final reading, did your interpretation/performance change once you had stopped making physical contact with the other characters on each of the colloquial words? In what way?

Now ask your actors to read the scene again in their pairs/groups. They may (unconsciously) incorporate elements of the discussion into their performance.

– Did this last reading change again? In what way?

5. REVISITING THE BASICS

Here are some important points to remember from this chapter:

- Colloquial words create connections between speakers from the same geographical region, generation, community or class.

- Playwrights often include colloquialisms to help create character identity, clarify the relationships between characters and construct an easily recognisable world.

- Researching a regional accent helps actors engage with the sound and rhythmic patterns in colloquial words.

- Researching the colloquial words within a text (including slang and expletives) helps to clarify meaning for the actor, as well as provide further clues about character, relationship and context.

- Practical experimentation with the colloquial words in a text will help actors become comfortable/familiar/at ease with them. If a character is comfortable using these words then the actor must be as well.

- Practical experimentation with the colloquial words in a text will help actors find a rhythm and energy that is realistic and truthful for that particular character, in that particular moment and for that particular world.

CHAPTER 7: VOICING THE VERBATIM

1. WHAT IS VERBATIM THEATRE?

Political theatre isn't a new concept and the twentieth century is littered with examples of plays drawing on real-life material from public events to create thought-provoking drama. However, there was a resurgence of politicised theatre in England during the 1990s; in particular, a style that has now become known as Verbatim Theatre. The theatre critic Michael Billington saw it as a natural reaction to perceived injusticies of the time: 'political theatre became a vital necessity rather than an optional luxury.'[44]

Verbatim texts are based on factual events, recording the speech from real-life interviews, first-hand testimonies and/or documented public enquiries. The playwright (sometimes in conjunction with the actors involved in the project) records interviews and/or personal testimonies from real people, which is then structured into 'a play'. Or the original text from a documented public inquiry is edited into a 'play' by the playwright (also known as 'tribunal plays'). I use the term 'play' loosely because they aren't in the same form or style of what we consider to be traditional drama. They do have characters (real people whose language and idiosyncratic speech rhythms have been written down verbatim) and they do have drama (drawn from real events and shaped by the playwright into a dramatic framework), however, that is where the similarity ends. Most notable is the role of the audience, whom the actors usually place in the role of interviewer, speaking directly to them and answering their imaginary questions.

2. KEY PLAYS AND PLAYERS

Tribunal plays have been the particular forte of **Nicolas Kent** (former Artistic Director of the Tricycle Theatre in Kilburn) and **Richard Norton-Taylor** (newspaper journalist). Commissioned and directed by Kent, produced and written (or edited) by Norton-Taylor, their plays include: *Half the Picture* in 1994 (a dramatisation of the Scott inquiry into the sale of arms to Iraq), *Srebrenica* in 1996 (focusing on the International Criminal Tribunal hearings into the Bosnian civil war), *The Colour of Justice* in 1999 (depicting the Macpherson inquiry which investigated how the Metropolitan Police handled the case of Stephen Lawrence, a black teenager stabbed to death in South London), *Justifying War* in 2003 (based on the Hutton inquiry into the death of Dr David Kelly the British/UN weapons inspector), *Bloody Sunday* in 2005 (focusing on the Saville inquiry into the events of Derry 1972 when civil rights marchers were killed by British soldiers), and, *Called to Account: the Indictment of Anthony Charles Lynton Blair for the crime of aggression against Iraq: a Hearing* in 2007 (which tested the evidence of the British Government's decision to declare war on Iraq through the first-hand testimonies from some of the key players). More recently *Tactical Questioning: Scenes from the Baha Mousa Inquiry* (2011) examined the British army's handling of detainees in Iraq.

Max Stafford-Clark's company Out of Joint produced: *A State Affair* by Robin Soans in 2000 (exploring the Bradford Estate portrayed in *Rita, Sue and Bob Too*, eighteen years after the play was written), *The Permanent Way* by David Hare in 2003 (focusing on the privatisation of British railways) and *Talking to Terrorists* by Robin Soans in 2005 (presenting the first-hand accounts of those involved in various terrorist movements). However, Stafford-Clark started experimenting with Verbatim Theatre back in 1976 with *Yesterday's News* (about the war in Angola), produced by his company Joint Stock (set up in 1975 with David Hare, William Gaskill and David Aukin). He also produced *Falkland Sound* in 1983, whilst Artistic Director of the Royal Court Theatre (providing first-hand testimonies of those affected by the Falkland War).

As well as his work with Out of Joint, **David Hare** has created: *Via Dolorosa* in 1998 (focusing on his journey through Israel and Palestine), *Stuff Happens* in 2004 (weaving fictional scenes with verbatim text around the events leading up to the Iraq War) and *The Power of Yes* in 2009 (where he uses the verbatim form to demystify the financial crisis).

As well as his work with Out of Joint, **Robin Soans** has created: *The Arab-Israeli Cookbook* in 2004 (a collection of stories and recipes from Arabs and Jews living side by side in the Middle East), *Life After Scandal* in 2007 (presenting interviews of those who have faced some sort of public scandal) and *Across the Divide* in 2007 (focusing on first-hand testimonies of people living in the Brent East constituency following the 1997 election). *Deep Heat: Encounters with the Famous, the Infamous and the Unknown* is a series of verbatim monologues, published in 2011.

Alecky Blythe set up the company Recorded Delivery after her first verbatim success *Come Out Eli* in 2003 (focusing on those affected by the Hackney siege of 2002). She uses a technique whereby actors are fed the lines through earphones during performances in order to recreate the exact speech rhythms of the characters. Her verbatim texts include: *Strawberry Fields* (2005), *All the Right People Come Here* (2005), *Cruising* (2006) and *The Girlfriend Experience* (2008). In 2011, her collaboration with composer Adam Cork at the National Theatre Studio, produced *London Road* (focusing on the community experience of residents on London Road, Ipswich where a series of prostitutes had been murdered in 2006). Cork took the speech rhythms of Blythe's verbatim text and set them to music, thereby creating a completely new style of musical theatre.

Other notable verbatim plays and playwrights from England include: *Guantanamo: 'Honor Bound to Defend Freedom'* (2004) by **Victoria Brittain** and **Gillian Slovo**, *Gladiator Games* (2005) by **Tanika Gupta**, *Deep Cut* (2008) by **Philip Ralph** and *The Riots* (2011) also by Gillian Slovo.

3. VERBAL FEATURES

Because verbatim texts provide a written form of verbal speech, transcribed from real speakers, they include all the features of everyday speech I've discussed so far in this book. Verbatim vocabulary is littered with colloquialisms, slang, expletives, jargon, clichés, rhetoric, lyricisms, trivia, irrelevances, fillers and other redundancies. Speech rhythm is defined by broken thoughts, unfinished phrases, repetitions, grammatical errors, word contractions and sound stutters. Here are a few thoughts regarding real versus invented speech from the playwrights themselves.

Robin Soans:

> ...when the bricks and mortar of a play are real conversations, people use such idiosyncratic and bizarre language that it is immediately recognisable as lacking in artifice. I interviewed a paparazzo for my recent play on scandal, and he said, 'If someone's snorting cocaine or picking their nose, I'll leave that alone, but a lot of photographers are looking for that...crack-sweaty-arse-pants...zoom in on armpits, all sorts of crap.' I doubt that many writers would or even could come up with the phrase 'crack-sweaty-arse-pants', but we know exactly what the photographer means; it has the undeniable ring of truth about it, as well as the sort of detail that is instantly recognisable and therefore binds us to the character.[45]

David Hare:

> Only a very great playwright would invent that soldier's line 'So. You want to talk,' whereas the soldier has said it effortlessly. All the time you're coming across lines that are almost impossible to invent.[46]

Alecky Blythe:

> ...how could I ever hope to write anything that comes close to the fantastically rich and multi-layered messiness of real speech?[47]

The difference between verbatim texts and fictional drama is that the verbal features have been *less manipulated* by the playwright. Although verbatim playwrights will tailor the material to highlight the political and create dramatic structure, they are less likely to edit out the idiosyncratic vocabulary/rhythms that help define character and their emotional state at the time of speaking (although this does vary across playwrights).

Alecky Blythe:

> The audio had been painstakingly transcribed with every 'um', 'er', stutter and non-sequitur lovingly preserved, because it is these that reveal the person's thought processes: there is always a specific reason why a person stutters on a certain word, and it is this detail that gives the characters such startling verisimilitude.[48]

However, Blythe changed her way of working for *London Road*: she allowed her characters to repeat more of their words/phrases. This provided greater rhythmic emphasis for Adam Cork to work with in composing the music. However, Blythe also found that the repetitions helped clarify the text for both actor and audience. Robin Soans works similarly.

Robin Soans:

> I might make small changes to the text for the sake of clarity or fluidity, but I take great pains to preserve the sense, tone and thrust of an interviewee's words. If, for the sake of an *and* or a *but*, what they say becomes much clearer, I have no qualms inserting such a word. Why alienate or confuse an audience for the sake of a monosyllable or two?
>
> As for all the *ums* and *ers*, the stutters and repetitions, I use them when they suit my purpose, and leave them out when they don't. This is only another form of editing. If one of my interviewees becomes very emotional, I can retain all the verbal inconsistencies to highlight that. But if they're telling a story and I want the narrative to trot on at a good pace, I'll pare their words down to what is necessary. I can't include everything that I'm told by my subjects, so I must choose what I think is the most representative sample.[49]

4. ORIGINAL PERFORMANCES

The primary concerns for actors and directors working with verbatim text have been:

- Capturing the language and rhythms of the original speakers

- Embodying the character of the original speakers (sometimes well-known people with public profiles)

- Maintaining the character and their speech patterns whilst addressing the audience directly

In some original productions, the actors completed many of the interviews themselves so had met and already studied their 'character'. In other productions, they were sent to meet the people they intended to portray. In this way they could build certain physical/vocal traits into their performances.

However, for the majority of companies, it seems that word and textual rhythms were the most important tools of all. Many gave their actors access to original recordings where they could imitate delivery. Imitation led to the discovery that the character and their emotional response to a situation could be automatically created from the words and rhythmic speech patterns that they used. It also helped actors avoid caricature and impersonation, particularly if their character was a well-known public figure.

By asking her actors to work with earphones so that the original recordings are fed to them during performance, Alecky Blythe feels she prevents the actors from settling back into their own speech rhythms and/or adding their own actorly interpretation to the textual rhythms ('the struggle to resist one's own natural rhythms is immense'[50]). The technique was pioneered by the American actress Anna Deavere Smith. Blythe thought that Deavere Smith's work 'demonstrated that language was the root of character. By copying their speech-patterns with such precision, the real person behind the performance shone through.'[51] However, when music was devised for her *London Road* text, Blythe was forced to remove the earphones and the actors simply learnt the speech/song rhythms, focusing on delivery with as little embellishment as possible.

Nicolas Kent insisted that his actors use microphones at the Tricycle Theatre so that they didn't need to project or theatricalise the text in any way ('The hyper-naturalism of everything being very low-key means it's nearer to the truth, I suppose. [52]). He also liked to work with the house-lights up so the audience felt closer to the events that were taking place on stage.

Because, in most cases (other than tribunal plays), the audience is 'cast' as the interviewer, the actors are required to directly address the audience. This can be confronting for both audience and actor. In addition, because the actors aren't involved in a rhythmic exchange of dialogue the nature of the text can be easily altered. Therefore, many companies have found that it is more important than ever for actors to rehearse (over and over again) rhythmic precision. In this way they will feel secure about reaching out to the audience, without losing the patterns they have painstakingly worked on in rehearsal.

5. PRE-REHEARSAL RESEARCH/PREPARATION

In most cases, you won't have the original recordings to work with so copying the speech rhythms of the real speakers isn't an option in your rehearsal process. Therefore, you and your actors will need to rely on the text; in particular, how the speech rhythms have been copied onto the page. Here are a few things your actors need to do before experimentation with the text in the workshop plan for this chapter.

(a) UNDERSTANDING THE VERBATIM PROCESS

Without access to the original recordings, it's a good idea for your actors to understand how the verbatim process works by carrying out their own small verbatim projects. Ask them to:

- Divide into pairs and record a short conversational exchange (you might like to set topics). Then ask each pair to swap their recording with another pair's recording so they won't be analysing their own rhythms. Get the pairs to transcribe the recording they've ended up with. This will help them to understand the way in which speech rhythm can be written down. Now ask them to try and recreate the actual conversation, in exactly the way in which it has been recorded, and then report on their findings.

(b) COLLECTING BACKGROUND INFORMATION

Your actors then need to gather background information about character, situation and circumstance from the actual text they will be using. This is crucial otherwise later work on the text will be empty and superficial. Ask them to:

- Read as much about the character and his/her background as they possibly can (if that information is available to them)

- Meet the character, if possible, and focus on any particular physical and vocal mannerisms

- Collect video clips off the internet, if meeting them isn't possible and the character is a public figure, in order to research their physical and vocal mannerisms

- Learn as much about the political/social situation that inspired the play as they possibly can (the specific events, the circumstances that led to the events, other characters that were involved)

(c) ANALYSING THE TEXT

Now it's time to focus more closely on the text itself. Ask your actors to:

- Read the text a number of times so they become moderately familiar with its rhythmic patterns (phrasing, pausing, stressing, pitching, tuning and pacing). Make sure they don't memorise them just yet

- Undertake exercises on the accent, if it is different to their own, as outlined in Chapter 6 of this book

- Undertake exercises on the character's voice as outlined in Chapter 4 of this book

- Undertake exercises on the colloquialisms, slang and expletives as outlined in Chapter 6 of this book

Now your actors can start focusing on the textual rhythms in greater detail by following the workshop plan for this chapter. This workshop will help them understand the reasons why their character uses particular speech features, and, allow them time to experiment with textual rhythms through practical exercise, before they embark on detailed memorisation.

Learning the text too early will set the rhythmic patterns in stone and they will be harder to change. Make sure all exploratory work is completed before the words/rhythms are committed to memory.

6. TEXT SAMPLES

Text Sample 1: Voicing the Verbatim

The following text has been taken from *Deep Cut* by Philip Ralph, which was commissioned by Sgript Cymru, produced by Sherman Cymru and first performed at Sherman, Cardiff, in 2008.

The story so far:

Between 1995 and 2002, four young soldiers died from gunshot wounds at their training base, the Deepcut barracks. Their deaths were announced as suicides by the Ministry of Defence, the government and the Surrey police, despite forensic evidence that put this in doubt. The families of these soldiers have been unable to find out what really happened and their calls for a public inquiry have fallen on deaf ears.

This play explores the story of eighteen-year-old Cheryl James from Llangollen and her parents' search for the truth about her death. Much of the text is based on first-hand testimonies, including that of another female soldier, 'Jonesy' from Rhyl, who joined up around the same time as Cheryl. Here, she talks about how she was recruited.

JONESY: I do believe that everyone who goes in the Army [has] got a reason. Passed my GCSEs and did an A-level. I liked school. But I got in with – well, it wasn't the wrong crowd, we were just a bit loud, I suppose, and we got into fights and we got into a really bad fight one night. We ended up in court and it caused horrendous arguments at home. (*Beat.*) I was just standing there thinking 'My God, I just don't want to end up doing this', you know? 'Cause I knew I wasn't stupid, I'd done my education. And I didn't want to go to university. My mum and stepdad couldn't have afforded [it] anyway. I just didn't know what I wanted to do.

I was 18 [and] I was walking home from school and I was like, 'Bloody hell, I've got no fags, I've got no money, I'm doing a shit job', and there was no jobs in the Job Centre and the one's that were [were] paying like eighty, ninety pounds a week at that time. I did want more. I'll be honest, I wanted more really. And I was walking past the Army careers, I thought, 'My God, I've never noticed that before.' And I went in and the guy in there was eating Kentucky Fried Chicken. He gave me some of his chips [and he] promised me the world and made me watch a video. Oh, God. That was great. So, I signed up there and then. He said I'd have a ball. And to be fair, he didn't lie to me that much, do you know what I mean? [How long did it take] before I signed my life away? Just under twenty minutes, I think.

I had to go and sign my Oath of Allegiance. You have to sign in front of an officer which was really impressive, I thought. And nobody believed I was going to go. Even my friends the night I was due to go in, throwing stones at my bedroom window. They were like, 'You don't want to go in there. It's crap!' but I said, 'I'm going.' That was it. Nothing was stopping me. Stood on the train station, my mum and sisters came [to see me off.] I was crapping myself. (*Beat.*) I arrived at Pirbright on a Sunday afternoon in April.

The main purpose of Pirbright is to make you leave. (*Laughs.*) 'Do you want to go home now?' We'd be like starving and pissed wet through and, you know, wondering why you signed that piece of paper and why did I just get won over by a few scabby Kentucky chips?

Deep Cut by Philip Ralph. Published by Oberon Books.[53]

Text Sample 2: Voicing the Verbatim

The following text has been taken from *Gladiator Games* by Tanika Gupta, which was first performed at the Crucible Studio in October 2005 and transferred to the Theatre Royal Stratford East in November 2005.

The story so far:

On the night of his release from Feltham Young Offenders Institution, Zahid Mubarek, a young British Asian, was murdered by his racist cellmate. Zahid had been sentenced to 90 days' imprisonment for the theft of six pounds' worth of razor blades and interfering with a car but his killer had a prison career spanning nine years and a history of racist violence. *Gladiator Games* traces the Mubarek family's pursuit of the truth. Imtiaz Amin is Zahid's uncle and only ten years older than him. The following monologue was reproduced from an original interview with Imitiaz.

IMITIAZ: Apparently from the court (*Hesitates.*) ...Tanzeel told me that when he was there – it was quite poignant looking back on it now – in hindsight because it was like when the Judge said 'take him down' or whatever, Zahid just turned round to his grandad and Tanzeel said in Punjabi, '*Me jara ow*', it was his way of saying, 'I'm going again'. He said just the expression on his face was, was, you know, er, it was like...they was never going to see him again. You know...er...

Long pause.

At the time, my nephew and my dad thought it was pretty much the way they deal with things here. And especially dad, he believes in the system. My father's point of view was look – he's going to the Young Offenders Institute – it's not full-blown prison. They've got to have things in place to rehabilitate er... (*He laughs sadly.*) have things in place to sort them out so that they can lead a more productive life. Had we known this much (*Measures a speck with his fingers.*) of what Feltham was about, really, you know, it would have been different. It would have been different. I was in Holloway Prison a couple of weeks ago, a visit for the prison law course I'm doing and I met a prison officer there. He said to me, 'You look remarkably familiar', and so I told him my name. He put his arm around me and said: 'Look, I'm really, really sorry about what happened. I was working at Feltham at the time and I knew Zahid. He was a smashing lad.' This was just a couple of months ago – it really hit me.

He was very much loved – despite his problems. He was very much loved.

Gladiator Games by Tanika Gupta. Published by Oberon Books.[54]

Text Sample 3: Voicing the Verbatim

The following text has been taken from *Life After Scandal* by Robin Soans, which was first performed at Hampstead Theatre, London in September 2007.

Life After Scandal is a series of intertwined interviews with people who have been involved in public scandals, including Jonathan Aiken, Edwina Currie, Craig Murray, Neil and Christine Hamilton, and, Charles and Diana Ingram. The play explores how people survive public humiliation and investigates a whole industry built on shame. MENAJI is part of the paparazzi but is able to see how ludicrous his job actually is.

MENAJI: Here we are…it's the beast…it's a Canon…it's a tool of the trade…it's a bit of a beast. I'm a paparazzo, but I'm not telling you my name. My camera does eight and a half frames a second, it's all digital…forget film, film's great, but too much aggravation… (*To BARMAN.*) …I'll have a beer…

Anything as long as it's not crap… (*To us.*) …it's a 2.8 70-mil to 200-mil zoom with auto-focus…now that means you only want the one lens…that's vital, you don't want to be fucking about changing lenses in the middle of the action. You don't carry a camera bag cos then everyone knows you've got a camera…you have a bag that looks like any sort of bag…you don't have any bits with you; you won't be far from your car…you can have all your shit in the car.

For your more powerful shots, you need a tripod, but usually in that kind of situation you're in a bush, or up a tree, on the beach, or behind a wall looking onto the beach.

So this is a zoom lens, good for a low light, and you can put a doubler on this if you want to get in close. You spend a lot of time outside someone's house, we call it the location, and you have to be there early before they leave.

There's always paparazzi cruising in their cars, following someone as they go about. Look, look at this…I was at an actress's house, outside her house, couple of hours ago…on a scout…followed her home on the off-chance…you never know who's gonna turn up…photographed this girl who turned up…don't know who she is…could be anybody…she didn't know I was photographing her…out the window of my car…scratching her thigh look…running her hand through her hair…look at this one…checking her mobile phone. Following is always better. I went through twelve traffic lights in a fortnight following Kate Moss…there may be other paparazzi following her…you don't want them getting 'the shot'. What you want is an exclusive. If someone's snorting cocaine or picking their nose, I'll leave that alone, but a lot of photographers are looking for that…crack-sweaty-arse-pants-zoom in on armpits, all sorts of crap. You only ambush someone if it's going to be difficult following them, or there's a back entrance out of a building and you can't cover it.

The ambush is when you jump out in front of them and blitz them. The cry is 'Go, go, go', and we all jump out.

You won't be quoting this under my name will you? They fucking do whatever they want to do whenever they want to do it. They buy the photographs off me, and then they just make up the headlines and the captions underneath…the story underneath is nonsense.

Life After Scandal by Robin Soans. Published by Oberon Books.[55]

7. WORKSHOP PLAN

This workshop won't succeed if your actors haven't completed the pre-rehearsal research/preparation beforehand, as described on pages 182-184 in this chapter.

It's important to note that the workshop has been designed for rehearsals where your actors don't have access to the original recordings and their only source material for the speech rhythms is the text itself.

The activities and exercises in this workshop are much more specific about rhythmic evaluation, as opposed to previous workshops that allowed a greater amount of creative interpretation from the actor. That is the nature of verbatim text.

Workshop Plan: Voicing the Verbatim

Objectives

- To understand why verbatim characters use particular speech features/rhythms

- To experiment with textual rhythms through practical exercise

Materials

You will need:

– Separate copies of the text extracts, as provided in the previous 'Text Extract' boxes, for each member of the workshop group

– Paper and highlighting pens.

Actor Preparation

Before the workshop, ask your actors to:

– Undertake a small verbatim project, transcribing real speech and then copying its rhythmic features (as outlined on pages 178-80 of this chapter)

– Read the play from which their chosen extract has been taken

– Collect background information relevant to the play/character they will be working on (as outlined on pages 182-3 of this chapter)

– Undertake accent research relevant to the play/character they will be working on (as outlined in Chapter 6)

– Undertake work on the character's voice, relevant to the play they will be working on (as outlined in Chapter 4)

– Undertake colloquial research relevant to the text sample they will be working on (as outlined in Chapter 6)

Activities and Exercises

1. Warming up

(a) Releasing, Grounding, Centring, Aligning, Breathing, Resonating

– Ask your actors to either run or jog around the space, keeping their arms and shoulders loose. At the sound of a clap, they must stop and flop over from the waist so they're hanging upside down (make sure their knees are bent). Ask them to shake out their arms down there with some sound (whatever comes out without thinking about it). Now get them to release a long 'fffff' sound. Ask them to repeat the 'fffff' sound but as they do so, coach them to roll up through the spine until they're standing in an aligned position. Their head should be the last part of their body to float up

– Repeat the previous exercise a number of times, using different sounds each time e.g. 'sssss', 'vvvvv', 'zzzzz', 'bwwwww' (blowing through the lips like a horse), 'mmmm' (humming) and long open vowel sounds

– Now ask your actors to take a walk around the space releasing 'fffff' sounds. Each time they need to breathe, they should stop, centre their weight, breathe in freely and easily, before setting off again. After a few minutes, coach them to vary the rhythm between short breath phrases and long breath phrases (perhaps one step and a short 'fffff' is followed by a number of steps and a longer 'fffff'). Once they seem comfortable ask them to try a different sound (of your choice). This may throw the rhythm so allow them time to get comfortable again before introducing another new sound.

(b) Articulation and Accent

– Lip stretches: Ask your actors to centre their weight and try silent and exaggerated 'ee – oo' movements with their mouths. Now ask them to try some upper lip sneering, lifting one muscle, then the other, followed by both together

– Tongue stretches: Again, ask your actors to remain centred. Coach them to stretch their tongues out of their mouths as far as they can go, followed by a stretch right to the back of the mouth (so the tongue is all scrunched up). They should try this sequence a number of times so the movement is quick, clean and easy. Get them to shake out their bodies afterwards to make sure they haven't picked up any unnecessary upper body tension

– Your actors should have a list of colloquialisms, slang and expletives, drawn from their text excerpt that they've been practising in the accent. Ask them to mouth these words, exaggerating the lip and tongue movements. Now get them to speak the list aloud but slowly and carefully so they can handle any difficult sound combinations easily. Finally, get them to pace it up to what they consider to be a slightly faster than normal speed. Make sure they aren't losing the accent (if this happens, get them to go back and mouth them).

2. Analysing the Rhythmic Features

– Ask your actors to pair up and read their chosen text aloud to each other a couple of times (no other instructions). Now get them to pinpoint (and mark on the text with the highlighter pens you have provided) all the features that disrupt the speaker's rhythmic flow, such as:

- broken thoughts

- unfinished phrases

- parenthesis (thoughts within thoughts)

- repetitions

– grammatical errors

– fillers

– silent hesitations

– stutters on particular sounds

– Ask them to read the text aloud again, being aware of where these features occur as they move down the page

– Now they need to discuss with their partner, *why* they think the character has used each of these particular rhythmic features

– Ask them to read the text aloud again, being aware of the reasons behind these features as they move down the page

– Get each pairing to share their findings with the rest of the group in a discussion format.

3. Experimenting with the Rhythmic Features

– Ask your actors to separate away from their partner into their own space. They need to stand, centre their weight on both feet (hip width apart), align their spine and release a few long 'fffff' sounds from their belly, before they start. The previous exercise should have helped them establish sense phrasing and pausing, now it's time to focus on the breath phrasing and pausing (detailed explanations are available back in Chapter 1). Ask them to read the text extract aloud again and note where the breaths naturally fall. They should mark these with a pencilled slash between the words on the page

– Get them to speak the text excerpt again but walk around the room whilst doing so but stopping at every pause (sense and breath). Get them to feel the timing of these (tiny breaks in the movement for sense pauses, longer breaks for breath pauses). Ask them to repeat the exercise so that differences between short and long phrases are comfortably handled. This exercise should help them to feel the textual rhythms through their body

– Now ask them to centre their weight again and speak the text in stillness. They should be able to maintain the rhythm without the movement

– Establishing the phrasing/pausing rhythm should have established where the nuclear stresses sit (more information on this is back in Chapter 1). Ask your actors to speak the text again, listen for the nuclear stress in each phrase and mark the syllable where it occurs on the page. Now get them to speak it again and over-exaggerate the stress of the nuclear syllable, giving it more emphasis than it needs. A final repetition aloud, focusing on meaning/emotion, should clarify the nuclear stress without your actors having to think about it

– Now your actors need to speak the text aloud, listening for the pitch movement on the nuclear stress (more information on this back in Chapter 1) and marking its direction with an arrow on the page. Give them some time to repeat the text a number of times, practising it in. Then ask them to forget about it and just concentrate on the meaning

– Encourage them to run or jog around the space, speaking a speeded up version of the text. As soon as they've finished speaking, ask them to stop moving, centre their weight and flop over from the waist so they're hanging upside down (make sure their knees are bent). They should release a long 'fffff' sound, then roll up the spine with another 'fffff' sound (just as they did in the warm-up). As soon as their head floats up they should start speaking the text extract again, focusing on meaning/emotion only. The pace should now operate at a much more natural and organic speed

– Finally, get them to present the pieces as direct address readings to the whole group (casting the audience as interviewer). This may distort the natural rhythmic flow. If so, get them to run around the space speaking it again and *then* repeat the still 'presentation' to the whole group.

4. Debriefing

Allow some time for a group debriefing session.

– What have you learnt about the character after working on their speech rhythm?

Now ask your actors to read the text excerpt again to the whole group. They may (unconsciously) incorporate elements of the discussion into their performance.

– Did this last reading change again? In what way?

8. REVISITING THE BASICS

Here are some important points to remember from this chapter:

- Verbatim Theatre texts are based on factual politicised events, recording the speech from real-life interviews, first-hand testimonies and/or documented public inquiries

- Verbatim Theatre texts often 'cast' the audience in the role of interviewer: the actors speak directly to them and answer their imaginary questions

- The verbal features in Verbatim Theatre texts have been *less manipulated* by the playwright than in fictional drama

- Verbatim vocabulary is littered with colloquialisms, slang, expletives, jargon, clichés, rhetoric, lyricisms, trivia, irrelevances, fillers and other redundancies. Verbatim speech rhythm is defined by broken thoughts, unfinished phrases, repetitions, grammatical errors, word contractions and sound stutters.

- Actors working with Verbatim Theatre texts need to: capture the language and rhythms of the original speakers; embody the character of the original speaker; and, maintain the character and their speech patterns whilst addressing the audience directly

- Practical experimentation with the words and rhythms in a Verbatim Theatre text will help actors realise the character and the character's emotional response to a situation/event

NOTES

1. Reckord, B. (1966), 'Foreword' to *Skyvers* in *New English Dramatists 9*. London: Penguin Books, pp. 77-8.

2. Ibsen, H. (1963), *Enemy of the People,* trans. by M. Meyer, London: Rupert Hart-Davis, p. 89.

3. Shaw, G. B. (1913), *The Quintessence of Ibsenism.* London: Constable and Company, p.3.

4. Shaw, G. B. (1914), *Misalliance, The Dark Lady of the Sonnets, and Fanny's First Play – with a Treatise on Parents and Children* by Bernard Shaw. Cambridge U.S.A.: The University Press, p. 243.

5. Tynan, K. (1975), *A View of the English Stage, 1944-63.* London: Davis-Poynter, p. 148.

6. Lacey, S. (1995), *British Realist Theatre: The New Wave in its Context 1956-1965.* London: Routledge, p. 28.

7. Ibid., p. 19.

8. Winterson, J., *My Hero: Shelagh Delaney* (*The Guardian* newspaper 18.09.10).

9. Billington, M. (2007), *State of the Nation: British Theatre since 1945.* London: Faber and Faber, p. 183.

10. Robinson, M. (2009), *The American Play, 1787-2000.* New Haven: Yale University Press, p. 107.

11. Ibid., p. 20.

12. Murphy, B. (1987), *American Realism and American Drama, 1880-1940* (Cambridge: Cambridge University Press, p. 193, taken from an interview recorded by Malcolm Mollan in the *Philadelphia Public Ledger*, January 22, 1922.

13. Robinson, M. (2009), p. 17, taken from Jackson R. Bryer (ed.) (1982), *The Theatre We Worked For: The Letters of Eugene O'Neill to Kenneth Macgowan.* New Haven: Yale University Press.

14. Bigsby, C.W.E. (1992), *Modern American Drama, 1945-1990.* Cambridge: Cambridge University Press, pp. 33-4, taken from A.J. Devlin (1986), *Conversations with Tennessee Williams.* Jackson: University Press of Mississippi.

15. Ibid., p. 153.

16. Ibid., p. 269, taken from Sessums, *Interview Magazine.* p. 78.

17. McGuire, P. (with B. Arnott & F.M. McGuire) (1948), *The Australian Theatre.* Clarendon: Oxford University Press, p. 150.

18. McCallum, J. (2009), *Belonging: Australian Playwriting in the 20th Century.* Strawberry Hills NSW: Currency Press, p. 33.

19. Ibid., p. 32, taken from Esson, *Ballades* p. 184.

20. Fitzpatrick, P. (1979), *After 'The Doll': Australian Drama since 1955*. London: Edward Arnold, p. 5, taken from Letter dated 15 June, 1926, in Vance Palmer (1948), *Louis Esson and the Australian Theatre*. Melbourne: Meanjin Press, p. 69.

21. Lawler, R. (1978), *Summer of the Seventeenth Doll*. Strawberry Hills NSW: Currency Press, p.xxvii (foreword).

22. Ibid., p.xxxiii-xxxiv (foreword).

23. Tynan, K. (1958), *The Observer Plays*. London: Faber and Faber, p. 11 (preface).

24. Reckord, B. (1966), *Skyvers* in *New English Dramatists 9*. London: Penguin Books, p. 85.

25. Esson, L. (1912), *The Woman Tamed* taken from *Three Short Plays*. Melbourne: Fraser and Jenkinson, p. 6.

26. Wesker, A. (1962), *Chips with Everything*. London: Jonathan Cape, p. 33.

27. Osborne, J. (1962), *Look Back in Anger*. London: Faber and Faber, p. 15.

28. Ibid., p. 22.

29. Ibid., p. 37.

30. Billington, M. (2007), p. 182.

31. Osborne, J. (1962), p. 11.

32. Bond, E. (1966), *Saved*. London: Methuen, p. 113.

33. Wesker, A. (1959), *Roots*. London: Penguin, p. 77.

34. Odets, C. (1994), *Waiting for Lefty and Other Plays*. New York: Grove Press, p. 65.

35. Chekhov, A. (2008), *Ivanov* in a version by Tom Stoppard. London: Faber and Faber, pp. 55-56.

36. Ibid., p. 61.

37. Tannen, D. (2007), *Talking Voices: Repetition, Dialogue, and Imagery in Conversational Discourse*. Cambridge: Cambridge University Press, p. 32.

38. Ibsen, H. (2003) *The Lady From the Sea* in a version by Pam Gems. London: Oberon Books, p. 59.

39. Williams, T. (1983), *Sweet Bird of Youth, A Streetcar Named Desire, The Glass Menagerie*. London: Penguin, p. 161.

40. Osborne, J. (1962), p. 27.

41. Sharpe, E. & Haydn Rowles, J. (2007), *How to Do Accents*. London: Oberon Books, p. 206.

42. Grosso, N. (1995), *Peaches* in *Coming On Strong: New Writing from the Royal Court Theatre*. London: Faber and Faber, p. 46.

43. Prichard, R. (1995), *Essex Girls* in *Coming On Strong: New Writing from the Royal Court Theatre*. London: Faber and Faber, p. 190.

44. Billington, M. (2007), p. 384.

45. Hammond, W. & Steward, D. (eds.) (2008), *Verbatim Verbatim: Contemporary Documentary Theatre.* London: Oberon Books, pp. 24-5.

46. Ibid., p. 51.

47. Ibid., p. 102.

48. Ibid., p. 96-7.

49. Ibid., p. 41-2.

50. Ibid., p. 80.

51. Ibid., p. 80.

52. Ibid., p. 156.

53. Ralph, P. (2008), *Deep Cut.* London: Oberon Books, pp. 38, 40-41.

54. Gupta, T. (2005), *Gladiator Games.* London: Oberon Books, pp. 105-106.

55. Soans, R. (2007), *Life After Scandal.* London: Oberon Books, ppp. 40-44, 47.

SUGGESTED READING

GENERAL REFERENCE

Bigsby, C.W.E. (1992), *Modern American Drama, 1945-1990.* Cambridge: Cambridge University Press.

Billington, M. (2007), *State of the Nation: British Theatre since 1945.* London: Faber and Faber.

Edgar, D. (2009), *How Plays Work.* London: Nick Hern Books.

Fitzpatrick, P. (1979), *After 'The Doll': Australian Drama since 1955.* London: Edward Arnold.

Hammond, W. & Steward, D. (eds.) (2008), *Verbatim Verbatim: Contemporary Documentary Theatre.* London: Oberon Books.

Harrop, J. & Epstein, R. (1990), *Acting with Style.* New Jersey: Prentice Hall.

Innes, C. (ed.) (1998), *The Cambridge Companion to George Bernard Shaw.* Cambridge: Cambridge University Press.

Lacey, S. (1995), *British Realist Theatre: The New Wave in its Context 1956-1965.* London: Routledge.

McCallum, J. (2009), *Belonging: Australian Playwriting in the 20th Century.* Strawberry Hills NSW: Currency Press.

McFarlane, J. (ed.) (1994), *The Cambridge Companion to Ibsen.* Cambridge: Cambridge University Press.

Murphy, B. (1987), *American Realism and American Drama, 1880-1940.* Cambridge: Cambridge University Press.

McGuire, P. (with Arnott, B. & McGuire, F.M.) (1948), *The Australian Theatre.* (Clarendon: Oxford University Press.

Parker, D. (ed.) (1987), *Essays on Modern American Drama: Williams, Miller, Albee, Shepard.* Toronto: University of Toronto Press.

Reckord, B. (1966), *Skyvers* (Preface) in *New English Dramatists 9.* London: Penguin Books.

Robinson, M. (2009), *The American Play, 1787-2000.* New Haven: Yale University Press.

CATHERINE WEATE

Rebellato, D. (1999), *1956 And All That: The Making of Modern British Drama*. London: Routledge.

Sharpe, E. & Haydn Rowles, J. (2007), *How to Do Accents*. London: Oberon Books.

Shaw, B. (1913), *The Quintessence of Ibsenism*. London: Constable and Company.

Styan, J.L. (1981), *Modern Drama in Theory and Practice 1: Realism and Naturalism*. Cambridge: Cambridge University Press.

Tannen, Deborah (2007), *Talking Voices: Repetition, Dialogue, and Imagery in Conversational Discourse*. Cambridge: Cambridge University Press.

Tynan, K. (1975), *A View of the English Stage, 1944-63*. London: Davis-Poynter.

Tynan, K. (1958), *The Observer Plays*. London: Faber and Faber.

Williams, M. (1977), *Australian Writers and their Work: Drama*. Clarendon: Oxford University Press.

PLAYS

EUROPEAN

Chekhov, A. (2004), *Plays: Ivanov, The Seagull, Uncle Vanya, The Cherry Orchard*, trans. by P. Carson. London: Penguin.

Chekhov, A. (2008), *Ivanov* in a version by Tom Stoppard. London: Faber and Faber.

Ibsen, H. (2008), *Four Major Plays: A Doll's House, Ghosts, Hedda Gabbler, The Master Builder,* trans. by J. McFarlane and J. Arup. Clarendon: Oxford Classics.

Ibsen, H. (1963), *Enemy of the People,* trans. by M. Meyer, London: Rupert Hart-Davis.

Ibsen, H. (2003) *The Lady From the Sea* in a version by Pam Gems. London: Oberon Books.

ENGLISH

Blythe, A. & Cork, A. (2011), *London Road*. London: Nick Hern Books.

Bond, E. (1966), *Saved*. London: Methuen.

Grosso, N. (1995), *Peaches* in *Coming On Strong: New Writing from the Royal Court Theatre*. London: Faber and Faber.

Gupta, T. (2005), *Gladiator Games*. London: Oberon Books.

Delaney, S. (1959), *A Taste of Honey*. London: Methuen.

Norton-Taylor, R. (ed.) (2011), *Tactical Questioning*. London: Oberon Books.

Osborne, J. (1962), *Look Back in Anger*. London: Faber and Faber.

Prichard, R. (1995), *Essex Girls* in *Coming On Strong: New Writing from the Royal Court Theatre*. London: Faber and Faber.

Ralph, P. (2008), *Deep Cut*. London: Oberon Books.

Reckord, B. (1966), *Skyvers* in *New English Dramatists 9*. London: Penguin Books.

Shaw, B. (1914), *Misalliance, The Dark Lady of the Sonnets, Fanny's First Play*. Cambridge U.S.A.: The University Press.

Shaw, B. (1988), *Heartbreak House*. London: Viking Penguin.

Shaw, B. (2005), *Plays Unpleasant: Widowers' Houses, The Philanderer, Mrs Warren's Profession*. London: Penguin.

Slovo, G. (2011), *The Riots*. London: Oberon Books.

Soans, R. (2011), *Deep Heat*. London: Oberon Books.

Soans, R. (2007), *Life After Scandal*. London: Oberon Books.

Wesker, A. (1960), *The Wesker Trilogy: Chicken Soup with Barley, Roots, I'm Talking About Jerusalem*. London: Jonathan Cape.

Wesker, A. (1962), *Chips With Everything*. London: Jonathan Cape.

AMERICAN

Albee, E. (1970), *Who's Afraid of Virginia Woolf?* London: Penguin.

Hansberry, L. (2001), *A Raisin in the Sun*. London: Methuen.

Hellman, L. (1979), *Six Plays by Lillian Hellman: The Children's Hour, Days to Come, The Little Foxes, Watch on the Rhine, Another Part of the Forest, The Autumn Garden* (New York: Vintage Books.

Herne, J.A. (2001), *Margaret Fleming*, published in M. Matlaw (ed.) *Nineteenth-Century American Plays*. New York: Applause 2001.

Inge, W. (1960), *Four Plays by William Inge: Come Back, Little Sheba, Picnic, Bus Stop, The Dark at the Top of the Stairs*. London: William Heinemann Ltd.

Miller, A. (2009), *Plays 1: All My Sons, Death of a Salesman, The Crucible, A Memory of Two Mondays, A View from the Bridge*. London: Methuen.

Odets, C. (1994), *Waiting for Lefty and Other Plays: Waiting for Lefty, Awake and Sing!, Till the Day I Die, Paradise Lost, Golden Boy, Rocket to the Moon*. New York: Grove Press.

O'Neill, E. (2006), *Anna Christie*. Lenoz, MA: Hard Press.

O'Neill, E. (1994), *The Iceman Cometh*. London: Nick Hern Books.

O'Neill, E. (1991), *Long Day's Journey Into Night*. London: Nick Hern Books.

Williams, T. (1983), *Cat on a Hot Tin Roof*. London: Penguin.

Williams, T. (1983), *Sweet Bird of Youth, A Streetcar Named Desire, The Glass Menagerie* London: Penguin.

AUSTRALIAN

Bailey, B. & Rudd, S. (1984), *On Our Selection: Dramatization of Steele Rudd's Books*. Strawberry Hills NSW: Currency Press.

Beynon, R. (1960), *The Shifting Heart*. Sydney: Angus & Robertson.

Dann, G. L. (1948), *Fountains Beyond*. Sydney: Australasian Publishing Co.

Esson, L. (2009), *Dead Timber and Other Plays*. Charleston, South Carolina: BiblioBazaar.

Esson, L. (1946), *The Southern Cross and Other Plays*. Melbourne: Robertson and Mullens.

Gray, O. (2000), *Burst of Summer*, published in K. Brisbane (ed.), *Plays of the 60s: Volume 1*. Strawberry Hills NSW: Currency Press.

Hewett, D. (1986), *This Old Man Comes Rolling Home*. Strawberry Hills NSW: Currency Press.

Lawler, R. (1978), *Summer of the Seventeenth Doll*. Strawberry Hills NSW: Currency Press.

Lawler, R. (1987), *The Doll Trilogy*. Strawberry Hills NSW: Currency Press.

Prichard, K.S. (1974), *Brumby Innes* and *Bid Me To Love*. Strawberry Hills NSW: Currency Press.

Pfisterer, S. (ed.) (1999), *Tremendous Worlds (Australian Women's Drama 1890-1960): The Apple* by Inez Bensusan, *Morning Sacrifice* by Dymphna Cusack, *Forward One* by Katharine Susannah Prichard, *No Family* by Miles Franklin, *Here Under Heaven* by Mona Brand, *Flood* by Eunice Hanger, *Jane, My Love* by Catherine Shepherd. Strawberry Hills NSW: Currency Press.

Roland, B. (1974), *A Touch of Silk*. Strawberry Hills NSW: Currency Press.

Seymour, A. (1988), *The One Day of the Year*. Sydney: Angus & Robertson.

SUGGESTED VIEWING

FILMS

ENGLISH

Look Back in Anger (Woodfall Films, 1958).

Saturday Night and Sunday Morning (Woodfall Films, 1960).

A Taste of Honey (Woodfall Films, 1961).

The Loneliness of the Long Distance Runner (Woodfall Films, 1962).

A Kind of Loving (Vic Films, 1962).

Billy Liar (Vic Films, 1963).

The Road to Coronation Street (ITV Studios Production, 2010).

AMERICAN

Golden Boy (Columbia Pictures, 1939).

A Streetcar Named Desire (Warner Bros, 1951).

Picnic (Columbia Pictures, 1955).

Bus Stop (20th Century Fox, 1956).

Cat on a Hot Tin Roof (Metro-Goldwyn-Mayer, 1958).

The Misfits (United Artists, 1961).

A Raisin in the Sun (Columbia Pictures, 1961).

Who's Afraid of Virginia Woolf? (Warner Bros, 1966).

CATHERINE WEATE

PART THREE:
NON-REALISTIC DRAMA

CHAPTER 8: DEMANDS AND CHALLENGES

1. DISTORTING REALISM

Dramatic texts are considered to be non-realistic when they distort realism. This can be achieved in a number of different ways, including all or even just one of the following:

- The *time* continuum may be disrupted
- Natural speech *rhythm* may be heightened, twisted or manipulated
- The *language* may be heightened, twisted or manipulated and be inappropriate for the character, situation and/or context
- A *character* may be representational, symbolic or inappropriate for the situation and/or context
- The *content/plot* isn't true-to-life
- The *presentation* breaks the boundaries of the 'fourth wall'

(a) TIME

Realistic drama tends to be in *linear time*. One event happens after another in the order they would have occurred in had they taken place in real life. It may be that the events happen in *real-time* across the play (i.e. the actual time it would take for these events to occur). Otherwise they can occur in *stretched time*, where the time frame is expanded across the course of the play, covering different time periods in the characters' lives (sometimes in the one day, sometimes a weekend or perhaps a number of years), however they will probably still occur in chronological order.

Non-realistic drama often disrupts linear time, manipulating the chronology of events to heighten audience perception of the subject, plot, situation or character(s). The playwright, David Edgar, separates non-linear time into three distinct categories: *disrupted time, double timescale* and *disconnected time.*

Disrupted time is simply linear time disturbed: flashbacks and flash forwards are common in disrupted time plays. Sometimes, however, playwrights choose to reverse the chronological events completely so the audience learns about the end of the story at the beginning of the play. In *Betrayal* (1978), Harold Pinter reverses some of the chronology so that we (as an audience) learn about an extra-marital affair backwards. The final scene is particularly revealing, outlining the start of the affair, when we already have prior knowledge of its final moments and aftershocks.

Double timescale is when a play moves between two stories set in completely different time periods, automatically commenting on each other in the process. Tom Stoppard sets his play *Arcadia* (1993) in a house in Derbyshire, and moves between scenes in the early nineteenth century and the modern day. The lives of the characters in each time zone are juxtaposed through this device as they search for knowledge (the nineteenth-century characters focusing on the future, the modern-day characters trying to reconstruct the past). Act One of *Clybourne Park* (2010) by Bruce Norris is set in a Chicago neighbourhood in 1959. Act Two is set in the same house but fifty years later, juxtaposing racial issues across two very different periods in time.

Disconnected time is when there are a number of different stories presented that have no immediate connection and it is up to the audience to draw their own conclusions. Clifford Odets used this device in *Waiting for Lefty* (1935). Although a trade union meeting about corruption in a taxi company frames the play, other scenes are seemingly unrelated. However, viewed as a whole, they focus the audience onto the left-wing political issues of the day, especially social inequalities during economic depression.

(b) RHYTHM

If realistic drama is all about recreating the rhythms of natural speech, non-realistic drama focuses on heightening, twisting or manipulating speech rhythm, thereby making it more prominent. Often it feels as if characters in non-realistic texts are *consciously* playing with rhythm. This effect is achieved by increasing word/phrase repetition, creating more dominant sound patterns and enhancing significant pauses (almost like a poem without actually setting the text into a verse structure). The more patterning there is in the text, the more marked the rhythm and the less realistic it feels.

Rhythmic patterning is particularly important (and prominent) in Samuel Beckett's *Waiting for Godot* (1953). Repetition is constant: the characters reiterate particular sounds, words and phrases throughout the play. This gives us the impression that they cannot move forward but just keep going round in circles.

The characters in Harold Pinter's plays use repetition, sound patterns and pauses to play verbal games with each other. The effect is poetical, without (necessarily) being lyrical. Pauses in particular, give definition to these games. He allows characters small silent hesitations within their speech (rather than using natural fillers such as 'ums', 'ahs' or 'ers') and then creates longer pauses at the end of a verbal exchange, marking a rhythmic episode and giving his characters time to regroup before entering into the next verbal skirmish.

Some contemporary non-realistic playwrights heighten rhythm by actually writing in a verse structure so that dialogue is set in verse lines. They feel that speech becomes far more dramatic and intense when presented in this way. The primary distinction between modern and classical verse plays is that there is less prescription in the verse form, less formulaic obeisance to metrical rules. Verse playwrights such as T.S. Eliot (whose plays appeared in the 1930s, 1940s and 1950s) and Tony Harrison (whose seminal works were written in the 1970s, 1980s and 1990s) vary the metrical beat to suit the moment. Sarah Kane, who drifts into verse during *4.48 Psychosis* (2000), uses a very loose verse structure to highlight and intensify emotion.

(c) LANGUAGE

In realistic drama, language provides us with specific information about a character's background, inner life and emotional state as well as place, situation and context. However, in non-realistic text, this isn't necessarily the case: the language may have actually very little to do with character and/or situation. The playwright may use language to create a particular sound quality (e.g. lyrical or staccato) regardless of the context in which it occurs. Or, the playwright may devalue language by using words that are completely meaningless for the context. Or, the playwright may use language to contradict the action that is taking place on stage.

There is continual contradiction between words and action in Samuel Beckett's *Waiting for Godot*. For example, Vladimir and Estragon may say 'Let's go' but they do not leave, giving us the impression that action is futile.

Ionesco wrote *La Cantatrice Chauve – The Bald Soprano* (1950) after having to learn banal statements whilst studying English. His language choices expose the empty platitudes, facile clichés and meaningless conversations within everyday life. The absurdity increases at the end of the play, building to a hostile climax, created through rhythmic sound patterns that quicken the tempo and highlight emotional intensity.

(d) CHARACTER

In realistic drama, characters are motivated: they have inner needs and drives based on their background, circumstances and the moment in which the play is set. In non-realistic drama, characters can be unrecognisable as human beings (sometimes portrayed as a creature or animal). Or they can be unrecognisable as *realistic* human beings: their inner needs and drives are not apparent and they do not react off situation appropriately (usually due to the absence of plot). Or, realistic human beings are placed in an environment/situation that they would never normally be exposed to within the real world ('let's see what happens if…').

In Edward Albee's *Seascape* (1975), a married couple, Nancy and Charlie, sit on a beach and talk about their lives, hopes and dreams. They are joined by another couple, Sarah and Leslie, who happen to be large, fantastical sea creatures. After the initial shock wears off, the two couples engage in conversation and, ultimately, the play explores the evolution and meaning of human life. Albee thought *Seascape* his most realistic play, even if some of the characters are lizard-like creatures from the sea. In Ionesco's *Rhinoceros* (1959), the inhabitants of a small town actually evolve into animals, in this case rhinoceroses, making a statement about mass political conformity in the aftershock of World War II.

Dan Rebellato's *Chekhov in Hell* (2010), follows the experiences of the Russian playwright Anton Chekhov after he wakes up in an NHS hospital in the twenty-first century. Chekhov was a keen observer of late nineteenth-century life and he employs the same detailed fascination with some of the more ridiculous and superficial elements of the contemporary world. It's a non-realistic character/plot device that focuses a mirror onto the incongruities in our own society.

(e) CONTENT/PLOT

In realistic drama, the content of the story is recognisable to the audience as having been drawn from real life. Non-realistic drama may include elements that could not possibly occur in the context of real life, such as the magical, the fantastical, the mythological, the supernatural, the futuristic, the absurd, the surreal, the symbolic or the alternative reality (where historical events are portrayed with a fictional twist). Non-realistic content/plots play on the unorthodox and the unconventional.

Caryl Churchill draws on folk and fairy tales in *The Skriker* (1994), where a shape-shifting sprite pursues two teenage mothers. The play focuses on the dark realities of the contemporary world that must answer to the horrors of the underworld.

Pirandello's *Six Characters in Search of an Author* (1921) is fantastical but in a completely different way. A group of actors are in the process of rehearsing a Pirandello play with their manager/director when six 'characters' enter, searching for an author who will tell their story. The original author abandoned them so they are unrealised and want to be brought to life. They are given the opportunity to act out their story with the company watching, arguing that they are more real than the actors who wish to represent them. Their story blurs the lines between fantasy and reality: even the director is unclear as to its truth.

(f) PRESENTATION

In realistic drama, actors create a representation of life on stage, separating the audience from the action by an invisible wall ('the fourth wall' of the traditional three-walled box in a proscenium arch theatre). This helps the audience believe they are watching a 'real' story, as if they are simply witnessing people getting on with their lives. In many non-realistic dramas, the fourth wall is broken and the characters speak to the audience directly. This presentational style helps the audience to understand they are watching a play, alienating them from any sense of reality.

Bertolt Brecht consciously broke the fourth wall in his plays so that the audience could operate as an analytic observer of the action rather than be swept away by it. Because his plays are didactic (meaning they contain a political/social/moral message) he did not want his audiences' judgement to be clouded by attachment to character. Therefore, he broke their emotional concentration by using narrators who spoke directly to them, creating characters who acknowledged their presence and incorporating song which broke up the action.

Likewise, Joan Littlewood's *Oh! What a Lovely War* (1963), collaboratively devised at Theatre Workshop in London's Stratford East, used a presentational style to focus audience attention on the devastating effects of World War I.

2. NON-REALISTIC MOVEMENTS

Categorising non-realistic plays can be difficult but there are a number of significant, clear and distinct movements that have influenced non-realistic drama. This list is by no means exhaustive.

(a) SYMBOLIST DRAMA

Most plays use symbols. J.L. Styan wrote:

> an object or a situation can immediately suggest an idea or a feeling that is greater than itself. A storm in a play, for example, has always symbolized displeasure in heaven and the anger of the gods, and whether in high tragedy or popular melodrama, the sight and sound of thunder and lightning speak ominously to an audience anywhere. A crown is a powerful symbolic property in Shakespeare, and held between the King and Bolingbroke in *Richard III*, it unmistakably points to the disputed authority over the kingdom. Such symbols have the virtue of being unshakably traditional and almost universal in impact, like red for danger or a voyage for life itself.[1]

Even the early realist playwrights dabbled with the use of symbolism. However, a group of European playwrights in the late nineteenth century and the early twentieth century developed dramas focusing almost exclusively on the symbolic as opposed to the representational, as a reaction against the rise of realism. Their plays relied heavily on the dramatisation of symbolic imagery.

They were influenced in particular by the composer Richard Wagner who was interested in exploring archetypes, myths, dreams, the supernatural and the mystical and sought to create music-theatre/opera that affected both the mind and the emotions. It was also influenced by the French symbolist poets, such as Mallarmé, Rimbaud, Valéry and Baudelaire who focused on revealing life indirectly through fantasy, dreams and rituals. Freud was another influence: his psychological in-depth character studies may have enlightened the realists but his research into symbols within dreams was used by the symbolists.

The Belgian **Maurice Maeterlinck** is considered the father of symbolist drama. His plays such as *The Intruder* (1890), *The Blind* (1890), *Interior* (1894) and *Pelléas and Mélisande* (1893) were fantastical, mystical, poetical and fatalistic. His follower, Frenchman **Paul Claudel**, was interested in the spiritual, divine and poetical in *The Hostage* (1911), *The Tidings Brought to Mary* (1912), *Break of Moon* (1906) and *The Satin Slipper* (1919-1924). The Russian, **Leonid Andreyev**, was also influenced by Maeterlinck in *The Life of Man* (1907). The Swede, **August Strindberg**, dabbled in symbolism with a series of dream plays, including *A Dream Play* (1902) and *The Ghost Sonata* (1907).

The French-Swiss artist, **Adolphe Francois Appia** and the Englishman, **Edward Gordon Craig**, re-thought the dynamics of stage design in order to meet the demands of symbolist drama, changing the way in which scenery, setting, costume, and lighting could be used to reflect the symbolic.

(b) EXPRESSIONIST DRAMA

The symbolist movement contributed to the expressionist movement, which also rose as a reaction against realist theatre during the early decades of the twentieth century, primarily in Germany.

Expressionistic drama manipulates reality so the audience can experience different perspectives or various angles of a story. For this reason, it is often fragmented into episodes, avoiding the flow of a 'well-made play'. Characters are not always named and are often generic representations of a particular stereotype ('The Father', 'The Mother' or 'The Son') sometimes reinforced by the use of mask. Choruses are common. Dialogue can be heightened and poetical in order to evoke a mood or emotion. Settings avoid realistic detail and, instead, rely upon images and themes drawn from the text. Like the symbolists, content can include dreams and nightmares from the subconscious mind, but it is more politicised, depicting some sort of bourgeois struggle against authority.

The movement in Germany was heavily influenced by **Georg Büchner**, **Frank Wedekind** and **August Strindberg** (who are now considered the forerunners of expressionistic drama). **Georg Kaiser** wrote about seventy plays and his politically inspired expressionistic masterpieces are considered to be *The Burghers of Calais* (1913), *From Morn to Midnight* (1917) and the 'Gas Trilogy' (*The Coral*, (1917), *Gas 1*, (1918), and *Gas II*, (1920)). Brecht admired his work but Nazi Germany did not and he was eventually banned and forced to flee the country, dying in exile. **Ernst Toller** wrote many of his plays whilst in prison, serving a long sentence for left-wing activities. Some of his most famous plays include *Masses and the Man* (1921), *The Machine Breakers* (1922) and *Hinkemann, the German* (1923). He too was exiled from Germany under Nazi rule.

The staging of expressionist drama required new ways of thinking, presenting and performing. The Austrian director, **Max Reinhardt**, was particularly interested in bringing the work of expressionist playwrights to the stage even asking the Norwegian expressionist **Edvard Munch** to design some of his German and Swedish productions. However, it was the Russian director, **Vsevolod Meyerhold**, who broke most significantly from the realist acting tradition. He had studied under Stanislavski and eventually succeeded him as head of the Moscow Art Theatre Studio (a smaller extension of MAT, committed to exploring alternative forms of theatre). Meyerhold increasingly leaned towards symbolist drama, closely followed by expressionist drama. He wanted actors to explore the style of a play, evoked through its language and movement. For this end, he encouraged actors towards a physical technique, whereby learning specific movements and gestures would trigger emotional responses (in opposition to Stanislavski's acting techniques where a character's inner emotions would trigger movement and gesture). At the same time, he made actors aware they were on a stage, in order to break down barriers and appeal more specifically to the senses of the audience.

The American director and designer, **Robert Edmond Jones**, worked with Reinhardt in Berlin and eventually established the Provincetown Players, in conjunction with George Cram Cook. This also meant he had some influence on **Eugene O'Neill**, who went on to produce the expressionistic plays, *The Emperor Jones* (1920) and *The Hairy Ape* (1922) amongst others. O'Neill became particularly interested in the writings of Strindberg, Wedekind and Kaiser.

Other American playwrights followed suit, balancing their realistic dramas with expressionistic experimentation. **Elmer Rice**'s *The Adding Machine* (1923), **Thornton Wilder**'s *Our Town* (1938) and *The Skin of Our Teeth* (1942), **Arthur Miller**'s *Death of a Salesman* (1949) and **Tennessee Williams**' *Camino Real* (1953), were laudable early American examples of the genre.

(c) DIDACTIC DRAMA

The symbolists and expressionists in turn influenced the development of didactic drama (sometimes called epic theatre, dialectical theatre or agitprop theatre) which sought to convey a strong left-wing social/political message to an audience through the adaptation of expressionistic techniques. The term agitprop comes from combining the words 'agitation' and 'propaganda' (there was a department of Agitation and Propaganda in the Pre-Soviet Russian Communist Party). In essence, the didactic playwrights borrowed the presentational style and episodic form of the expressionists but were less interested in the emotional and sentimental in order to convey their political message.

Erwin Piscator was one of the early proponents. Although he originally came from Germany, he left when the Nazis rose to power in the early 1930s and ended up directing in Moscow, followed by New York. He returned to Germany in the 1950s. One of his most famous dramas is *The Good Soldier Schweik* (1928). **Bertolt Brecht** was influenced by Piscator, working alongside him before he left Germany.

Piscator's and Brecht's idea of epic theatre (although Brecht later preferred the term dialectical theatre) was to challenge or inspire audiences into social/political/moral action. They believed this couldn't be achieved through the representational style of realistic drama, preferring instead a presentational style that forced audiences to disengage from their emotions, observe the action analytically and see the situation for what it truly was. Structurally, this meant breaking the narrative into episodic (or epic) scenes and using choruses, narrators, songs, dances and audio-visual media that spoke to the audience directly. In this way audiences became critically detached by constantly being made aware of watching a performance (rather than being drawn into a realistic world). This emotional distance was also helped by the techniques Brecht developed for actors in the Berliner ensemble, where characters were 'presented' rather than 'embodied'. His actors were shown how to narrate the action so that the story (rather than the emotional life of the character) became the key focus. Brecht's techniques became known as *verfremdungseffekt* or the alienation effect. His most famous texts include: *The Threepenny Opera* (1928), *Life of Galileo* (1938-9), *The Good Person of Setzuan* (1938-41), *Mother Courage and Her Children* (1939) and *The Caucasian Chalk Circle* (1943-5). In turn, Brecht's work influenced the Germans **Max Frisch**, **Friedrich Dürrenmatt** and **Peter Weiss** (who was later nationalised as a Swede).

Whilst in America, Piscator had some influence on the Group Theatre in New York and **Lee Strasberg** produced his work. His style also fed into the American version of the 'Living Newspaper', originally devised by the Bolsheviks in Russia. In 1930s America, it was produced by the Federal Theatre Project, under the directorship of **Hallie Flanagan Davis** with initial help from the playwright **Elmer Rice**, as a reaction against the Great Depression. It combined journalistic facts with dramatised events and was a forerunner of late twentieth-century verbatim theatre.

Brecht visited England twice with the Berliner Ensemble (1956 and 1965), inspiring directors such as **Peter Brook** at the Royal Shakespeare Company, **George Devine** and **William Gaskill** at the Royal Court and **Ewan MacColl** and **Joan Littlewood** at Theatre Workshop in Stratford East (Littlewood even played Mother Courage in the first English staging). Theatre Workshop was committed to creating didactic theatre for working-class audiences, using a range of European styles (including Brecht, Meyerhold and Appia). Littlewood thought that realism was the responsibility of the individual actor, not necessarily the way in which theatre should be constructed and, therefore, established her own acting company with a training programme. Productions were drawn from both classical and contemporary repertoire, particularly championing the work of the Irish playwright, Brendan Behan. However, their most famous work, *Oh! What a Lovely War* (1963) was devised by the company in the Brechtian tradition. The piece was composed of sketches, songs and audio-visual effects in a presentational, epic style, in order to highlight the horrors of World War I.

The English playwright, **John Arden**, initially wrote in the realist tradition, producing plays such as *Live Like Pigs* (1958) but changed course after seeing the work of the Berliner Ensemble. Consequently, *Serjeant Musgrave's Dance* (1959), an anti-war drama, was heavily influenced by the politics and structure of Brechtian works (including songs and direct-address to the audience). **Edward Bond** also dabbled in Brechtian devices in his later plays (influenced by William Gaskill at the Royal Court), eschewing his realist roots.

(d) ABSURDIST DRAMA

Absurdist drama developed out of the French surrealist art movement of the 1920s and French existentialist philosophy in the 1940s. However, time and circumstance were the defining influences: the combination of post-war disillusionment and a decline in religious faith contributed to a growing sense of futility. Life had become meaningless for the absurdists because human beings were living in a void, faced with an inexplicable and bleak world without logic. The development of the cold war in the 1950s strengthened these feelings.

Therefore, the term 'absurdist' meant more than the ridiculous. The playwright Eugene Ionesco described it as 'devoid of purpose... Cut off from his religious, metaphysical and transcendental roots, man is lost; all his actions become senseless, absurd, useless.'[2]

Audiences were asked to experience the absurdity of the human condition through illogical texts that were difficult to pin down to specific meanings. Most did not include a linear plot development or psychological characterisation. Physical features were strong, with dancing, clowning and acrobatics but there were also games, songs and jokes in the vaudeville tradition. It was thought that laughter alleviated the pain of living. However, Freud felt that human beings actually enjoy abandoning the logical, finding the comic, delighting in the nonsensical, reliving their childhood.

Importantly, there weren't any rules. Some absurdist plays start out realistically enough, giving a false impression, only to dissolve into the ridiculous and nonsensical. Language can be poetical, clichéd and/or gibberish, often dispersing into patterns of sounds. Martin Esslin in *The Theatre of the Absurd* calls it 'anti-literary…turning away from language as an instrument for the expression of the deepest levels of meaning.'[3]

This was entirely true of **Eugene Ionesco**'s absurdist plays. Of Romanian/French origin, he lived most of his life in Paris. *La Cantatrice Chauve* was written in 1948 (translated as *The Bald Prima Donna* in England and *The Bald Soprano* in America) and first performed in 1950 at the Théâtre de Noctambules. The text explores the absurdities in commonly used language, turning ordinary conversation into meaningless dialogue. Audiences found it hilarious, despite the fact it had been written as a serious piece of theatre.

Other well-known plays of Ionesco include *The Lesson* (1951), *The Chairs* (1952) and the full-length play *Rhinoceros* (1959). In *The Lesson*, a professor becomes enraged with a young student, whom he deems unworthy when she cannot master simple subtraction or understand his nonsensical lecture on language. Eventually, he brutally murders her and she turns out to be his fortieth victim that same day. The play ends with yet another student knocking on his door. Here, the absurdist language becomes an instrument of power. In March 1955, it became the first Ionesco play to be staged in England. Audiences swung between amusement, shock and anger.

The Russian/French **Arthur Adamov**, started out as an absurdist but ended up producing Brechtian-inspired works, eventually settling for social realism. His first absurdist play, *La Parodie* (*The Parody*), was written in 1947. In it, he parodies the world by focusing on a pessimist and an optimist who are suitors to the same girl: their failures highlight the futility of human endeavour. Heavily influenced by Strindberg's *A Dream Play*, Adamov was often inspired by his own dreams or he revised texts after new dreams occurred. In *Professor Taranne* (1953), he includes an actual transcript of one of his own dreams. However, it is *Le Ping-Pong* (*Ping-Pong*) that Martin Esslin describes as 'one of the masterpieces of The Theatre of the Absurd'. It was written in 1955 and explores the obsessions of two men with a pinball machine: ultimately, they lose their values, their ideologies and even their identity because of it.

Not everyone classifies the French playwright, **Jean Genet**, as an absurdist. However, his plays *The Maids* (1946), *The Balcony* (1955) and *The Blacks* (1955) did indeed possess absurdist features: the parodying of social identity, the distortion and devaluation of language, and, the inclusion of dreams, fantasies and rituals.

Samuel Beckett was an Irish playwright who moved to Paris before World War II. This meant that his work was shaped by early twentieth-century Irish literature and theatre, French symbolism and existentialism, plus the experience of living in a European city beset by war followed by post-war ennui. His most famous work *En Attendant Godot* (*Waiting for Godot*) was first performed in Paris in 1953, followed by London in 1955 (not long after Ionesco's *The Lesson*) and America in 1956. The playwright David Edgar notes the similarities between *Waiting for Godot* and *Look Back in Anger* that were produced in London around the same time.

> In the mid-'50s, London audiences probably didn't notice that two groundbreaking new plays both had five characters and one set, and included long speeches, a crucial offstage character, music-hall turns, people taking off their trousers, elements of the first half being echoed in the second, nothing much happening, and the two protagonists spending the play trying to leave and ending up agreeing to stay. The reason why playgoers are unlikely to have spotted these similarities between *Waiting for Godot* and *Look Back in Anger* is because they employ completely opposite strategies to represent the conditions of their time.[4]

In fact, English audiences were baffled by *Waiting for Godot*. There was no clear message or resolution. There was no linear plot development (it circled around, repeating itself). There was no clear content (characters waited or were bored from waiting). The marked use of silence (balancing out speech to create a rhythmic pattern) was unnerving and audiences sometimes heckled in these moments, unsure of what to do or how to act themselves. One critic, Ivor Brown of the *Observer*, thought it might be a theatrical hoax. The critic, Michael Billington, says:

> ...as proof he cited the various definitions of the play offered to him by its champions. Brown actually lists nine competing points including the ideas 'That it was a superb tragedy: that it was a superb comedy. That two of the characters are facets of the same person: that all the characters are the same person. That it cheerfully lifted the heart and struck resounding notes of hope: that it was a fine piece of pessimism proper to the doomed and dismal world we live in.' For a conservative critic like Brown these contradictions were proof that Beckett's play was meretricious nonsense. What he didn't consider was that these varying interpretations were all simultaneously possible...[5]

Some of Beckett's other successful plays include *Endgame* (1957), *Krapp's Last Tape* (1958), and *Happy Days* (1961) plus the radio plays *All That Fall* (1957) and *Embers* (1959). He received the Nobel Prize for Literature in 1969.

Absurdism did not take hold in America in the same way as it had done in Europe, partially because post-war disillusionment wasn't as severe, and, partially because an early commitment to realist acting technique was difficult to shake off. However, one of the few exceptions was the playwright **Edward Albee**, who experimented with Ionesco-like absurdist content and characters within realistic settings.

The English playwright, **Harold Pinter**, was influenced by Beckett's poetical absurdism. On the surface, his plays seem realistic but he often presents us with absurd situations and dialogue that resembles the rhythmic precision of a musical score. In an interview with Kenneth Tynan, he said '...I think what I try to do in my plays is to get to this recognisable reality of the absurdity of what we do and how we behave and how we speak.'[6]

Tom Stoppard's *Rosencrantz and Guildenstern Are Dead* (1967) is also indebted to Beckett. Hamlet's two schoolfriends who were simple plot devices without much to do in Shakespeare's play are given the time and space to question their existence, their purpose, even their identities. Like *Waiting for Godot*'s two central characters, they are left waiting with time to fill.

(e) VERSE DRAMA

There is nothing new about plays written in verse (as focused on in my previous book *Classic Voice*) but many contemporary playwrights have also chosen to work with it, adapting the form to meet the needs of a modern world. Indeed, in Europe, many symbolist, expressionist, didactic and absurdist playwrights wrote in structured verse, or, created a poetic format that closely resembled verse.

A revival of the English verse play occurred in the nineteenth century: the romantic poets, such as **Shelley, Wordsworth, Keats, Coleridge, Swinburne** and **Tennyson**, used Shakespeare as their model (although they weren't considered particularly successful). In the 1930s, **W.H. Auden** and **Christopher Isherwood** mixed up prose and verse in their left-leaning plays. However, the most popular English verse play revivals were in the 1940s and 1950s with playwrights who chose as their message the redemptive power of Christian religious faith. These playwrights were driven by the political climate and (once again) a reaction against the rise of dramatic realism.

In 1883 Ibsen wrote 'Verse has been most injurious to dramatic art. A scenic artist whose department is the drama of the present day should be unwilling to take a verse into his mouth.'[7] and happily concluded that it would die out. However, verse plays in the 1940s and 1950s were highly fashionable and saw long West End runs (and in some cases, long Broadway runs) playing to packed houses. Part of their popularity wasn't just because the themes of faith, hope and love spoke to politically disillusioned middle-class audiences, it was also the way in which playwrights of the period restructured the verse form so that it more closely resembled natural speech rhythm. Rather than just copying the forms of classical antiquity and the Renaissance (as the nineteenth-century playwrights had tried to do), they adapted it for contemporary characters and audiences without resorting to prose.

The poet **T.S. Eliot** spoke and wrote prolifically on the subject. His plays include: the incomplete *Sweeney Agonistes* (two fragments were published together under the one title in 1932), *Murder in the Cathedral* (1935), *The Family Reunion* (1939), *The Cocktail Party* (1949), *The Confidential Clerk* (1953) and *The Elder Statesman* (1958). Eliot championed the verse play because he felt that poetic rhythm 'intensifies the drama'[8] and heightens the dramatic experience, affecting listeners on an unconscious level just like music. For him, the prose of playwrights such as Ibsen and Chekhov was limited. However, the problem was to find a way of working in verse that was appropriate for character 'capable of unbroken transition between the most intense speech and the most relaxed dialogue.'[9]

> What we have to do is to bring poetry into the world in which the audience lives and to which it returns when it leaves the theatre; not to transport the audience into some imaginary world in which poetry is tolerated.[10]

He developed his verse structure over time: when working on *The Family Reunion* (1939) he tried

> ...to find a rhythm close to contemporary speech, in which the stresses could be made to come wherever we should naturally put them, in uttering the particular phrase on the particular occasion. What I worked out is substantially what I have continued to employ: a line of varying length and varying number of syllables, with a caesura and three stresses. The caesura and the stresses may come at different places, almost anywhere in the line; the stresses may be close together or well separated by light syllables; the only rule being that there must be one stress on one side of the caesura and two on the other. In retrospect, I soon saw that I had given my attention to versification, at the expense of plot and character.[11]

However, with *The Cocktail Party* (1949) he laid down the rule for himself 'to avoid poetry which could not stand the test of strict dramatic utility:

with such success, indeed, that it is perhaps an open question whether there is any poetry in the play at all.'[12]

Other popular verse playwrights of the period, who wrote with similar philosophies, include **Ronald Duncan**, with *This Way to the Tomb* (1945), and, **Christopher Fry** with *A Phoenix Too Frequent* (1946), *The Lady's Not for Burning* (1948) and *Venus Observed* (1950). However, the movement died out as the absurdist dramas of Beckett and Ionesco, and the New Wave realism of Osborne and Wesker, rose to the forefront of British theatre. Glenda Leeming in *Poetic Drama* wrote:

> …Fry's later works include the surreal dream-based *A Sleep of Prisoners* (1951) and the loosely episodic *Curmantle* (1962); potentially there could have been a transition to verse plays within the absurdist framework, but Fry was not in tune with that world view, and the West End phase of the poetic drama movement closed there. [13]

However, there were English poets still prepared to experiment with verse drama, such as **Ted Hughes**, **Tony Harrison** and, more recently, **Glyn Maxwell**.

3. VOCAL DEMANDS

Like realism, the vocal demands of non-realistic dramatic texts lie within the language and the way in which that language has been structured rhythmically. However, word and rhythm can vary enormously, depending on style and genre. Even within style and genre there is variation, for example, the language and rhythmic structure of one absurdist text can feel very different from that of another absurdist text, even when they have both been written by the same playwright. This is because contemporary playwrights who write non-realistically tend to experiment with distorting realism in order to make their point, convey a message, evoke an emotion, create a particular type of character or simply tell a story. So it's a little harder to pin the linguistic features down to paper without talking about a specific text.

Analysis of a non-realistic text might include finding language that is heightened, lyrical, poetical, staccato, repetitive, contradictory, symbolic, political, rhetorical, devalued, illogical and, in some cases, completely meaningless. But it also might mean finding realistic language.

Realistic rhythms are rarer. You might find natural speech rhythms that have been heightened ever so slightly or perhaps formalised into verse with strong musical beats or even configured into a free verse without a strong musical beat. There will be repetitions, sound and word patterns plus careful placement of silences/pauses.

This means that, when speaking these texts aloud, the voice must be incredibly flexible and sensitive, capable of making minute split-second adjustments according to word and rhythm. Here are some questions that pinpoint the specific vocal challenges to come.

- If a playwright sets his/her story in a seemingly real context with characters who have true-to-life features but then plays around with language and rhythmic structure to heighten audience perception, how does the actor adjust their process to bring the text to life vocally?

- If an absurdist playwright uses nonsensical language with seemingly meaningless word and sound patterns, how does the actor approach it vocally? Should these elements be made more prominent i.e. heightened in performance? Or played naturalistically? Or parodied?

- If a verse playwright structures their play in formalised rhythms but dramatically shifts the rhythmic beat to suit character, relationship and moment, how does the actor keep re-adjusting themselves rhythmically? And how does the actor deal with inhabiting and communicating contemporary characters who are speaking poetically?

For this reason, the following three chapters will discuss and provide practical work for:

- **Marrying the Realistic with the Non-Realistic**

- **Expressing the Absurd**

- **Talking in Verse**

CHAPTER 9: MARRYING THE REALISTIC WITH THE NON-REALISTIC

Characters that seem authentic, situations that appear truthful but word and rhythm that have been distorted. This chapter will focus on how actors need to adapt their voices to meet the demands of both the realistic and non-realistic.

Because there tends to be massive stylistic variation between the way in which different non-realistic texts use word and rhythm, let's begin by focusing on the texts themselves, in particular the work of Harold Pinter and Howard Barker.

1. PINTER: VOCAL DEMANDS

Although Pinter's writing reveals the realistic, it also includes the existential and absurdist (consistent with post-war thinking). This means his plays focus on issues of identity in an uncertain world (often comically). The characters seem real, usually caught up in circumstances beyond their control, but it is the way their language has been rhythmically structured that sets them apart.

Pinter tends to heighten the absurdity of everyday speech. Realists use repetition, hesitations, dis-fluency, illogicality, incomprehension, interruptions, overlapping and unfinished speech but Pinter formalises them into a rhythmic structure: in other words, highlights them by placing them in specific patterns so that the audience can hear them more clearly.

Part of the way he does this is by creating verbal skirmishes, a little like verbal fencing matches. In many ways they resemble the verbal fencing of the Restoration playwrights (which I wrote about in *Classic Voice*) although these battles are sparer, shorter and more stylised. Characters try to outmanoeuvre one another, fight for supremacy and/or score points against their opponent. The most common way for a character to win a game is through the undercut. Undercutting usually stops the other character short because it is difficult to formulate a response. So a pause or a silence is needed to reassess the situation. These skirmishes tell us a great deal about the characters, their relationship to each other and their situation at this particular point in time. So although Pinter heightens, stylises and formalises speech patterns, they operate in similar ways as realist text, revealing subtextual information.

Pinter is known and celebrated for his use of pauses. All speech patterning requires a balance between sound and silence but Pinter formalises this in his plays, creating distinctly timed moments when sound is absent. As human beings we don't like marked silences, we prefer to fill them with sound, often using speech fillers and redundancies which are reassuring and comforting to us. Pinter milks our feelings of tension and alarm in his structured use of silence, focusing on three different types:

- The hesitation

  Hesitations occur when a character wavers during the flow of speech, perhaps when they are unsure of where they are headed or when they are losing control of a situation or if they are trying to hide something. These tiny silences replace the sound hesitations or redundancies or fillers that we usually use during everyday speech, such as 'um', 'ah' or 'mm'. Usually, they are marked with three dots, as in '…' or a dash, as in '–'.

- The pause

  Pauses are longer than hesitations and are indicated by the actual word 'pause' in the text. They represent moments when a character or characters are regrouping (tactically) in the verbal battle, in other words reassessing the situation before trying something new.

- The silence

  Silences are longer again. They are marked by the actual word 'silence' in the text. Usually, they occur after one character has delivered an undercut and mark the end of a verbal skirmish where a point has been scored. The listener or receiver cannot respond and needs a moment to think about how to proceed. The space is filled with reverberations of what the speaker has just said.

These hesitations, pauses and silences have a direct effect on speech rhythm, as well as the overall rhythmic flow of the scene, so they must be handled with precision if the verbal exchanges are to work.

Other elements in the text that help stylise the speech rhythm are phrasing, punctuation and repetition. Pinter, like any other playwright, repeats words and phrases but, in many cases, he increases the repetition far more than usual in everyday speech patterning. This not only helps his characters reiterate their point but it also has a comic affect.

Therefore, actors must treat Pinter's texts like a finely tuned piece of music. Everything that is written down on the page is there for a reason and must be played. However, it's also important not to embellish. Actors should only focus on what they've been given in the text. This means: not 'filling out' characters with the minutiae of realistic detail; not over-emoting; and, not trying to fill the hesitations, pauses and silences with 'acting' business. All of this muddies the clarity and sparseness of Pinter's text.

Voices must be acutely responsive to the structure and style so flexibility and precision are essential. Extensive verbal rehearsal on the text is the only way in which to develop and maintain these elements.

2. PINTER: TEXT SAMPLE

Pinter: Text Sample: Marrying the Realistic with the Non-Realistic

The following text has been taken from Scene Three of Harold Pinter's *Betrayal*. It was first performed at the National Theatre, London in November 1978, directed by Peter Hall.

The story so far:

Jerry and Emma have been having an affair for seven years. They are both married to other people with two children each by their married partners. Emma is married to Robert, Jerry's best friend. They have regularly met in a flat that was established for their clandestine meetings but eventually realise they are using it less and less. In this scene, they both see that the affair is over.

The play explores various kinds of betrayal within relationships and was inspired by Pinter's own affair with Joan Bakewell over a similar period of time. Interestingly, Pinter reverses some of the chronology so that we (as an audience) learn about the affair backwards.

Flat. 1975. Winter

JERRY and EMMA. They are sitting.

Silence

JERRY
What do you want to do then?

   Pause

EMMA
I don't quite know what we're doing, any more, that's all.

JERRY
Mmnn.

   Pause

EMMA
I mean, this flat...

JERRY
Yes.

EMMA
Can you actually remember when we were last here?

JERRY
In the summer, was it?

EMMA
Well, was it?

JERRY
I know it seems –

EMMA
It was the beginning of September.

JERRY
Well, that's summer, isn't it?

EMMA
It was actually extremely cold. It was early autumn.

JERRY
It's pretty cold now.

EMMA
We were going to get another electric fire.

JERRY
Yes, I never got that.

EMMA
Not much point in getting it if we're never here.

JERRY
We're here now.

EMMA
Not really.

   Silence

JERRY
Well, things have changed. You've been so busy, your job, and everything.

EMMA
Well, I know. But I mean, I like it. I want to do it.

JERRY
No, it's great. It's marvellous for you. But you're not –

EMMA
If you're running a gallery you've got to run it, you've got to be there.

JERRY
But you're not free in the afternoons. Are you?

EMMA
No.

JERRY
So how can we meet?

EMMA
But look at the times you're out of the country. You're never here.

JERRY
But when I am here you're not free in the afternoons. So we can never meet.

EMMA
We can meet for lunch.

JERRY
We can meet for lunch but we can't come all the way out here for a quick lunch. I'm too old for that.

EMMA
I didn't suggest that.

    Pause

You see, in the past...we were inventive, we were determined, it was...it seemed impossible to meet...impossible...and yet we did. We met here, we took this flat and we met in this flat because we wanted to.

JERRY
It would not matter how much we wanted to if you're not free in the afternoons and I'm in America.

    Silence

Nights have always been out of the question and you know it. I have a family.

EMMA
I have a family too.

JERRY
I know that perfectly well. I might remind you that your husband is my oldest friend.

EMMA
What do you mean by that?

JERRY
I don't *mean* anything by it.

EMMA
But what are you trying to say by saying that?

JERRY
Jesus. I'm not *trying* to say anything. I've said precisely what I wanted to say.

EMMA
I see.

Pause

The fact is that in the old days we used our imagination and we'd take a night and make an arrangement and go to an hotel.

JERRY
Yes. We did.

Pause

But that was…in the main…before we got this flat.

EMMA
We haven't spent many nights…in this flat.

JERRY
No.

Pause

Not many nights anywhere, really.

Silence

EMMA
Can you afford…to keep it going, month after month?

JERRY
Oh…

EMMA
It's a waste. Nobody comes here. I just can't bear to think about it, actually. Just… empty. All day and night. Day after day and night after night. I mean the crockery and the curtains and the bedspread and everything. And the tablecloth I brought from Venice. (*Laughs.*) It's ridiculous.

Pause

It's just…an empty home.

JERRY
It's not a home.

Pause

I know…I know what you wanted…but it could never…actually be a home. You have a home. I have a home. With curtains, etcetera. And children. Two children in two homes. There are no children here, so it's not the same kind of home.

EMMA
It was never intended to be the same kind of home. Was it?

Pause

You didn't ever see it as a home, in any sense, did you?

JERRY
No, I saw it as a flat…you know.

EMMA
For fucking.

JERRY
No, for loving.

EMMA
Well, there's not much of that left, is there?

Silence

JERRY
I don't think we don't love each other.

Pause

EMMA
Ah well.

Pause

What will you do about all the…furniture?

JERRY
What?

EMMA
The contents.

Silence

JERRY
You know we can do something very simple, if we want to do it.

EMMA
You mean sell it to Mrs Banks for a small sum and…and she can let it as a furnished flat?

JERRY
That's right. Wasn't the bed here?

EMMA
What?

JERRY
Wasn't it?

EMMA
We bought the bed. We bought everything. We bought the bed together.

JERRY
Ah. yes.

EMMA stands.

EMMA
You'll make all the arrangements, then? With Mrs Banks?

Pause

I don't want anything. Nowhere I can put it, you see. I have a home, with tablecloths and all the rest of it.

JERRY
I'll go into it, with Mrs Banks. There'll be a few quid, you know, so…

EMMA
No, I don't want any *cash*, thank you very much.

Silence. She puts her coat on.

I'm going now.

He turns, looks at her.

Oh here's my key.

Takes out keyring, tries to take key from ring.

Oh Christ.

Struggles to take key from ring. Throws him the ring.

You take it off.

He catches it, looks at her.

Can you just do it please? I'm picking up Charlotte from school. I'm taking her shopping.

He takes key off.

Do you realise this is an afternoon? It's the Gallery's afternoon off. That's why I'm here. We close every Thursday afternoon. Can I have my keyring?

He gives it to her.

Thanks. Listen. I think we've made absolutely the right decision.

She goes.

He stands.

Betrayal by Harold Pinter. Published by Faber and Faber in *Harold Pinter: Plays Four.*[14]

3. PINTER: TEXT ANALYSIS

In this text sample, the relationship between Emma and Jerry has been carefully constructed through sounds, words, phrase length, punctuation, hesitations, pauses and silences. It's made up of a series of verbal skirmishes, highlighting their struggle to continue (and end) the affair.

The scene begins with a silence (so the audience can note there is trouble ahead). Then two false starts occur (with two sets of pauses) before they launch into a longish verbal battle. The exchange is pacey with short, sharp phrases. Jerry tries to score a point with 'It's pretty cold now' but Emma blocks it by ignoring him and continuing. The scene continues until she undercuts with 'Not really.' A 'silence' marks her small victory.

Jerry starts the next skirmish with a different tactic, focusing on why he thinks the affair is failing (because Emma isn't free). His 'and everything' indicates that he doesn't have the courage to provide more detail. Emma half-heartedly argues the point before admitting with a tiny 'No' that he is right. Then, she tries to turn the blame onto Jerry as well. He argues the point. Emma pauses to assess the situation and changes tack. Her opening gambit includes a number of hesitations while she thinks the situation through. Her final line, full of active verbs and repetition, creates a strong ending to her speech: 'We met here, we took this flat and we met in this flat because we wanted to.' Jerry undercuts this by blaming them *both* for their failure to meet on a regular basis. Silence.

The next verbal skirmish begins by focusing on their respective families as the excuse. Jerry mentions Emma's husband as being his oldest friend, suggesting (rather than having the courage to state outright) that this is another reason for them to finish, indicating his guilt. Emma picks up on this and, as they argue about it, use self-repetition and allo-repetition, which creates a strong rhythmic exchange. They then blame the flat itself. Three reassessment pauses occur during this skirmish, plus a number of hesitations. Jerry undercuts again. Silence.

There are two long speeches (complete with hesitations) in the first part of the next skirmish, followed by a short, sharp, pacey battle. In the space of this exchange there are repeated words and sounds that sharpen the rhythm (e.g. the 'uh' sound in 'fucking' and 'loving'). This is a key battle as it highlights how they view their relationship: discussion of the flat is symbolic (the word 'home' is repeated nine times). Emma undercuts and wins the point for this round. Silence.

The next short exchange pinpoints the end of the affair. First of all, Jerry's line 'I don't think we don't love each other', includes an interesting double negative (he would've used the positive directly if he had truly wanted to draw her back in). Emma doesn't take the bait and replies with a resignation and a pause. Her next lines about 'furniture' and 'contents' (almost like a contract or inventory) take Jerry by surprise, ending in the 'silence'.

The silence has given Jerry time to consider and they both enter into practical (if not hurtful) arrangements. There are three mentions of the 'bed'. Emma finishes the exchange with horror at an offer of *cash* (note the italics). In this silence, she puts her coat on: one of the rare moments when Pinter indicates there can be action in a silence.

The next struggle is over the key, trying to disengage it from the key ring, but all the lines are Emma's. She fills the silence with her speeches. The last words of the relationship are hers. Jerry remains mute. But the action with the key ring helps structure the rhythm of her lines. There is a strong, decisive and emphatic beat in her final three sentences. Clearly, Emma doesn't regret the outcome. She started the scene with this decision in mind and drove it through to a satisfactory conclusion.

4. PINTER: WORKSHOP PLAN

This workshop can be successfully realised without the participants having prior knowledge of the text as a whole. In fact, it can be a starting point of discovery about the characters and their situation *before* full-scale rehearsals commence. The text is interchangeable, any scene between two Pinter characters, involving a series of verbal skirmishes, can be used.

Pinter: Workshop Plan: Marrying the Realistic with the Non-Realistic

Objectives

- To experiment with word and rhythm in a Pinter text

- To understand how word and rhythm in a Pinter text create character, relationship and situation

Materials

You will need:

– Separate copies of the text extract, as provided in the previous 'Pinter: Text Sample' box, for each member of the workshop group (or your choice of Pinter text excerpt that includes two characters involved in verbal skirmishes).

Activities and Exercises

1. Warming up

Releasing, Grounding, Centring, Aligning, Breathing, Resonating and Articulating

- Ask your actors to place their feet a little wider than hip-width apart and swing one arm, forwards and backwards. Once they've established a rhythmic flow, ask them to soften or bend their knees on each downward beat of the arm movement. The whole body should be free and the arm movement shouldn't be stiff (especially on the backwards trajectory). Now ask them to be conscious of their breath releasing in a rhythm (in and out through the mouth) in time with the arm movement. Once they've established a rhythmic flow for the breath, get them to add the word 'whoooosssssshhhhh' to each out-breath (full voice, not whispered). Don't ask them to stop, just get them to let the movement become smaller and smaller until the arm comes to a rest beside the body. This should have released some tension on one side of the body so get them to repeat the exercise with the other arm to even up

– Now ask your actors to repeat the exercise but this time with a hum ('mmmmm'), keeping the lips loosely together. They can then try a few swings on each of the

---

following sound sequences – 'mmmOO', 'mmmOH', 'mmmAW', 'mmmAH', 'mmmAY', 'mmmEE'. Their face should feel 'buzzy' and 'tingly' by the end of the exercise

– Get them to repeat the arm swings again but using the following lines (feed each one to them at regular intervals). Of course at this point they won't know they're from the text sample. Ask them to really use their lips and tongue (to the point of exaggeration). The arm swing will help them to release sound into the space

It's pretty cold now.

Well, things have changed.

So how can we meet?

your husband is my oldest friend.

It's not a home.

We bought the bed together.

I don't want any *cash*.

I'm going now.

here's my key.

2. Exploring Rhythmic Structures

– Hand out copies of the sample text and ask your actors to read it in their heads. Then ask them to try it aloud with a partner so they're familiar with the movements their lips and tongue will need to make

– Ask each pair to repeat the text aloud but, this time, verbalise every punctuation mark, hesitation, pause, silence and stage direction, as well as the dialogue. This will help them to realise the importance of everything written on the page. Then, ask them to repeat the exercise with only the characters' words and note any changes from their first reading

– Ask them to repeat the text aloud again but this time clap at each hesitation, pause and silence (you will need to explain the three types of Pinteresque pauses). They must decide how many claps are needed in each space (e.g. less for hesitations, more for pauses, even more for silences). They might need to try this a few times through to refine their decisions. Then, ask them to repeat the scene again without the clapping and note how weighted the silences feel

– Introduce the idea of verbal skirmishes (although you may have already discussed this whilst working on pauses) and ask them to note where each skirmish starts and ends. Get them to verbalise the reasons behind these beginnings and endings before trying the text aloud again

– Ask them to repeat the text but each time a character tries to win a point, they must use a finger (on the word that best expresses that point) to gently/lightly poke the other character in the arm. The movement must be quick and light so that the rhythmic pace isn't disrupted. This will help them with their character's tactics and how they express them through speech stress. Ask them to repeat the scene again without the finger poking and note any changes from their first reading.

3. Debriefing

Allow some time for a group debriefing session.

– What have you learnt about how the text extract is structured?

– What have you learnt about character, relationship and situation in the text excerpt after working on rhythmic structures?

Now ask your actors to read the scene again in their pairs. They may (unconsciously) incorporate elements of the discussion into their performance.

– Did this last reading change again? In what way?

5. BARKER: VOCAL DEMANDS

Howard Barker uses complex and visceral language in his plays to explore themes of power, sexuality and human motivation: he calls it the 'Theatre of Catastrophe'. Packed with imagery and dense with metaphor, his texts include words that are beautiful, ugly, violent, sometimes comic and often ambiguous. Word meaning isn't always clear and can be spoken/heard/felt in a variety of different ways with multiple interpretations.

However, this isn't the only reason why Barker's texts are considered non-realistic: he feels 'form' is as politically powerful as 'content' and that the subtle exploration of human behaviour can only be expressed through the form that he gives it. This means creating rhythms that are unrecognisable as everyday speech. He distorts syntax, displacing words so that realistic grammatical order is broken; he disrupts phrasing, grouping words together in odd patterns (sometimes like free verse) and doing away with most punctuation (the occasional 'pause' is written as a word); and, he plays around with word/phrase repetition.

For actors, clarifying the rhythm means clarifying the emotional content. For audiences, listening in to the rhythms means being drawn into these strong emotions. In Barker's own words:

> My challenge to naturalism is located in my commitment to a poetic discourse. A densely metaphorical, indeed rhythmic form of speech is something important to me. I always like to quote Nietzsche: "If you don't understand the rhythm of the sentence, you can't understand the meaning of it." For an actor, that's an instinct. For me, rhythm is crucial. When I hear an actor grasp the rhythm, I know he is almost certainly in control of meaning.[15]

Therefore, there are two very specific vocal demands within the dramatic texts of Howard Barker. Actors need:

1. Vocal strength (to communicate powerful, often violent, words/ images, and/or extreme emotions, sometimes presented in bold, capitalised print).

2. Vocal flexibility (to communicate the anti-realistic rhythms, presented through distorted syntax, disrupted phrasing and continual repetition).

Vocal strength means engaging with the powerful lower body muscles so that they take the weight of the voice (and sound isn't pushed from the more delicate muscles in the throat, which can cause vocal damage). At the same time the actor must be focused on the word/image/emotion so that a connection between mind and body takes place. A karate expert who chops a brick in half with his hand, doesn't rely totally on his hand to execute the action, otherwise the fine bones in it would break, but works with strong muscles all the way down the body to achieve his purpose, plus a mind-body focus. The vocal equivalent of breaking a brick in two requires the same strategy. Although there are some simple exercises that prepare actors for strong vocal work in the workshop warm-up, I don't believe detailed work on vocal violence can be documented in written form, as it can be too easily misinterpreted in the testing process and put actors at risk. If you are planning sustained pressure on the vocal folds in a production then do call in an expert for specialist help. For this reason, most of my focus in the workshop plan is with increasing flexibility.

Vocal flexibility means engaging with the rhythmic flow of the words, which is different from the usual patterns we create. For this reason, Barker states that his texts are for speaking not reading in the head. Speaking one of his texts aloud for the first time can be challenging and stumbling is usual. The mouth is thrown by the jumble of images, metaphors, repetitions, undefined phrasing and lack of punctuation. But on consequent readings, the mind, heart and body become more attuned to the text. The rhythms start to make sense and deeper levels of meaning are drawn out. Here, Barker talks about his work with actors at his theatre company, the Wrestling School:

> I must have a certain kind of actor around me. He or she has to above all possess a musical sense of speech, its patterns, its rhythms. My texts contain long, disrupted, doubling-back, speeches. Only a skilled voice-user, an actor with a passion for his own voice, can lead us through these exotic groves of poetic idiom. With these I can lift the text to the power of a musical experience.[16]

6. BARKER: TEXT SAMPLES

Barker: Text Sample 1: Marrying the Realistic with the Non-Realistic

The following text has been taken from 'The Investor's Chronicle' in *13 Objects* by Howard Barker. It opened at the Birmingham Rep in October 2003 and was directed by the playwright himself.

The story so far:

A collection of thirteen short self-contained plays explore how people make emotional (and sometimes disturbing) investments in inanimate objects. In 'The Investor's Chronicle' we find a rich man who is threatening to burn a Holbein painting that he's just bought at auction.

A rich MAN holds a portrait by Holbein.

MAN: I'm burning it
(Pause.)
I think
I try to be honest

I think
Even as I bid for it
As I lifted my fingers off my knee
(I love those auctioneers they see the slightest movement it might have been a nod
but I just lift my fingers off my knee)
I knew it would be burned by me
Yes
The blood rushed to my face
My heart beat quicker and this wasn't nerves this wasn't the anxiety of bidding in a
public place the thrill of the accumulating figures
(This went in tens of thousands incidentally)
It was my terrible desire rising
It was my animal leaning on its chain
(Pause.)
They were all
Oh it was pitiful
All after it the thin curators the dribbling collectors even yes an actor in dark glasses
I don't know his name a million women wet themselves for him an American I don't
know his name he sat stone still he was acting probably he never stops I left him far
behind I left him at a million and a half he got up silently and silently he left he had
no curiosity he had to make a film a million and a half so much for his love of art
I smiled I particularly resent the proximity of actors actors belong in restaurants I
permitted myself one thin smile
(Pause.)
Holbein
(Pause.)
Holbein
(Pause.)
1553
(Pause.)
And it isn't as if I don't know art
Oh
The
Contrary
(Pause. He takes out a hip flask, unscrews the top and sprinkles whisky over the painting.)
Holbein is my favourite
Twenty years I waited for him
AND THE PUBLICITY
I won't quote
BILLIONAIRE RECLUSE
That's me
PAYS FOUR-POINT-FIVE MILLION FOR

Oh these figures get me down what do they know about art it's arithmetic to them
the more noughts on the end the more appreciative they are
CONNOISSEURS MY
(He takes out a cigarette lighter.)
ANUS
(Pause. He ignites a flame.)
Holbein
(Pause.)
1553 they say I've got my doubts he was in Ghent in 1553 and yet the subject is an
Englishwoman of course he could have travelled or so might she but 1554 is more
accurate in my opinion but let the experts always let the experts let them let them I
say
(He is about to put the flame to the picture but stops.)
And the frame's nice
The frame is pear inlaid with ivory
Which won't burn obviously
The ivory
Only the pear
The ivory
(Pause.)
I'll kick that into the flower bed
(Pause, then he lets the flame snuff out.)
I hate them all
I hate
I hate them all
(Pause.)
Not Holbein
Oh no
Not him
THOUGH HIM I MIGHT HAVE IF WE'D MET
I don't rule it out
A snob he was no doubt
He might have peered at me down his long nose he might have revealed under those
heavy eyelids a contempt for me
(Pause.)
I hate them all but
(Pause.)
And I try to be honest
I do try
(Pause.)
That is not the reason I am burning it
I'M NOT A SCHOOLBOY

WHAT DO YOU TAKE ME FOR SOME SNOTTY VANDAL
SPRAYING HIS NAME ACROSS A BROTHEL WALL
I AM A BILLIONAIRE
(Pause.)
It said so in the papers
(Pause.)
I am burning
Not
A
Painting
No
Oh
No
I am burning all the human filth who make this painting no longer a painting at all

'The Investor's Chronicle' from *13 Objects* by Howard Barker. Published by Oberon Books in *Howard Barker: Plays Two.*[17]

Barker: Text Sample 2: Marrying the Realistic with the Non-Realistic

The following text has been taken from 'South of that Place Near' in *13 Objects* by Howard Barker. It opened at the Birmingham Rep in October 2003 and was directed by the playwright himself.

The story so far:

A collection of thirteen short self-contained plays explore how people make emotional (and sometimes disturbing) investments in inanimate objects. In 'South of that Place Near' we find a woman with a postcard from her lover. He has asked her to join him but the address on the postcard has been smudged and she has no way of knowing where to find him.

WOMAN: The post office
The trickery of the post office
The trickery and malevolence of the post office
The trickery malevolence and criminal mismanagement of the post office
Is legendary is it not
THEY DELIBERATELY CONCEAL THE ORIGINS OF LETTERS
How can they in an age of such sophisticated and sensitive machinery contrive to
SMUDGE THE CANCELLATION MARK
It's deliberate
Oh yes
It's human intervention

Some clerk read this some sorter I don't know some minor I don't know some operative at the very lowest levels read it bored perhaps thought oh a postcard I'll read that stopped the machine oh yes they can be stopped trod on a button stopped it paused and read squinting short-sighted put his glasses on read my read his the few untidy words and thought I'll smudge I'll cause the name of this place to be rendered utterly illegible not just difficult but utterly oh utterly he must have smiled he must have known and smiled at my inevitable frustration laughing loud triumphant smudging card from nowhere

JOIN ME

JOIN ME

SAYS MY LOVE

(*Pause.*)

Picture of a mountain and a cable car and underneath the legend the mountain and the cable car as if it wasn't obvious but I don't criticize I keep my passionate resentment for those who most deserve it

HOW MANY MOUNTAINS

SNOW-CAPPED MOUNTAINS

HOW MANY SNOW-CAPPED MOUNTAINS HAVE A CABLE CAR

And it's antique

The card

Typically he sent an antique card black and white or grey to be precise no brilliant colour splashed with names of the resorts no discreet ever discreet the mountain and the cable car the stamp is Swiss that helps ha a Swiss mountain with a cable car ha and even if the mountain has not changed the cable car certainly has

JOIN ME

JOIN ME

Oh I want to

Oh I so want

'South of That Place Near' from *13 Objects* by Howard Barker. Published by Oberon Books in *Howard Barker: Plays Two*.[18]

7. BARKER: TEXT ANALYSIS

The Investor's Chronicle opens with a man holding a Holbein portrait. His first statement is bald, stark and more than a little frightening: 'I'm burning it', followed by a 'pause', giving us time to let the information sink in.

What follows, is a (distorted) narrative of how he recently purchased the painting. The language is peppered with his emotional excitement about the auction and his need to possess the object ('It was my terrible desire rising/It was my animal leaning on its chain') plus his contempt for the curators and other bidders ('the dribbling collectors'). However, it is also the rhythms that draw us in to his story. Some of it is written in free verse (word patterns down the page), some of it is written in prose (word patterns across the page). He seems to become more colloquial and inconsequential when venturing into prose, saving the more powerful, more emotive moments for the free verse lines. However, repetition is constant throughout both forms ('I think/I try to be honest/I think'). The free verse patterns help us see the phrasing but in the prose, words tumble over each other without punctuation. However, once spoken aloud it isn't hard to find flow, and therefore, sense.

After describing the auction, the man permits himself a moment of enjoyment: repeating the name of the painter and underlining the antiquity of the painting, all separated out with 'pauses'. The pace is snail-like in its relish. Even 'Oh/The/Contrary' is split over different lines, making a distinct point.

Then, he's off again, this time describing the publicity he received over the purchase, giving us five capitalised lines (indicating heightened moments) interspersed with lower-case lines, making them stand out even further. Within those capitalised lines, we learn the figure he actually paid, which remains unfinished/interrupted ('PAYS FOUR-POINT-FIVE-MILLION FOR'). This section of text is also interspersed with the cigarette lighter, being taken out and ignited.

He then provides us with his knowledge as an art connoisseur. Expressed in prose, the flow and pace give us insight into his feelings of superiority. The key repetitions are 'let' and 'expert'. This knowledge is undercut with a statement lacking in expert knowledge ('And the frame's nice'), which stops him from putting the flame into the picture. He considers what will burn and what won't, finishing with how he'll kick the ivory into the flower bed.

A pause follows and he allows the flame to go out. However, his repetitive 'hate' lines give us the first direct indication of why he wants to burn the picture. He excludes Holbein from this hate although qualifies it by saying he might hate him if he'd met him. This line is capitalised and the syntax is distorted, however, in a curious way it makes the thought cleaner, less complex.

He takes time, building up to the core reason why he's burning the painting, using short free verse lines, capitalised heightened lines, more pauses than usual and even a phrase split over a series of lines, one word on each ('I am burning/Not/A/Painting/No/Oh/No'). His reason is finally given, quickly and succinctly, in prose.

'South of That Place Near' opens with four lines that build (repetitively) one on top of the other, like building blocks. They are (rhythmically) satisfying to speak aloud and help the woman to alleviate some of her frustration through blame. It builds to a line where she can happily make her point through the heightened emotion of capital letter speaking ('THEY DELIBERATELY CONCEAL THE ORIGINS OF LETTERS'). Two lines on, she provides us with even more information, again in capital letters ('SMUDGE THE CANCELLATION MARK').

Like the man in 'The Investor's Chronicle', she too moves between free verse lines (down the page) and prose (across the page). The first large prose passage is her imagination running riot on what might have happened at the post office. Her prose runs on and on as her mind runs on and on. She stops short to read from the postcard, where her lover has written in repetitive free verse. Her words are emotional (capitalised again) as we come to the crux of her anger and frustration: that her lover wants her to join him and she has no idea where he is ('JOIN ME, JOIN ME, SAYS MY LOVE'). The last three words give it the feel of a renaissance poem, highly romanticised, contrasting strongly with the previous (imagined) machinations at the post office.

Her words run on in prose again as she tries to find clues on the postcard's front picture. Again, she stops short with three capitalised lines, reiterating the form of the opening, each line adding further information through a satisfying repetition.

The next large prose passage revisits the picture on the card and its failure to provide any clues: her mind is running on again. She stops herself short with her lover's words again ('JOIN ME/JOIN ME'). We are drawn into her emotions through a repetitive plea with muddied syntax ('Oh I want to/Oh I so want'). This syntax places 'want' as the final word, giving it emotional weight and strength.

8. BARKER: WORKSHOP PLAN

This workshop is more successful if the participants don't have prior knowledge of the text before commencement. Let them stumble on their first reading and give them the chance to articulate why. Then, introducing exercises that help clarify the rhythmic structures (and, therefore, the sense and emotion) will be empowering. Once again, these texts are interchangeable with any other Barker monologues.

Barker: Workshop Plan: Marrying the Realistic with the Non-Realistic

Objectives

- To release and relish powerful words/images, freely and easily, from within a Howard Barker text.

- To experiment with the rhythms of a Howard Barker text.

- To understand how rhythmic structures in a Howard Barker text create deeper levels of meaning and emotion.

Materials

You will need:

– Separate copies of the text extracts, as provided in the previous 'Barker: Text Samples' box. You may choose to use just one excerpt for participants or vary both around the group.

Activities and Exercises

1. Warming up

Releasing, Grounding, Centring, Aligning, Breathing, Resonating and Articulating

– Ask your actors to get down on the floor on all fours. Make sure they place their hands in line with their shoulders and their knees in line with their hips. Their head should be dropped and the neck released. They need to let go of their stomach muscles towards the floor. Now ask them to pull in their stomach muscles (very briefly) so their back arches and then release it down, letting go of the breath at the same time. Get them to repeat this action five times

– Whilst they are still in this position (with released stomach muscles), ask them to release a 'fffff', then a 'sssss', then a 'vvvvv', followed by a 'zzzzz'. Each sound should be on a separate breath. Now feed them some of the strong images from the text to repeat out loud (examples are below). Coach them to take the words to their

---

central core. Ask them to repeat the exercise (still feeding them the lines) but get them to play with the sound articulation (letting each word roll around the mouth), finding the essence of the words

– They should now release back into a prayer stretch (kneeling but sitting back on their legs, forehead on the floor, arms outstretched in front of them). There will be a stretch from their fingertips, right through to their lower back

– Now ask them to come up into a crouching position on their toes but with the palms of their hands flat on the floor, their head up (so there is a, relatively, straight through-line of the spine) and their tail-bone dropped. They now need to breathe into the strong lower back muscles. Ask them to repeat 'fffff', 'sssss', 'vvvvv', 'zzzzz' all on separate breaths but concentrate on opening up those lower muscles. If they are unsure about this, separate them out into pairs and get their partner to place a flat hand on their lower back (just above the bottom) to see if they can feel the rise and fall of the breath. Now feed them the same lines again but ask them to think them from the back muscles. On the repeat they need to play around with the sound articulation again. If they've been working in pairs then get them to swap over

– They should now spend time, from their crouching position, rolling up the spine to a standing position. Make sure their head is the last thing that floats up

– Once up, they need to centre their weight and align their spine (as in previous workshops), repeat the 'fffff', 'sssss', 'vvvvv', 'zzzzz' and text phrases from their central core. If you see/feel/hear them tightening up around the throat during this process, ask them to roll up and down through the spine whilst speaking the lines before repeating in an upright position again.

Sample phrases for the warm-up.

It was my terrible desire rising
My animal leaning on its chain

I hate them all
I hate
I hate them all

I am burning all the human filth…

Oh I want to
Oh I so want

2. Exploring Rhythmic Structures

– Hand out copies of the sample text(s) and ask your actors to read it in their heads. Then ask them to try it aloud in their own space and time

– Generate a discussion on their first thoughts about speaking the text aloud (e.g. what worked, what didn't work)

– Now ask them to speak it again but make deliberate phrasing choices. They may need to double-back occasionally to repeat sections so that they make more sense. They may choose to mark the phrasing with a pencilled slash

– Get them to repeat the text with their phrasing decisions but, before they do, feed in the idea of the phrase being formed by their intonation pattern rather than distinct silent pauses. They will need the occasional tiny silence to take a breath: make sure they know exactly where these occur. Longish pauses should be taken only where 'pause' is indicated in the text

– Get them to repeat the text with their phrasing decisions again but, before they do, feed in the idea that the capitalised words represent strong emotions (not necessarily an increase in vocal volume, although that might work too)

– Team the group into pairs and ask one actor in each partnership to speak the text aloud with their decisions, immediately followed by the second actor. They can then compare any differences and why they might have occurred

– Now ask them (still in pairs) to find as many examples as they can of unusual metaphors, distorted syntax, disrupted phrasing and repetitions. Get them to make notes so that each pair can feed back to the group in the debriefing.

3. Debriefing

Each pair should feed back to the group as a whole in the debriefing session, answering the following questions:

– What have you learnt about language and rhythm in the text extract?

– How do they contribute to your understanding of the character's behaviour/ motivation?

Now ask your actors to read the extract again in their pairs (one after the other). They may (unconsciously) incorporate elements of the discussion into their performance.

– Did this last reading change again? In what way?

9. REVISITING THE BASICS

Here are some important points to remember from this chapter:

- Some non-realistic playwrights include both the realistic and the non-realistic in their dramatic texts. Characters may seem authentically motivated but the words and rhythms they use are distorted, with the intention of enhancing or intensifying certain elements of their behaviour.

- Harold Pinter heightens the absurdity of everyday speech by creating specific and formalised rhythmic patterns for his characters. These rhythmic patterns are structured into short verbal skirmishes, where each character tries to outmanoeuvre his/her opponent. Undercutting is a common way of winning a verbal skirmish: pauses and silences provide definition and repetition moves the game forward.

- Howard Barker creates rhythms that are unrecognisable on the page as everyday speech. Syntax is distorted, phrasing is disrupted, punctuation (generally) is absent and repetition is prolific.

- Both Pinter and Barker texts require vocal flexibility and precision if the rhythmic demands are to be met. However, Barker texts also require vocal strength and connection if the visceral, powerful and, sometimes violent, language is to be communicated successfully.

- Practical experimentation with the words and rhythms in a Pinter or Barker text will help actors discover deeper levels of meaning, ultimately informing their work on character and situation (just like in a realist text).

CHAPTER 10: EXPRESSING THE ABSURD

In the previous chapter we saw how some playwrights use non-realistic language and rhythms to provide us with information about a character's behaviour. However, what happens when language and rhythm *don't* help us make sense of what's going on? Then, of course, we have a full-blown absurdist text.

Without characters (in a realistic, psychological sense of the word) then the audience cannot identify with what is being portrayed on stage. They are alienated far more than they would be in a Brechtian play, where humanity still exists. It is easier, therefore, for the audience to see absurdism as grotesque and comic, despite the bleak world view that brought it into existence. In addition, because the audience can't relate, empathise, sympathise or even comprehend, they are more directly affected by the sound patterns in words and rhythms. Martin Esslin, in *The Theatre of the Absurd,* says:

> The Theatre of the Absurd…in abandoning psychology, subtlety
> of characterization, and plot in the conventional sense, gives the
> poetical element an incomparably greater emphasis. [19]

Words, and the way in which they operate rhythmically, don't always make sense in an absurdist world. Instead of asking 'what do they mean?' we need to ask 'why are they there?' which automatically leads us to larger issues about the absurdist view of the state of the world and humanity's place within it. We may still laugh but we will also see the horror boiling up from beneath.

All of this can be found in the texts of Samuel Beckett and Eugene Ionesco.

1. BECKETT: VOCAL DEMANDS

Vocal sound was important to Beckett. He liked to direct his own works and used the voice like an instrument, finely tuning the way in which actors dealt with his texts. His writing is specific in its use of sound, word and rhythm; therefore he wanted his actors to approach it in the same way. On occasion he even wrote with the vocal quality and verbal ability of certain actors in mind.

He also experimented with radio plays, where he could play even more with a vocal score.

By devaluing the language his characters speak (most of whom have difficulty in expressing themselves) he ensured that sound rose to the forefront of audience experience/perception. On stage, this often operated in tandem with movement (such as vaudevillian sight gags): characters who are frustrated in their linguistic communication resort to bodily communication instead. Therefore, sound play is usually balanced out with physical play.

Dialogue includes characters: struggling to find the right words; arguing with each other; shouting commands; contradicting, misunderstanding or ignoring each other; or, simply forgetting what either they or somebody else has just said. Dialogue can be a game that characters play or it can break down completely, ending up in silence.

Monologues are usually incoherent and disjointed, often indicating that a character has difficulty in communicating with other human beings.

The words themselves can be: illogical for the context, contradictory to onstage action, nonsensical, meaningless and clichéd.

Rhythmic patterns are created by: repeating sounds, words and phrases, creating sound/word association games, distorting syntax, stressing a strong metrical beat and using a variety of pauses, such as: '...', ' – ', 'pause', 'long pause', 'silence' and 'long silence'. Sound is absent to reinforce rhythmic patterns, create dramatic tension and remind the audience that the characters operate in a void (just like that of the post-war world).

Sometimes Beckett's sounds, words and rhythms massage the ear, at other times their dissonance is jarring.

Just like Pinter and Barker, actors need vocal flexibility and precision to bring a Beckett text to life. However, they also need a sense of vocal playfulness and a willingness to explore outside of their comfort zone. They must be able to make a connection to individual words and images, even if they don't make sense within the context of delivery. They must 'go with the flow' of the meaningless. Above all, they mustn't parody or 'send up' the text. This only creates a satirical intonation pattern that the audience will listen to above and beyond any other sound, word or rhythm they communicate.

2. BECKETT: TEXT SAMPLE

Beckett: Text Sample: Expressing the Absurd

The following text has been taken from *Waiting for Godot* by Samuel Beckett. It was written in the late 1940s and first performed in French in 1953. The first English performance was at the Arts Theatre, London, in August 1955, directed by Peter Hall.

The story so far:

There is no story. Vladimir and Estragon wait for someone called Godot for two days and fill their time by talking, arguing, singing, game-playing, sleeping and considering suicide. Other people enter into their world (Pozzo, Lucky and a boy) however it is their waiting which characterises the play. It is possible to draw social, religious and political conclusions from the text, however Beckett himself said: 'Why people have to complicate a thing so simple I can't make out.' The Irish critic Vivian Mercer once wrote in a review that it was a play where 'nothing happens, twice'. In this scene, Vladimir and Estragon have just had yet another meaningless and pointless argument.

VLADIMIR:	You're a hard man to get on with, Gogo.
ESTRAGON:	It'd be better if we parted.
VLADIMIR:	You always say that, and you always come crawling back.
ESTRAGON:	The best thing would be to kill me, like the other.
VLADIMIR:	What other? *(Pause.)* What other?
ESTRAGON:	Like billions of others.
VLADIMIR:	*(Setentious.)* To every man his little cross. *(He sighs.)* Till he dies. *(Afterthought.)* And is forgotten.
ESTRAGON:	In the meantime let us try and converse calmly, since we are incapable of keeping silent.
VLADIMIR:	You're right, we're inexhaustible.
ESTRAGON:	It's so we won't think.
VLADIMIR:	We have that excuse.
ESTRAGON:	It's so we won't hear.
VLADIMIR:	We have our reasons.
ESTRAGON:	All the dead voices.
VLADIMIR:	They make a noise like wings.

ESTRAGON:	Like leaves.
VLADIMIR:	Like sand.
ESTRAGON:	Like leaves.
	Silence.
VLADIMIR:	They all speak together.
ESTRAGON:	Each one to itself.
	Silence.
VLADIMIR:	Rather they whisper.
ESTRAGON:	They rustle.
VLADIMIR:	They murmur.
ESTRAGON:	They rustle.
	Silence.
VLADIMIR:	What do they say?
ESTRAGON:	They talk about their lives.
VLADIMIR:	To have lived is not enough for them.
ESTRAGON:	They have to talk about it.
VLADIMIR:	To be dead is not enough for them.
ESTRAGON:	It is not sufficient.
	Silence.
VLADIMIR:	They make a noise like feathers.
ESTRAGON:	Like leaves.
VLADIMIR:	Like ashes.
ESTRAGON:	Like leaves.
	Long silence.
VLADIMIR:	Say something!
ESTRAGON:	I'm trying.
	Long silence.
VLADIMIR:	*(In anguish.)* Say anything at all!
ESTRAGON:	What do we do now?

VLADIMIR:	Wait for Godot.
ESTRAGAON:	Ah!
	Silence.

Waiting for Godot by Samuel Beckett. Published by Faber and Faber.[20]

3. BECKETT: TEXT ANALYSIS

This is a well-known and much-quoted piece from Beckett's *Waiting for Godot*. It is a predictable choice for this chapter but its rhythmic artistry can't be ignored in a book that focuses on vocal patterning.

Since the 1950s, academics have attempted to make sense of this scene, but perhaps we should simply revel in the sound of its lyrical, rhythmical beauty (as Beckett intended) rather than try and place it within a context. However, like them, I can't resist some analysis: it is human nature to attach meaning to language.

The world of *Waiting for Godot* is uncertain: the characters are waiting for a person or thing or god, in the form of the unseen Godot, which can be translated into a need, a want, a desire, a belief and/or a faith. Eventually we (the audience) understand that this event, this coming of Godot, will never occur: waiting is futile and, therefore, existence is pointless. This links with a depressingly bleak post-war world where the absurdists saw humanity in a meaningless void.

The characters use sound and word to fill space and time. In the text sample, words are heightened and evocative: there is the war/holocaust allusion with the killing of 'billions', the 'dead voices' and 'ashes'; there is the religious allusion with 'To every man his little cross…'; and, there is the poetic imagery of 'wings/leaves/sand', 'whisper/rustle/murmur' and 'feathers/leaves/ashes'. The poetic imagery is incredibly suggestive: it conjures up sounds in our head. It doesn't matter if we read, speak or listen to these words, we can still hear them.

However, it isn't just the words that draw us in to these images: it is the combination of poetic imagery with rhythmic patterning that works on our senses. The repetition of particular sounds in words, the repetition of the words themselves, the repetition of a particular metrical beat, the repetition of particular line lengths and the repetition of pauses/silences/long silences (there are eight in total) is also incredibly powerful. Small changes to this rhythmic pattern keep our aural interest (too much of the same and we would probably tune out). No wonder this short excerpt is constantly quoted.

However, after such a powerful communication, energy drains away, there is nothing more to be said and a 'long silence' occurs. Vladimir implores Estragon to speak (twice) but words aren't possible. So what to do in this hiatus? Return to the waiting.

4. BECKETT: WORKSHOP PLAN

Your workshop participants may already know the text sample, given its fame, but it doesn't matter. The more you work on this text, the more you will find; so even if it is familiar to them there will still be new discoveries. Such is the complexity of Beckett's writing.

Beckett: Workshop Plan: Expressing the Absurd

Objectives

- To explore the language in a Samuel Beckett text through sound/word play
- To experiment with the rhythmic patterns in a Samuel Beckett text

Materials

You will need:

— Separate copies of the text extract, as provided in the previous 'Beckett: Text Sample' box.

Activities and Exercises

1. Warming up

Releasing, Grounding, Centring, Aligning, Breathing and Resonating

— Ask your actors to stretch their bodies any way they like, yawning out loud at the same time. Ask them to stretch and yawn again but use a completely different type

---

of stretch that creates a contrasting body shape. Repeat with a third stretch/yawn, different again

– Now ask your actors to find a space of their own and plant their feet firmly into the floor, hip width apart (they may like to do a bit of stomping first to make sure their feet are well connected to the floor). Without moving their feet from this position, ask them to shake out their body as much as they possibly can (it will end up looking like an extreme cold shiver). Now ask them to repeat the shaking with the mouth open and the breath releasing. Repeat the shake again but vocalise that breath into a sigh. Repeat again but place the lips gently together and shake out a hum ('mmmmm'). The last series of shakes should start on a hum then release into vowels: 'mmmOO', 'mmmOH', 'mmmAW', 'mmmAH', 'mmmAY', 'mmmEE'. Their faces should feel 'buzzy' and 'tingly' now

These exercises are appropriate for the text excerpt being used in this workshop. However, if you are using Beckett text that involves strong vocalisation, which is highly likely, then do revisit the initial warm-up exercises in the Howard Barker workshop plan in Chapter 9, which open up strong, lower body muscles to support the weight of the voice.

Articulating

– Choose three or four simple nonsensical tongue-twisters (that focus on different sound combinations) and ask your actors to practise them in their own space away from the rest of the group until their brains and mouths are operating in sync. Now divide the group into pairs with each partnership standing and facing each other. They need to centre, ground, align and make sure they are breathing from the centre of their bodies (using a few long 'fffff' sounds to check). Ask each pair to choose one of the tongue twisters and see how fast they can say it as a team: rhythmically, in time together. Every so often, instruct the whole group to shake out, breathe and start again (to ensure that physical tensions aren't building up). Eventually they will find a particular idiosyncratic rhythm that will help them master the exercise. They may find that a rhythmic movement or physical beat helps as well

– Now ask them to keep the same tongue-twister but change to a different rhythm (which will throw them out of sync). On mastering the rhythmic change, ask them to separate and move around the room until they find a new partner and 'announce' their version of the tongue-twister to them. Ask them to repeat this exercise to a number of different people. Encourage them to be completely serious throughout: playing the tongue-twisters as if they hold meaning and are sensible communications. If time permits, you might like them to repeat the process using the other tongue twisters.

2. Playing with Sound/Word/Image

– The Word Orchestra.

Set up your actors in rows with one person at the front as 'conductor'. The conductor then physically 'conducts' and the group must react with sound (either vowel or consonant) in accordance with the conductor's movement. Now give them a word from the text e.g. *kill*. Repeat the same exercise with the same conductor but instead of using isolated sounds of their own they may only use the word given to them, changing the way in which they play with it under direction from the conductor's movement. Try the exercise using all of the following words from the text:

Kill
Billions
Dies
Dead
Wings
Leaves
Sand
Whisper
Rustle
Murmur
Feathers
Ashes

Then start feeding in some phrases from the text, such as:

To every man his little cross
It's so we won't think
It's so we won't hear
All the dead voices
They make a noise like wings
They make a noise like feathers

Encourage the conductor to really play with his/her movement. Encourage the orchestra to really play with the sounds in the words and rhythms in the phrases, whilst following the conductor's movements. If the orchestra starts to strain vocally then stop for a moment, get them to flop over from the waist (knees bent) and shake the upper body out before rolling up through the spine to standing, whilst releasing a long 'fffff' sound.

– Physicalising Words.

Slowly feed your actors the list of words from the previous exercise. Ask them to vocalise each in turn and create a movement that (they feel) physicalises the essence of the sound energy (i.e. short, sharp sounds within the word may need a short, sharp movement, and multiple syllables may need a series of movements). There is no need for them to follow the literal meaning of the word but do make sure they speak and move at the same time. Be aware they may need time and space for exploration before you move onto the next word

Ask the group to go back to their original partner and teach their word movements to them as precisely and meticulously as they can. Then ask them to choose around five of the most successful and put them together to create a word poem that can be physically performed by both of them. They can disrupt the order in any way they like, repeat words at any point, speak together or one at a time but, importantly, they must try to maintain a sense of rhythmic fluency

Now ask them to repeat their word poem but without the movements. Their delivery should retain the quality of the original movement (the movement will have helped them find an appropriate vocal dynamic). It's a good idea for each pair to perform their work to the rest of the group. Initiate a discussion on the different types of vocal qualities/energies that emerged throughout the showing.

3. Exploring Rhythmic Structures

– Hand out copies of the sample text and ask each pair to read it aloud a number of times in their own space and time. They should connect quite easily to some of the words after the previous exercises. By the second or third reading they will begin to sense the strong rhythm. Coach them to only observe silence where it is indicated in the text (as the pauses and silences provide a rhythmic framework) but try not to enter into a discussion about it at this point in time

– In order for your actors to feel the rhythmic shifts/changes, they need to feel the beat through their bodies. Ask your actors to speak the text again in their pairs but this time they should let the rhythm dominate, stamping their feet on the strong stresses whenever they speak. They might like to try this exercise a couple of times so that it can be handled smoothly and fluently. Only then will rhythmic changes become clear. Now ask them to forget the stamping exercise, repeat the text again, returning their thoughts to word play. The rhythm will be there for them without them having to think about it

– The very LAST thing to do is to initiate a discussion on context, themes and absurdist world view, using the information provided earlier in this chapter and in Chapter 8. Now ask them to try the text again in their pairs so that the discussion can inform their performance.

3. Debriefing

Allow some time for a group debriefing session:

– Did your last reading change in any way?

– Which are the most powerful, evocative words in this text extract?

– How does Beckett create the rhythm?

– Can you pinpoint the rhythmic changes throughout the text? Why do they occur?

Now ask your actors to read the scene again in their pairs. They may (unconsciously) incorporate elements of the discussion into their performance.

5. IONESCO: VOCAL DEMANDS

In 1958, a very public argument broke out between Kenneth Tynan (theatre critic) and Eugene Ionesco (absurdist playwright) in the pages of *The Observer*. Tynan argued for the realists whilst Ionesco defended the non-realists. Ionesco justified his plays by stating that the language of society was 'nothing but clichés, empty formulas and slogans'.[21] He thought that it was the duty of true theatre to reflect this so 'the words themselves must be stretched to their utmost limits, the language must be made almost to explode, or to destroy itself in its inability to contain its meaning.'[22]

This evocative description sums up perfectly the way in which Ionesco uses words in his plays: they are there to express his anguish at the human condition. When they were first staged it came as a complete surprise to him that audiences found his works comic: he had written them as tragedies.

Like Beckett, his words can be illogical, meaningless and clichéd. He uses nonsensical proverbs and epigrams, foreign words or common foreign phrases (usually in English) that French audiences wouldn't necessarily understand and violates the 'turn-taking rule' so that characters speak their lines out of sequence. His texts often dissolve into a complete jumble of sound and word, losing meaning altogether. In many cases, this can mirror the verbal play of childhood, where his characters regress into a world of comfort and familiarity.

The patterning and repetition of both sound and word is an important element of this verbal play and contributes to strongly marked rhythms. The less sense present, the more Ionesco plays with sound and rhythm, creating an energy that is heightened, insistent and, sometimes, frantic.

Vocally, his texts require verbal discipline and rigorous rehearsal. Communicating nothing at all can be demanding. However, like Beckett, actors need to work outside of their comfort zone, taking risks and playing vocally. It is important that they don't try for the comedy or humour that they might perceive from the meaningless language. It must be taken in all seriousness and played for 'real'.

Ionesco often includes heightened emotions that aren't linked to any specific psychological moment: you will see directions in the subtext for shouting and screaming. This is incredibly difficult for actors because it means that a strong vocal response can't be connected to word, thought or emotion and so vocal straining and pushing are more common. Exercises for the powerful lower body breathing muscles are helpful in redirecting the strain away from the throat, as explained in Chapter 9 with the Howard Barker text. However, if in doubt, call in a vocal specialist for advice and practical application. Also, be careful in rehearsal. The human voice can't stand the strain of too much push before swelling or bleeding occurs in the vocal chords/folds. Better to rehearse vocally strong sections of text just once in a day, otherwise you may find that your actors lose their voices or, worse, face vocal damage.

6. IONESCO: TEXT SAMPLE

Ionesco: Text Sample: Expressing the Absurd

The following text has been taken from *La Cantatrice Chauve* (*The Bald Soprano*) by Eugene Ionesco (translated by Donald M. Allen). It was first produced in Paris at the Théâtre des Noctambules in May 1950. It has been permanently staged at the Théâtre de la Huchette since 1957.

The story so far:

Ionesco wrote *La Cantatrice Chauve* (*The Bald Soprano*) after having to learn banal statements whilst studying English. He channelled this experience into a comedy, exposing the empty platitudes, facile clichés and meaningless conversations within everyday life.

Mr and Mrs Smith are the quintessential middle-class English couple, who live in London. They've invited Mr and Mrs Martin over for dinner, despite having eaten already. This section of text takes place at the very end of the play when their conversation becomes more and more absurd, disintegrating into hostility.

MRS. MARTIN: I'll give you my mother-in-law's slippers if you'll give me your husband's coffin.

MR. SMITH: I'm looking for a monophysite priest to marry our maid.

MR. MARTIN: Bread is a staff, whereas bread is also a staff, and an oak springs from an oak every morning at dawn.

MRS. SMITH: My uncle lives in the country, but that's none of the midwife's business.

MR. MARTIN: Paper is for writing, the cat's for the rat. Cheese is for scratching.

MRS. SMITH: The car goes very fast, but the cook beats batter better.

MR. SMITH: Don't be turkeys; rather kiss the conspirator.

MR. MARTIN: Charity begins at home.

MRS. SMITH: I'm waiting for the aqueduct to come and see me at my windmill.

MR. MARTIN: One can prove that social progress is definitely better with sugar.

MR. SMITH: To hell with polishing!

(Following this last speech of Mr. Smith's, the others are silent for a moment, stupefied. We sense that there is a certain nervous irritation. The strokes of the clock are more nervous too. The speeches which follow must be said, at first, in a glacial, hostile tone. The hostility and the nervousness increase. At the end of this scene, the four characters must be standing very close to each other, screaming their speeches, raising their fists, ready to throw themselves upon each other.)

MR. MARTIN: One doesn't polish spectacles with black wax.

MRS. SMITH: Yes, but with money one can buy anything.

MR. MARTIN: I'd rather kill a rabbit than sing in the garden.

MR. SMITH: Cockatoos, cockatoos, cockatoos, cockatoos, cockatoos, cockatoos, cockatoos, cockatoos, cockatoos, cockatoos.

MRS. SMITH: Such caca, such caca, such caca, such caca, such caca, such caca, such caca, such caca, such caca.

MR. MARTIN: Such cascades of cacas, such cascades of cacas, such cascades of cacas, such cascades of cacas, such cascades of cacas, such cascades of cacas, such cascades of cacas, such cascades of cacas.

MR. SMITH: Dogs have fleas, dogs have fleas.

MRS. MARTIN: Cactus, coccyx! crocus! cockaded! cockroach!

MRS. SMITH: Incasker, you incask us.

MR. MARTIN: I'd rather lay an egg in a box than go and steal an ox.

MRS. MARTIN (*Opening her mouth very wide*): Ah! oh! ah! oh! Let me gnash my teeth.

MR. SMITH: Crocodile!

MR MARTIN: Let's go and slap Ulysses.

MR SMITH: I'm going to live in my cabana among my cacao trees.

MRS. MARTIN: Cacao trees on cacao farms don't bear coconuts, they yield cocoa! Cacao trees on cacao farms don't bear coconuts, they yield cocoa! Cacao trees on cacao farms don't bear coconuts, they yield cocoa!

MRS. SMITH: Mice have lice, lice haven't mice.

MRS. MARTIN: Don't ruche my brooch!

MR. MARTIN: Don't smooch the brooch!

MR. SMITH: Groom the goose, don't goose the groom.

MRS. MARTIN: The goose grooms.

MRS. SMITH: Groom your tooth.

MR. MARTIN: Groom the bridegroom, groom the bridegroom.

MR. SMITH: Seducer seduced!

MRS. MARTIN: Scaramouche!

MRS. SMITH: Sainte-Nitouche!

MR. MARTIN: Go take a douche.

MR SMITH: I've been goosed.

MRS. MARTIN: Sainte-Nitouche stoops to my cartouche.

MRS SMITH: "Who'd stoop to blame?...and I never choose to stoop."

MR. MARTIN: Robert!

MR. SMITH: Browning!

MRS. MARTIN, MR. SMITH: Rudyard.

MRS. SMITH, MR. MARTIN: Kipling.

MRS MARTIN, MR. SMITH: Robert Kipling!

MRS. SMITH, MR. MARTIN: Rudyard Browning.

MRS. MARTIN: Silly gobblegobblers, silly gobblegobblers.

MR. MARTIN: Marietta, spot the pot!

MRS. SMITH: Krishnamurti, Krishnamurti, Krishnamurti!

MR. SMITH: The pope elopes! The pope's got no horoscope. The horoscope's bespoke.

MRS. MARTIN: Bazaar, Balzac, bazooka!

MR. MARTIN: Bizarre, beaux-arts, brassieres!

MR. SMITH: A, e, i, o, u, a, e, i, o, u, a, e, i, o, u, i!

MRS. MARTIN: B, c, d, f, g, l, m, n, p, r, s, t, v, w, x, z!

MR. MARTIN: From sage to stooge, from stage to serge!

MRS. SMITH (*Imitating a train.*): Choo, choo, choo, choo, choo, choo, choo, choo, choo, choo, choo!

MR. SMITH: It's!

MRS. MARTIN: Not!

MR. MARTIN: That!

MRS. SMITH: Way!

MR. SMITH: It's!

MRS. MARTIN: O!

MR. MARTIN: Ver!

MRS. SMITH: Here!

(*All together, completely infuriated, screaming in each other's ears. The light is extinguished. In the darkness we hear, in an increasingly rapid rhythm:*)

ALL TOGETHER: It's not that way, it's over here, it's not that way, it's over here, it's not that way, it's over here, it's not that way, it's over here!

(*The words cease abruptly. Again, the lights come on. Mr. and Mrs. Martin are seated like the Smiths at the beginning of the play. The play begins again with the Martins, who say exactly the same lines as the Smiths in the first scene, while the curtain softly falls.*)

La Cantatrice Chauve (The Bald Soprano) by Eugene Ionesco. Translated by Donald M. Allen and published by Grove Press in *The Bald Soprano and Other Plays*.[23]

7. IONESCO: TEXT ANALYSIS

If, as we learnt earlier in this book, realistic language helps create the identity of a character, then meaningless language devalues character so that identity is lost. In this extract from the end of the play, the Smiths and the Martins can't communicate anymore. They speak without purpose, use words that are meaningless, lines that are interchangeable (their allocation seems random) and rhythms that aren't part of everyday speech. They have not only lost their identity, they have lost their humanity. They don't know who they are or understand their place in the world.

Ionesco puts the banality of language on display. It looks haphazard but, in actual fact, has been carefully crafted: there are specific types of verbal play. In the first section, characters play with proverbs and epigrams, dealing them out like hands in a card game. They may *sound* like proverbs and epigrams but not as we know them. Usually, epigrams express an opinion or a piece of advice or a judgement about some aspect of human nature by someone who is, or is trying to be, wise. Repetition, paradox and antithesis are essential to creating the form. The epigrams used by the Smiths and the Martins may have meaningless content but the form is intact, which is how we recognise them. The characters are also trying to be wise, working to top each other with their pontificating wisdom. The game is broken by Mr Smith's startling 'To hell with polishing!'. There is a moment of stupefied silence.

The characters start up again nervously and the remainder of the scene builds in emotional tension, ending in shouted hysterics. They are frustrated in their inability to communicate. Ultimately, however, it is emotion without substance, without meaning.

Initially, this section starts with epigrams/proverbs but soon descends into a series of repeated words or repeated phrases. In most cases, speakers pick up on sounds/words used by previous speakers, changing them into something slightly different. It becomes a game of sound/word association (with the occasional rhyme thrown in) resembling strange tongue twisters. The dominant sounds are hard plosive consonants (/ k / with cockatoos, caca, cascades, cacas, cactus, coccyx, crocus, cockaded, cockroach, incasker, incask, crocodile, cabana, cacao, coconuts, cocoa, cartouche; / g / with groom, goose, bridegroom, gobblegobblers; and, / b / bazaar, Balzac, bazooka, bizarre, beaux-arts, brassieres).

This resembles the speech play of small children. The lines become more and more childlike as the scene progresses: they do not want to engage with the adult world so childhood is a much safer and comforting place. There are tongue-twisters, the playing with particular sounds and even the familiar chants of the school room (listing poets, repeating the vowel letters in order or reciting most of the consonant letters in order). There are even moments when the characters regress to babbling, rhythmically repeating the same sounds and syllables that babies find pleasurable (such as 'caca' or 'choo').

Lines are occasionally split between characters. Most importantly, the final line of the play is introduced to the audience through shared delivery (one word or syllable per character). It's a way of making 'It's not that way, it's over here' even more prominent. Vocally, it builds to a crescendo of sound (where the characters are 'screaming'), then the lights go out and the line is repeated rapidly in unison. It is an evocative yet chilling moment in the dark. Suddenly sound stops. Is this the end of the play/end of the world? When the lights come on again, the audience is returned to the opening scene, although the Smiths are now played by the Martins. The story is cyclical: the characters (whom are interchangeable) have come full circle.

8. IONESCO: WORKSHOP PLAN

Participants in this workshop do not need prior knowledge of the whole play text; however, it can also be run equally well if they do.

Ionesco: Workshop Plan: Expressing the Absurd

Objectives

- To explore the absurdist language in a Eugene Ionesco text through sound/word play

- To explore the patterns in a Eugene Ionesco text through rhythmic play.

Materials

You will need:

– Separate copies of the text extract, as provided in the previous 'Ionesco: Text Sample' box

– Tongue-twister handout (including phrases drawn from the text)

– Packs of cards

Activities and Exercises

1. Warming up

Releasing, Grounding, Centring, Aligning, Breathing and Resonating

– Ask your actors to stand with their feet hip width apart but with one foot slightly more forward than the other. They should place their weight a little further on the front foot and soften their knees, as though they are about to spring forward. Now get them to do some quick and light panting, feeling the action of the diaphragm in the centre of the body, followed by a long and released 'fffff' sound (to release any tensions they might have picked up). Repeat this exercise a few times to ensure that the diaphragm and abdominals are awake and ready for action

– They should now release a long 'fffff', 'sssss', 'vvvvv', 'zzzzz' and 'mmmmm' (all on different breaths from low in the body). Hopefully their 'springing' position will help them to access the lower body muscles. If they start to look/feel uncomfortable then get them to shake out and swap their feet around

– Ask them to bounce out some sounds from their lower breathing muscles: 'mmmOO', 'mmmOH', 'mmmAW', 'mmmAH', 'mmmAY', 'mmmEE'. They need to concentrate on creating a light, bouncy energy. The push should come from the lower body, not the upper throat. If you feel there is too much tension there, get them to shake out again before repeating.

Articulating

– The sample text extract is one big tongue-twister so choose some lines from it for the articulation warm-up (preferably ones that focus on different sound combinations). Have them printed out on a piece of paper for ease of reference (don't give them the text to work with). Ask your actors to practise them in their own space away from the rest of the group until their brains and mouths are operating in sync. Now divide them into groups of four. They need to centre, ground, align and make sure they are breathing from the centre of their bodies (using a few long 'fffff' sounds to check). Ask each group to choose one of the tongue-twisters and see how fast they can say it as a team: rhythmically, in time together. Every so often, instruct the whole group to shake out, breathe and start again (to ensure that physical tensions aren't building up). Eventually they will find a particular idiosyncratic rhythm that will help them master the exercise. They may find that a rhythmic movement or physical beat helps as well

– Now ask them to pick up their tongue-twister handout again and have a conversation only using the phrases/sentences printed on the sheet. They can be used in any order and repeated as many times as they like. If they trip up, ask them to repeat the line that caused them difficulty. Coach them to really use their lips and tongue. They must concentrate on playing the lines seriously. Stop and re-start if they start to play the humour or dissolve into laughter.

2. Playing with Sound/Word/Rhythm

– Ask your actors to stay in their groups of four and give them the text extract to read in their heads. Because of the articulatory demands, get them to mouth the words silently (so their lips and tongue know/understand the movements they will need to make). Finally, get them to speak it aloud as a group (without comment)

– Now ask them to take the first section of text, from 'I'll give you my mother-in-law's slippers if you'll give me your husband's coffin' to 'To hell with polishing'. Hand out a pack of cards to each group and ask them to deal them out to all four 'players'. Feed in the idea that these epigrams/proverbs are being played as a game of cards, each line is a hand that is being played to win, topping the previous one. Now ask them to physically play a card each time they have a line. They will need to decide on the energy in which they play their hand (which will affect their vocal energy) and the point in the line (which particular syllable) they actually throw down the card. You will find that, on the whole, they will choose a nuclear stress

– Get them to repeat the previous exercise but this time ask them to build the energy/vigour of the physical action, which will feed into the vocalisation

– Repeat the exercise again but without the cards. The lines should retain the rhythmic energy of the card game without the physical action. Encourage them to play the verbal game in all seriousness

– Now ask them to focus on the next section, from 'One doesn't polish spectacles with black wax' to 'choo, choo, choo'. Get them to try the card game exercise again then put the cards to one side. On the next reading, the first three lines should retain elements of the card game as they are still epigrams/proverbs. On each of the remaining lines they must choose a physical children's game to play whilst speaking e.g. pat-a-cake (clapping the palms of their hands to another person's palms and then clapping their hands together, then back to their partner's palms) or tag (where one person is 'it' and tries to 'tag' the others, thereby making them 'it') or hopscotch or follow the leader or jump rope (without the rope). This will be tricky with the paper in their hands but, if they can manage, it helps them to play with the words. Encourage them to keep changing the game. Get them to try this a few times through to find the right game for the lines (it should mirror the rhythmic energy)

– Finally, ask them to try the text without the physical games. The lines should retain the verbal play. On a few repetitions they will be able to find the text's natural build in rhythmic energy

– The very LAST thing to do is to initiate a discussion on what they think is happening in this scene (incorporating the absurdist world view, using the information provided earlier in this chapter and in Chapter 8). Encourage them to think outside of the box, especially if this is their first sight of a section of the play. Now ask them to try the whole text extract through (including the final section) so that the discussion can inform their performance. Don't allow them to repeat the final section more than once because of the vocal strain it may induce.

3. Debriefing

Allow some time for a group debriefing session:

– Did your last reading change in any way?

– What were your biggest challenges in the speaking of this text?

9. REVISITING THE BASICS

Here are some important points to remember from this chapter:

- Absurdist playwrights use words and rhythms that are incomprehensible, illogical and nonsensical to communicate their vision of a bleak world without meaning. Audiences cannot identify with characters who speak in this way so they tend to view them as grotesque and comic.

- Samuel Beckett and Eugene Ionesco devalue language in their plays: their characters have difficulty in expressing themselves. Because audiences cannot make sense of what is being said they are more likely to be affected by sounds, words and rhythmic patterning.

- Actors need vocal flexibility and precision to bring these texts to life. They also need to be vocally playful and explore outside of their comfort zone.

- Actors mustn't parody or 'send up' the text, even if they think there is comedy to be played. The words may seem funny but the message behind them is tragic. Playing the humour will only create a satirical intonation pattern that the audience will listen to above and beyond sound, word and rhythm.

- Actors need to develop vocal strength in order to deal with heightened emotions from frustrated characters. These emotions aren't (necessarily) linked to any specific psychological moment so connections can't be made. Therefore, technical skill is paramount.

- Practical experimentation with the words and rhythms in a Beckett or Ionesco text will *not* help actors discover deeper levels of meaning in character and situation but it will help them understand the way in which sound has been patterned poetically as well as the world view that inspired it.

CHAPTER 11: TALKING IN VERSE

The language within a play can be *poetic* but it doesn't necessarily mean that it is *verse*. Plays in verse shape words into patterns on the page, play around with the order of grammatical syntax and use a specific rhythmic arrangement.

But why create plays in verse at all? Why develop characters who speak in verse? What is the point? For many playwrights, across thousands of years of history, verse has helped heighten the dramatic experience: the rhythms and language of verse can have a powerful effect on audience emotion. However, the most complex issue that has always faced playwrights writing in verse or poets writing drama is: how to structure the vagaries of human speech within the verse form. Verse is about words whereas drama is about people embodying those words.

The Ancient Greeks and the Renaissance Italians felt that a structured verse form suited the heightened emotions of tragedy whereas prose, or a more fluid type of free verse, was more appropriate for comedy and the speech of common, less noble characters.

The Elizabethans/Jacobeans started out using a strict form of blank verse, the metre of which mirrored the beat of the human heart and loosely resembled natural speech rhythm. As time wore on, however, they adapted the structure of blank verse to meet more of the demands of character/situation, changing line lengths, metrical beats and grammatical syntax to suit their purpose.

The nineteenth-century verse dramatists felt that prose was unsuitable for serious subject matter because it was too close to everyday speech so they were more likely to conform to traditional metrical rules. Perhaps this is why their plays weren't popular: they never found a form that married real speech with the intensity of verse.

The mid-twentieth-century verse dramatists thought it important to adopt a verse form that was as close to everyday speech as possible, whatever the subject matter. To achieve this they used variations of traditional metrical forms, without strict adherence to the number or positioning of beats in a line, creating rhythms that were more appropriate for character and situation.

The late twentieth-century/early twenty-first-century verse dramatists have been even less formulaic, constantly changing and evolving the way in which they work with form. Their verse is more likely to fall into the category of *free verse*. Of course there are exceptions, not every contemporary verse playwright uses free verse. Tony Harrison has a penchant for rhyming couplets in some of his plays, as does Torben Betts. Steven Berkoff has, on occasion, used metrical verse beats and traditional rhyme schemes. However, in this chapter, I will be focusing on the way in which contemporary verse playwrights use free verse and the way in which actors can lift it off the page for an audience.

1. VOCAL DEMANDS

It is a common misconception that free verse is unstructured. Line lengths vary, rhythmic beats are less metrical or regular (mirroring the irregularities of prose/speech) and rhyme is absent. However, the words are still shaped into patterns on the page which affects the rhythmic structure. In dramatic free verse, these patterns usually correspond to the thoughts and emotions of character, relationship and situation.

Free verse is often described by its detractors as 'chopped-up prose'. Not true. Take a look at the following extract from Ted Hughes' modern version of the ancient verse drama *The Oresteia*. Here, Clytemnestra explains how she killed her husband Agamemnon.

> I pondered this for a long time.
> And when the moment for action came
> I made no mistake. See, my work
> Perfected. I don't disown it.
> Every possibility of error
> I wrapped in a great net –
> Not a fish could have slipped from the shoal.
> His struggles merely tightened the tangle.
> Then, at my leisure, choosing the best places
> On his helpless body

CATHERINE WEATE

> I pushed the blade into him. Once, twice.
>
> Twice he screamed. You heard him.
>
> Then his eyes stared elsewhere.
>
> His body arched like a bow being strung,
>
> Every muscle straining for life.
>
> I placed the point for a third and final time
>
> And drove the blade clean through him.[24]

Now take a look at the following text, where I've re-patterned the same words into prose.

> I pondered this for a long time. And when the moment for action came, I made no mistake. See, my work perfected. I don't disown it. Every possibility of error I wrapped in a great net – not a fish could have slipped from the shoal. His struggles merely tightened the tangle. Then, at my leisure, choosing the best places on his helpless body I pushed the blade into him. Once, twice. Twice he screamed. You heard him. Then his eyes stared elsewhere. His body arched like a bow being strung, every muscle straining for life. I placed the point for a third and final time and drove the blade clean through him.

Speak the two extracts aloud (preferably the prose first) and you will hear that the patterning makes a difference. It changes the spoken rhythm, particularly stress and intonation. The verse shape heightens the emotions, whereas the prose shape blunts them. The difference is partially bound up with the line endings.

End-stopped lines are where the sense and rhythm stop at the end of the line, which is usually indicated by a punctuation mark in the text. *Enjambed lines* are where the sense of a line of verse continues on into the next line without punctuation marks. In the Ted Hughes' excerpt, there is enjambment on lines 2, 3, 5, 9, 10 and 16. The final words in enjambed lines become significant ('came', 'work', 'error', 'places', 'body' and 'time'). When an enjambed line occurs, speakers need to preserve the meaning without losing the shape of the verse: a *suspensory pause* solves the problem. The last word (or the last stressed syllable) needs to be carried over into the next line, suspended by pitch and length. In other words, instead of a pause of silence at the end of the line, *there is a pause on the word itself*, thereby doing away with the need for silence.

So, using suspensory pauses on 'came', 'work', 'error', 'places', 'body' and 'time' makes them more prominent. This prominence is lost when reading the text as prose and the interpretation becomes quite different. Suspending or stressing 'came' indicates that it is the arrival of the moment that is important to Clytemnestra. Suspending or stressing 'work' tells us that she saw the killing of her husband as a 'job' and we hear her pride in doing it well. 'Error' was her fear and provides us with insight into her motivation for 'work perfected'. 'Places' is nasty: it tells us that she thought carefully/logically about where to stab. This is backed up by the suspended/stressed 'body'. The final enjambed line gives us a feeling of movement, of action. However, we also feel 'time' suspended: her hesitation on this word recreates the moment just before she 'drove the blade clean through him.'

In traditional classical verse that has metrical beats, *a caesura* or *caesural pause*, is often used midline (usually indicated with punctuation marks in the text). It helps to balance the rhythmic metre of an enjambed line, often occurring in the middle of the line or the one after. This isn't necessarily the case in free verse although you can see how Hughes makes regular use of caesural pauses around enjambed lines, which creates drama at key moments.

Therefore, punctuation becomes much more important in free verse than in prose. As we learnt in Part One, prose punctuation doesn't necessarily mirror speech phrasing: there are anomalies. In free verse, the punctuation tends to create a pattern of silences.

So what about the actor? If the rhythmic structure lies in the way in which words and silences have been patterned on the page then actors need to take these patterns as their guide. This will help them find the rhythmic structure and, therefore, the pausing, phrasing, stressing, intonation and key changes. Ignoring the patterns will, ultimately, muddy the thoughts and emotions of the character.

2. KANE: TEXT SAMPLE

Kane: Text Sample: Talking in Verse

The following text has been taken from *4.48 Psychosis* by Sarah Kane. It was first performed at the Royal Court Jerwood Theatre Upstairs in London in June 2000.

The story so far:

4.48 Psychosis explores the inner thoughts of an unknown speaker across a series of pre-dawn (4.48 a.m.) moments. Character and plot are left vague so the audience focus, more acutely, on the speaker's emotional state. Kane committed suicide not long after the text was completed and it was first performed after her death.

I dread the loss of her I've never touched
love keeps me a slave in a cage of tears
I gnaw my tongue with which to her I can never speak
I miss a woman who was never born
I kiss a woman across the years that say we shall never meet

     Everything passes
     Everything perishes
     Everything palls

    my thought walks away with a killing smile
    leaving discordant anxiety
    which roars in my soul

No hope No hope No hope No hope No hope No hope No hope

A song for my loved one, touching her absence
    the flux of her heart, the splash of her smile

In ten years time she'll still be dead. When I'm living with it, dealing with it, when a few days pass when I don't even think of it, she'll still be dead. When I'm an old lady living on the street forgetting my name she'll still be dead, she'll still be dead, it's just
               fucking
                   over

                    and I must stand alone

My love, my love, why have you forsaken me?

She is the couching place where I never shall lie
and there's no meaning to life in the light of my loss

>Built to be lonely
>to love the absent

>Find me
>Free me
>>from this

>>>>corrosive doubt
>>>>futile despair

>>>>horror in repose

>Iy can fill my space
>fill my time
>but nothing can fill this void in my heart

>The vital need for which I would die

>>>>>>Breakdown

4.48 Psychosis by Sarah Kane. Published by Methuen in *Sarah Kane: Complete Plays*.[25]

3. KANE: TEXT ANALYSIS

In *4.48 Psychosis*, Kane's fusion of content and form is striking. The text extract presented here is a particularly good example.

CONTENT

The speaker expresses her fear of loneliness and the ultimate human goal to share life with somebody else. She speaks about the future love that she will never see, the unborn love, the absent love, the lost love and the dead love. The final lines are telling as her lonely despair leads her to thoughts of death, which in turn leads to her 'Breakdown'.

- The language is raw, in tune with her emotions:

  dread, loss, slave, cage, gnaw, perishes, palls, killing, discordant, anxiety, roars, dead, corrosive, futile, despair, horror, void, die.

- However, there are flashes of beauty in the darkness:

  A song for my loved one, touching her absence

    The flux of her heart, the splash of her smile

- Even something a classical poet might have written:

  My love, my love, why have you forsaken me?

- But the light and the dark are also juxtaposed:

  a killing smile

  it's just fucking over and I must stand alone/My love, my love, why have you forsaken me?

- Repetition is constant. Words run around her head like a broken record:

  I dread.../I gnaw.../I miss.../I kiss...

  Everything passes/Everything perishes/Everything palls

  No hope No hope No hope No hope No hope No hope No hope

  ...she'll still be dead.../...she'll still be dead.../...she'll still be dead, she'll still be dead...

  When I'm living with it, dealing with it, when a few days pass when I don't even

  think of it...

  My love, my love...

  Find me/Free me

  I can fill my space/fill my time/but nothing can fill this void in my heart

FORM

Kane uses a mixture of verse and prose. The patterns and shapes she creates on the page are just as important as the words in expressing meaning. They have been carefully structured so that our attention is drawn towards particular words, combinations of words and/or phrases. In addition, they help us feel the rhythm of her thoughts/emotions, which are jumbled together in her mind, fighting for space. Here is an overview of the structure:

- Five long, flowing, unpunctuated lines in a semi-regular beat

- A line space

- Three indented short lines in a semi-regular beat (contrasting with the beat of the previous lines)

- A line space

- Three indented lines in free verse without a regular beat

- A line space

- A single line of the same repeated phrase, creating a repetitive, regular beat

- A line space

- Two lines (one indented) with a lyrical, poetical beat to match the beauty of the content

- A line space

- A prose paragraph with a strongly marked rhythm because of its repetitive phrases. It finishes with a line falling down the page. The last clause (about standing alone) is separated out with extra line spaces.

- A line space

- A single line in a traditional rhythm that matches the classical content

- A line space

- Two long, flowing, unpunctuated, free verse lines

- A line space

- Two indented, short lines

- A line space

- One phrase, separated out into different clauses, falls down the page. The indentation size and number of line spaces between the clauses, vary. The final clause ('horror in repose') is separated out, all alone.

- A line space

- Three lines of free verse, two shorter, one longer

- Two line spaces

- One line of free verse, separated out, all alone

- Two line spaces

- The last word is indented well over to the right of the page. 'Breakdown' refers to an emotional breakdown but the verse has also broken down, spluttering to a stop.

This extract is a balancing act between light images and dark images, sounds and silences, long lines and short lines, regular beats and irregular beats, and, left to right text as opposed to falling down the page text. Alongside the constant repetitions of sound, word and phrase, it confronts the ear on so many different levels. Although it isn't easy to speak aloud, especially with such disturbing content, it is rhythmically exciting and almost satisfying.

4. MAXWELL: TEXT SAMPLE

Maxwell: Text Sample: Talking in Verse

The following text has been taken from *The Forever Waltz* by Glyn Maxwell. The European premiere was first performed at the Smirnoff Baby Belly, Edinburgh in August 2005.

The story so far:

MOBILE arrives in the underworld, searching for his ex-lover, EVIE. Unfortunately he can't remember anything about himself or how he arrived at this point. WATTS, a mysterious guitar-wielding guide helps him to remember. In this scene, MOBILE remembers EVIE's wedding day, where he couldn't resist turning up to see her and the man she decided to marry. His pain is evident throughout their exchange and it's clear that he still loves her. When her new husband starts playing the song that was MOBILE and EVIE's song when they were together, MOBILE grabs the wedding cake knife and stabs her to death. No wonder his mind wanted to forget.

EVIE: Oh my lord.

MOBILE: The same.

EVIE: I knew you'd come though.
Life was perfect, it was on the cards.

MOBILE: How could I not? We go back, you and I,
come a long way.

EVIE: We do, we'll always be,
you know –

MOBILE: You know –

EVIE: There'll always be what there was.

MOBILE: That's absolutely true.
There always is what there was. My philosophy.

EVIE: Nobody tried to stop you.

MOBILE: Nobody did.

EVIE: I wouldn't want that.

MOBILE: A smart chap with a gift,
nobody's going to stop me.

EVIE: Nobody could!
        Who ever could? It's good to see you, John.
        What have you got me there.

MOBILE: Well it's a surprise,
        isn't it? Where's the gentleman of the hour?

EVIE: Oh, he's I don't know.

MOBILE: Is he out there?

EVIE goes quickly to the window and signals to say 'Don't play, don't play the song'.
MOBILE goes to the window. EVIE draws him back.

        He's musical.

EVIE: Like you!

MOBILE: Just like me.

EVIE: Perhaps that was my fantasy all along,
         to be a rock-star girl, I didn't mind
         who sang the songs!

MOBILE: Is he going to sing a song?

EVIE: Oh I hope not, they're hopeless.

MOBILE: They look like they're ready to play. What do they play?

EVIE: Nothing you'd recognise.

MOBILE: They look very cool.
         A very cool ensemble.

EVIE: Should I open my present, John?

MOBILE: I don't think so.
         You open it and it's over.
         Nothing to look forward to.

EVIE: But then no one
         would ever open anything.

MOBILE: When we met,
         what did we laugh about?

EVIE: What?

MOBILE: When we met, what did we laugh about?

EVIE: John, I don't know. It's sort of long ago.

MOBILE: That rhymed, did you hear, but then it's your wedding day.
Things are going to rhyme.

EVIE: You've been sitting there
some time, haven't you John?

MOBILE: Oh many years.
Best years of our lives, did you not notice?
You coughed and they went by. They made you ill.

EVIE: I loved our time together.

MOBILE: Did you love it?
Take it out on a date. Give it chocolates.
Put its hand where you want it.

EVIE: I want you always,
John, to be my friend.

MOBILE: Excellent news.

EVIE: What we had was what we had, and it was special,
and I'll never forget —

MOBILE: Except what we laughed at.

EVIE: Except what we laughed at, yes. Can I open my present?

MOBILE: You mean *can you open my present*
and then John can you leave.

EVIE: Be my friend, John,
it isn't easy for anyone if you're here.

MOBILE: It's easy for me.

EVIE: Then do a thing for me.
Do it out of pity.

MOBILE: Out of pity?
On the day of days?

EVIE: Not pity, do it out of
selflessness. Why are you looking at me?

MOBILE: Why am I looking at you? Selflessness.
I am leaving my self.

EVIE: That's a start, can your self leave too?
Only a joke.

MOBILE: I was catching your eye again.
I was catching it like the old days but unlike
the old days it will not catch mine at all.

EVIE: I'm looking at you, John. Out of love.

MOBILE: Far out of love.

EVIE: I don't mean out of love,
I mean, *from* love.

MOBILE: Very, very far from love.

EVIE: You twist and twist. I'm trying to reach, can you see?
It's my wedding day. *This* is all I am.
I tried to be a person who was good,
who never hurt a soul.

MOBILE: Oh I tried that.

EVIE: He is who I chose.
He is who I picked.

MOBILE: Whom I picked.

EVIE: Go home, John, go home.

MOBILE: What about your present?

EVIE: Will you go if I open this?

MOBILE: I'll go if you open it.

EVIE: Go straight away?

MOBILE: Quick as a flash. Smile.

MOBILE uses his cell phone to take a picture of EVIE.

You didn't smile. Smile this time.

EVIE: And you'll go.

MOBILE: Smile.

*She does, he takes another picture. He gives her the gift and looks
at the picture he took.*

EVIE: Thank you John.

MOBILE: Like the crocodile.

The Forever Waltz by Glyn Maxwell. Published by Oberon Books.[26]

5. MAXWELL: TEXT ANALYSIS

The dialogue in this scene is written in free verse, which provides insight into the relationship between Evie and Mobile on Evie's wedding day to another man. Despite her discomfort and his bitterness, there is memory and intimacy in their shared verse lines.

> EVIE: Nobody tried to stop you.
>
> MOBILE: Nobody did.
>
> EVIE: I wouldn't want that.
>
> MOBILE: A smart chap with a gift,
>
> nobody's going to stop me.
>
> EVIE: Nobody could!
> Who ever could? It's good to see you, John.

However, it is also telling when verse lines aren't shared. In the following scene, Mobile gives Evie the opportunity to share his lines, but she blocks him, disconnects from him, starting her lines afresh. Clearly she doesn't want to connect to his words.

> MOBILE: When we met,
> what did we laugh about?
>
> EVIE: What?
>
> MOBILE: When we met, what did we laugh about?
>
> EVIE: John, I don't know. It's sort of long ago.

Following the verse pattern of the dialogue will, therefore, help bring character, relationship and situation to life. It also gives the scene pace and flow. Re-write it as prose and the rhythm becomes stilted and broken when it is spoken aloud. Try these two different versions.

E: Oh my lord.

M: The same.

E: I knew you'd come though. Life was perfect, it was on the cards.

M: How could I not? We go back, you and I, come a long way.

E: We do, we'll always be, you know –

M: You know –

E: There'll always be what there was.

M: That's absolutely true. There always is what there was. My philosophy.

EVIE: Oh my lord.

MOBILE: The same.

EVIE: I knew you'd come though.
                 Life was perfect, it was on the cards.

MOBILE: How could I not? We go back, you and I,
                 come a long way.

EVIE: We do, we'll always be,
                 you know –

MOBILE: You know –

EVIE: There'll always be what there was.

MOBILE: That's absolutely true.
                 There always is what there was. My philosophy.

The verse makes it easier for actors to lift the words off the page as they are given such clear guidelines through the shapes and patterns.

6. WORKSHOP PLAN

Participants in this workshop do not need prior knowledge of the texts being presented.

Workshop Plan: Talking in Verse

Objectives

- To explore the language, shapes and patterns in contemporary free verse drama

- To discover how the language, shapes and patterns in free verse drama lift inner thought and emotion off the page.

Materials

You will need:

– Separate copies of the Ted Hughes Clytemnestra speech, in both verse and prose, as provided earlier in this chapter

– Separate copies of the 'Kane: Text Sample' and 'Maxwell: Text Sample', as provided earlier in this chapter

– Lists of words from the Ted Hughes and Sarah Kane texts on separate handouts (see 'warming up' for suggestions).

Activities and Exercises

1. Warming up

Releasing, Grounding, Centring, Aligning, Breathing, Resonating and Articulating

– Ask your actors to stand centred and aligned (as described in Chapter 4 – feet hip width apart, weight balanced between both feet, weight balanced between the toes and heels, knees unlocked, lengthened spine, released stomach muscles). Now ask them to try some silent breathing from low in their bodies. Once this breath has deepened and lengthened, get them to place the lips gently together, drop the back of the tongue and hum ('mmmmm'), feeling the vibration on the lips. Keeping their feet rooted to the floor, ask them to shake out their upper body whilst still humming: this should loosen it up a little, increasing the vibration. Now ask them to tense various parts of their bodies whilst they are humming and check how it affects the sound e.g. clenching a fist, locking the knees, tightening the stomach muscles, clenching the buttocks, pointing the toes on one foot. Ask them to release the tension slowly, letting it drain away, feeling free and easy, before moving on to the next tense body part

– Ask the group to divide into pairs and provide each partnership with two handouts: one a word list from the Hughes text excerpt and the other a word list from the Kane text extract. For example:

Hughes – *pondered, moment, action, mistake, work, perfected, error, slipped, struggles, tightened, tangle, places, helpless, body, pushed, blade, screamed, stared, arched, strung, straining, drove, clean*

Kane – *dread, loss, slave, cage, gnaw, perishes, palls, killing, discordant, anxiety, roars, dead, corrosive, futile, despair, horror, void, die, breakdown*

– Ask each actor to speak their word list aloud in their own space and time (away from their partner). Coach them to explore the individual sounds in each word, letting them roll around their mouths, really using their lips and tongues. This will help them to explore deeper meanings

– Now ask them to repeat their word list aloud (still in their own space and time) but, this time, trying the tensing and releasing exercise whilst they're speaking. Keep coaching them to release the tension slowly, letting it drain away, before moving on. If you find there is too much vocal pushing in the room when bodies are tensed ('screamed' is a tricky word), get your actors to just shake their bodies out and move on

– Ask everybody to return to their partners and stand centred and aligned, facing one another. They need to decide who the speaker is and who the listener before they start. Speakers can then read out their word list, working to capture the essence of each word before moving on to the next. Listeners should have their eyes closed. When the reading is finished, listeners should try and guess what they think the text (that these words came from) is about. Ask the pairs to swap over and repeat the exercise with the other list of words.

2. Exploring Shapes and Patterns in Free Verse Drama

– Give each actor a copy of the Ted Hughes verse extract, re-written as prose, and ask them to read it in their heads to make sense of it and then aloud to listen to it. Give them some background information about context, if you feel it necessary. They may wish to discuss (with their partner) the relationship between the subject matter and their previous guesses about the word list

– Now give them copies of the Ted Hughes verse extract, structured in the original verse. Again, ask them to speak it aloud

– Ask each pair to discuss the difference between the two readings. *What changed as a result of the text being written in a different form?* Get them to report back to the group as a whole

– Explain (if it hasn't come up already) end-stopped lines, enjambed lines, suspensory pauses and caesural pauses. Get them to try the verse text again (to their partner) with this new information in mind

– Give each actor a copy of the Sarah Kane text sample and ask them to read it in their heads to make sense of it and then aloud to listen to it. Of course they will recognise some of the words. They may wish to discuss (with their partner) the relationship between the subject matter and their previous guesses about the word list

– Ask each pair to discuss how the shape of the verse influences the way in which it is said. Coach them to keep speaking it as they discuss (so it isn't just an intellectual exercise). You can then get them to share their findings with the whole group and ask for sample readings from volunteers to illustrate their decisions

– Give each actor a copy of the Glyn Maxwell text sample and ask them to read it in their heads to make sense of it and then try it aloud as a duologue. Give them some background information about context, if you feel it necessary

– Once again, ask each pair to discuss how the shape of the verse influences the way in which it is said (trying it aloud in order to consolidate decisions). You can then get them to share their findings with the whole group and ask for sample readings from volunteers to illustrate their decisions.

3. Debriefing

Although there have been a number of group discussions throughout this workshop, still allow some time for a debriefing session. You can ask these questions in relation to one of the texts or all three.

– What have you learnt about character, relationship and situation from the way in which the verse has been structured?

Now ask your actors to read the text sample(s) again. They may (unconsciously) incorporate elements of the discussion into their performance.

– Did this last reading change again? In what way?

7. REVISITING THE BASICS

Here are some important points to remember from this chapter:

- Plays in verse shape words into patterns on the page, play around with the order of grammatical syntax and use a specific rhythmic arrangement

- Playwrights tend to use verse in order to heighten the dramatic experience: the rhythms and language of verse can have a powerful effect on audience emotion

- Plays written in *free* verse are defined by the way in which the words are shaped into patterns on the page, which affects the rhythmic structure. However, line lengths vary, rhythmic beats aren't necessarily metrical or regular (mirroring the irregularities of prose/speech) and rhyme is absent.

- Line endings (end-stopped and enjambed) and pauses (suspensory and caesural) are particularly important to the word patterning in dramatic free verse and provide actors with important clues about stress and intonation

- Actors need to be guided by the patterns and shapes in dramatic free verse. In this way, they will be able to explore deeper levels of meaning in character, relationship and situation.

NOTES

1. Styan, J.L. (1981), *Modern Drama in Theory and Practice 2: Symbolism, Surrealism and the Absurd.* Cambridge: Cambridge University Press, p. 3.

2. Esslin, M. (1962), *The Theatre of the Absurd.* London: Eyre and Spottiswood, p. 17.

3. Ibid., p. 234.

4. Edgar, D. (2009), *How Plays Work.* London: Nick Hern Books, p. 4.

5. Billington, M. (2007), *State of the Nation: British Theatre since 1945.* London: Faber and Faber, p. 82.

6. Esslin, M. (1962), pp. 211-212.

7. Donoghue, D. (1959), *The Third Voice: Modern British and American Verse Drama.* Princeton: Princeton University Press/Clarendon: Oxford University Press, in a quote from *The Correspondence of Henrik Ibsen,* trans. ed. by Mary Morison (1905). London: Hodder and Stoughton, p. 367. Letter dated 25th May 1883.

8. Eliot, T.S. (1951), *Poetry and Drama:* The Theodore Spencer Memorial Lecture, Harvard University, November 21, 1950. London: Faber and Faber, p. 19.

9. Ibid., p. 31.

10. Ibid., p. 27.

11. Ibid., p.27.

12. Ibid., p.32.

13. Leeming, G. (1989), *Poetic Drama.* Basingstoke: Macmillan, p. 10.

14. Pinter, H. (1991), *Betrayal* in *Plays Four.* London: Faber and Faber, p. 195.

15. Menegaldo, G. (1997), *Challenging Conventions: An Interview with Howard Barker.* Poitiers: University of Poitiers: online interview.

16. Ibid.

17. Barker, H. (2006), 'The Investor's Chronicle' from *13 Objects* published in *Howard Barker: Plays Two.* London: Oberon Books, p. 296.

18. Barker, H. (2006), 'South of That Place Near' from *13 Objects* published in *Howard Barker: Plays Two.* London: Oberon Books, p. 310.

19. Esslin, M. (1962), p. 294.

20. Beckett, S. (1979), *Waiting for Godot.* London: Faber and Faber, p. 62.

21. Esslin, M. (1962), p. 95.

22. Ibid., p. 144.

23. Ionesco, E. (1958), *La Cantatrice Chauve* (*The Bald Soprano*) trans. by D.M. Allen and

published in *The Bald Soprano and Other Plays*. New York: Grove Press, p. 39.

. Hughes, T. (1999), *The Oresteia: Agamemnon*. London: Faber and Faber, p. 68.

25. Kane, S. (2001), *4.48 Psychosis* published in *Sarah Kane: Complete Plays*. London: Methuen, p. 218.

26. Maxwell, G. (2005), *The Forever Waltz*. London: Oberon Books, p. 65.

SUGGESTED READING

GENERAL REFERENCE

Barker, H. (1997), *Arguments for a Theatre*. Manchester: Manchester University Press.

Billington, M. (2007), *State of the Nation: British Theatre since 1945*. London: Faber and Faber.

Edgar, D. (2009), *How Plays Work*. London: Nick Hern Books.

Eliot, T.S. (1951), *Poetry and Drama*. London: Faber and Faber.

Eliot, T.S. (1953), *The Three Voices of Poetry*. Cambridge: Cambridge University Press.

Esslin, M. (2001), *The Theatre of the Absurd*. London: Methuen.

Harrop, J. & Epstein, R. (1990), *Acting with Style*. New Jersey: Prentice Hall.

Leeming, G. (1989), *Poetic Drama*. Basingstoke: Macmillan Education.

Rabey, D.I. & Gritzner, K. (eds.) (2006), *Theatre of Catastrophe: New Essays on Howard Barker*. London: Oberon Books.

Rebellato, D. (1999), *1956 and all that: The Making of Modern British Drama*. London: Routledge.

Styan, J.L. (1981), *Modern Drama in Theory and Practice 2: Symbolism, Surrealism and the Absurd*. Cambridge: Cambridge University Press.

Styan, J.L. (1981), *Modern Drama in Theory and Practice 3: Expressionism and Epic Theatre*. Cambridge: Cambridge University Press.

MODERN VOICE

287

Unwin, S. (2011), *The Well Read Play.* London: Oberon Books.

Weate, C. (2009), *Classic Voice: Working with Actors on Vocal Style.* London: Oberon Books.

PLAYS

Adamov, A. (1962), *Two Plays: Professor Taranne, Ping Pong.* London: John Calder.

Albee, E. (1976), *Seascape.* London: Cape.

Arden, J. (1982), *Serjeant Musgrave's Dance.* London: Methuen Drama.

Barker, H. (2006), *Plays Two: The Castle, Gertrude – The Cry, Animals in Paradise, 13 Objects.* London: Oberon Books.

Beckett, S. (2006), *The Complete Dramatic Works of Samuel Beckett.* London: Faber and Faber.

Bovell, A. (2009), *Speaking in Tongues.* London: Nick Hern Books.

Bovell, A. (2009), *When the Rain Stops Falling.* London: Nick Hern Books.

Brecht, B. (2010), *Collected Plays: Five (Life of Galileo, Mother Courage and Her Children).* London: Methuen Drama.

Brecht, B. (2010), *Collected Plays: Six (The Good Person of Szechwan), The Resistable Rise of Arturo Ui, Mr Puntila and his Man Matti).* London: Methuen Drama.

Brecht, B. (2010), *Collected Plays: Seven (Visions of Simone Machard, Schweyk in the Second World War, Caucasian Chalk Circle, Duchess of Malfi).* London: Methuen Drama.

Churchill, C. (1994), *The Skriker.* London: Nick Hern Books.

Duncan, R. (1971), *Collected Plays: This Way to the Tomb, St. Spiv, Our Lady's Tumbler, The Seven Deadly Virtues, The Rehearsal, O-B-A-F-G, The Gift.* London: Hart-Davis.

Eliot, T.S. (2004), *Complete Poems and Plays.* London: Faber and Faber.

Fry, C. (2007), *Plays One: The Lady's Not for Burning, A Yard of Sun, Siege.* London: Oberon Books.

Fry, C. (2007), *Plays Two: Venus Observed, The Dark is Light Enough, Curtmantle.* London: Oberon Books.

Fry, C. (2007), *Plays Three: The Firstborn, The Boy with the Cart, A Phoenix Too Frequent, Thor with Angels, A Sleep of Prisoners, Caedmon Construed, A Ringing of Bells.* London: Oberon Books.

Genet, J. (2009), *The Balcony.* London: Faber and Faber.

Genet, J. (2009), *The Maids.* London: Faber and Faber

Harrison, T. (1985), *Theatre Works 1973-1985.* London: Penguin Books.

Hughes, T. (1999), *The Oresteia.* London: Faber and Faber.

Ionesco, E. (1958), *The Bald Soprano and Other Plays.* New York: Grove Press.

Ionesco, E. (2000), *Rhinoceros, The Chairs, The Lesson.* London: Penguin Books.

Kane, S. (2001), *Complete Plays: Blasted, Phaedra's Love, Cleansed, Crave, 4.48 Psychosis, Skin.* London: Methuen Drama.

Maxwell, G. (2005), *The Forever Waltz.* London: Oberon Books.

Miller, A. (2000), *Death of a Salesman.* London: Penguin Books.

Norris, B. (2011), *Clybourne Park.* London: Nick Hern Books.

Odets, C. (1994), *Waiting for Lefty and Other Plays.* New York: Grove Press.

O'Neill, E. (1997), *Anna Christie, The Emperor Jones, The Hairy Ape.* New York: Random House.

Pinter, H. (1996), *Plays One: The Birthday Party, The Room, The Dumb Waiter, A Slight Ache, The Hothouse, A Night Out, The Black and White, The Examination.* London: Faber and Faber.

Pinter, H. (1991), *Plays Four: Old Times, No Man's Land, Betrayal, Monologue, Family Voices, A Kind of Alaska, Victoria Station, One for the Road, Mountain Language.* London: Faber and Faber.

Pirandello, L. (2002), *Six Characters in Search of an Author.* London: Nick Hern Books.

Rebellato, D. (2010), *Chekhov in Hell.* London: Oberon Books.

Rice, E. (1992), *The Adding Machine.* London: Samuel French.

Stoppard, T. (2000), *Rosencrantz and Guildenstern Are Dead, Jumpers, Travesties, Arcadia.* London: Faber and Faber.

Strindberg, A. (1976), *Plays One: The Father, Miss Julie, The Ghost Sonata.* London: Methuen Drama.

Strindberg, A. (2001), *Plays Two: The Dance of Death, A Dream Play, The Stronger.* London: Methuen Drama.

Theatre Workshop, Littlewood, J., Lewis, S., (2006), *Oh! What a Lovely War.* London: Methuen Drama.

Toller, E. (2011), *Plays One: Transformation, Masses Man, Hoppla, We're Alive!* London: Oberon Books.

Wilder, T. (2000), *Our Town and Other Plays.* London: Penguin Books.

Williams, T. (1990), *The Rose Tattoo, Camino Real, Orpheus Descending.* London: Penguin Books.

White, P. (1985), *Collected Plays Volume One: The Ham Funeral, Season at Sarsaparilla, A Cheery Soul, Night on Bald Mountain.* Strawberry Hills NSW: Currency Press.

CATHERINE WEATE